ENGLISH DEISM:
ITS ROOTS AND ITS FRUITS

ENGLISH DEISM:
ITS ROOTS AND ITS FRUITS

BY

JOHN ORR, A.B., A.M., B.D., Ph.D.

Professor of Bible,
Westminster College
New Wilmington, Pa., U. S. A.

WM. B. EERDMANS PUBLISHING COMPANY
GRAND RAPIDS, MICHIGAN
1934

FOREWORD

THE author became interested in the subject of deism while doing graduate study in the University of Berlin. While making use of the splendid library facilities of Berlin, he perceived that works in English on English deism do not equal in excellence the works on the same subject by such German authors as Lechler and Noack. Though the works of Leland and Farrar are valuable, they cannot be regarded as adequate treatments of English deism. The author believes there is need for a work on English deism which will trace its roots, objectively depict its development and decline and indicate its influence upon later thought. In this tripartite work, he seeks to supply that need. Parts I and II, with only slight modifications and emendations in their present printed form, constituted the author's Ph. D. dissertation at the University of Pittsburgh. Helpful criticism of the manuscript of these two parts of the present work were received from Dr. M. R. Gabbert, head of the department of philosophy of the University of Pittsburgh. Part III, which deals with the influence of English deism upon later thought, has been added to the original dissertation to complete the present work.

The greatest difficulty in the task of preparing such a work as this is the gaining of access to the many old, out-of-print books needed. The author acknowledges his indebtedness for valuable assistance to the following librarians: the librarians of the Universities of Berlin, Chicago, Pennsylvania and Pittsburgh; the librarians of Princeton, Western, Pittsburgh-Xenia and Chicago Theological Seminaries; the librarians of The Library of Congress, of Carnegie Library of Pittsburgh and of Westminster College, Pennsylvania.

CONTENTS

PART II
ENGLISH DEISM

PART III
THE FRUITS OF ENGLISH DEISM

PART I

THE ROOTS OF ENGLISH DEISM

CHAPTER I

INTRODUCTION

THE terms "deism" and "deist" need definition. Prior to the seventeenth century they were used interchangeably with the terms "theism" and "theist," respectively. The Greek word for god was *theos*. The Latin word for god was *deus*. It was not strange that the words derived from the two ancient languages were commonly used as equivalent in meaning. Language, however, is not static, and words change their meanings with the passage of years. Theologians and philosophers of the seventeenth century began to give a different signification to the words "theist" and "deist" and to the corresponding words "theism" and "deism." As early as 1563, the Swiss theologian Viret wrote, in his *Instruction Chretienne,* of persons who called themselves "deists."[1] The description added by him of the beliefs and attitudes of these persons might well have been used of eighteenth century English deists. According to the distinction in the meaning of terms that usage gradually recognized, theists and deists held some beliefs in common but at other points held views radically different. As against the atheist, both asserted belief in one supreme God, the Creator. As against the pantheist, they agreed that God is personal and distinct from the world. But the theist taught that God remained actively interested in and operative in the world which he had made, whereas the deist maintained that God endowed the world at creation with self-sustaining and self-acting powers and then abandoned it to the operation of these powers acting as second causes.[2]

In logical consistency with his main position, the theist has usually believed in a divine revelation, in divine interference in the form of miracles with the operation of second causes, in predictive prophecy, in the giving by God of posi-

---

[1] ROBERTSON, JOHN M., *A Short History of Freethought Ancient and Modern.* New York, Macmillan Co., 1899. p. 262.

LELAND, JOHN, *A View of the Principal Deistical Writers that have appeared in England in the last and present Century. With Observations upon them, and some account of the answers that have been published against them.* London. Printed for T. Cadell, Jr. and W. Davies; 1798. Fifth Edition; 2 vols. Vol. I, p. 2.

[2] FLINT, ROBERT, *Anti-Theistic Theories.* Edinburgh and London, William Blackwood and Sons; 1879. p. 442.

tive religious ordinances, in providence and in prayer as an
efficacious thing.   These beliefs have been common to the
three great theistic religions, Judaism, Christianity and
Mohammedanism.   Most Christian theists have also believed
in the incarnation of God in Jesus Christ.

As logical corollaries of his doctrine that the Creator has
not interfered with the laws which he gave to the world at
its creation, the deist has denied special revelation, miracles, supernatural prophecy, providence and the incarnation
and deity of Christ.   He has generally also rejected the
rites, ordinances and institutions of positive religions, holding them to be the inventions of self-seeking men and not
of divine origin.

Because of his fundamental tenet, the deist has usually
been charged with teaching that God is an "absentee God."
Thus Dr. A. H. Strong defines deism as "the view that represents the universe as a self-sustained mechanism from
which God withdrew as soon as he had created it."[3]   Some
deists would not have admitted such a statement of their
belief to be correct. They would have said that they believed
that God does operate in the world but only through natural
laws and not in any supernatural way.   For this reason,
Flint not only recognizes the old use of the word "deist" as
equivalent to "theist" and the later usage of the word to
denote one who holds the "absentee" conception of God, but
also recognizes the use of the word to denote the man who
believes that God is operative in the world in a natural but
not in a supernatural way.   This latter type of deism, Flint
calls "historical deism."[4]   However, since both the deists
who would confess to belief in an absentee God and those
who would assert belief in a present God acting only through
natural laws, believe that those laws were given at creation
and not modified since, there does not seem enough difference between these types of deists to justify a third definition of the terms "deist" and "deism."   The difference is
really that some deists have been more radical in their
deism than others.

The work of the deists, as thus distinguished from theists,
had a positive and a negative aspect.   On the positive side,
the deists championed their conception of God and their
theory of his relation to the world.   They also presented the
content of what they usually called the religion of nature.

[3] STRONG, A. H., *Systematic Theology*.   Philadelphia, The Judson
Press; 1912.   p. 414.
[4] FLINT, *Anti-Theistic Theories*, p. 443.

e of this as rational religion or the re-
ometimes they referred to it as the
me of them gave to it the name "Chris-
at it was original and uncorrupted
t was claimed that it was the original
a to be found, more or less concealed
various religions of priestly invention,
f the world. Some deists gave con-
this natural religion. Others gave it
All insisted on its rational and essen-
er. In the writings of most of the
ally given to presenting the positive
⸺ ⸺ of deism was very limited although it was that
element that gave deism its distinctive character.

The negative element in the works of the deists was very
much more prominent and took much more space in their
writings than did the positive element.[5] For this reason no
adequate presentation of English deism could be made without giving extended notice to this negative part of their
work. On the negative side, the deists repudiated such particular positive religions as Judaism, Christianity,[6] and
Mohammedanism with their institutions, rites and doctrines.
This required arguments attacking these religions and parts
of them. It also called for an explanation of how these
religions with their various institutions, rites and doctrines
came into being. Christianity, being the dominant religion
of the occidental world within which deism arose, received
most attention from the deists. Some of them made their
chief attacks upon contemporary forms of Christianity.
Others attacked the Christianity of the New Testament
itself. The attacks upon Judaism were aimed almost entirely at the teachings of the Old Testament. Though the present day historian of the English deistic movement may
regard it as a fault in the work of the deists that they gave
so large a part of their writings to corollaries of their main
proposition rather than to the setting forth and defense of
the main position itself and to negative attacks upon the
positions of others rather than to a positive defense of their
own position, he must himself give much space to their
discussion of the corollaries and to their negations if he

---

[5] Wollastson, one of the less prominent English deists, was exceptional in that his work was almost entirely positive in character.
[6] Some deists openly repudiated Christianity and spoke ill of Christ
himself while others claimed to be seeking to destroy what they regarded
as corruptions of a primitive pure and worthy Christianity which they
identified with natural religion.

would impart to his readers the true character and flavor of their works.

There is also another reason for giving much attention to the negative element in the work of the deists. In military warfare, an army's position may be entirely untenable unless certain positions held by the enemy are attacked and taken. Under such circumstances the army cannot hope to maintain itself by defending its own position against attacks of the enemy. Its best defense is a vigorous offensive, a destroying attack upon the positions held by its enemy. The same may be true in intellectual warfare. Though deists nowhere directly state that they felt such a situation had arisen in their warfare with rival philosophical and religious views, their method plainly suggests that they realized that unless they could destroy the positions held by their opponents they could not maintain their own position. If the Bible were indeed a special revelation from God, if miracles were actually wrought and prophecies requiring supernatural inspiration were actually spoken, if Jesus Christ was indeed the incarnate Son of God, virgin-born and raised from the dead, if the institutions, ordinances, rites and doctrines of the Christian church were God-given through inspired men, then the main position of the deists that God did not interfere with the world which he had made or interrupt the operation of those natural laws which were given at the creation would be untenable. Since belief in at least the greater number of these things was taught by most branches of the contemporary Christian church, the deist could hardly hope to win men from these churches to his own viewpoint without first destroying their faith in these beliefs. He felt also the necessity of justifying himself in his own rejection of them. The attempt to do so constituted a large part of the negative portion of the writings of most of the deists even as the negative portion constituted a large part of their total works.

But in the hands of the people was the venerated Bible with its miracles, prophecies, doctrines, rites and ordinances. The existence of this book and of these particular contents of it called for explanation. Faith in its trustworthiness must be broken down if its teachings were to be rejected. The setting of one part of the Bible against another part, of one of its great teachers against another, would tend to do this. Upsetting one's faith in the canonicity of parts of the Scriptures would have a like effect. But most effective of all would be a proof that the authors or the transmitters and guardians of the book or both were crafty, dishonest, self-seeking men who could not be trusted to put only truth into the book and to keep it pure from corruptions during the long period of its transmission to the modern age. Some of the anti-clericalism that characterized the writings of nearly all of the deists may well have been due to repugnance at the actual faultiness of some of the clergy. Some of it may have been just that natural dislike that arises when men find themselves on opposite sides when an issue is at stake upon which they feel deeply. In so far as the anti-clerical part of the writings of the deists sprang from either of these grounds it would have no special interest for this thesis. Many others who were not deists have been anti-clerical. But some of the anticlericalism in the writings of the deists evidently has a more direct and important relation to deism itself. The charge of selfishness and fraud against the clergy was the main method by which the deists sought to discredit the authority of the Church and of the Bible which taught things that the deist must reject if he was to remain a deist. Viewed from this angle, the anticlerical writings of the deists constituted an important element in the history of deism and, as such, calls for frequent notice in this work. The setting of one part of Scripture against another, the attacks upon the canon of Scripture and the attacks upon the character of the clergy were with the deists all part of an effort to get rid of an authority that taught positions inconsistent with deism.

Occasionally a present day writer makes use of the term "deist" in the old sense of the word as equivalent with the term "theist." Such usage is confusing and should be avoided. In this treatise the term deist will always be used to denote one who admits a Creator but does not admit that the Creator has interfered with the operation of natural laws since the creation, and who advocates a rationalistic religion of nature as against any religion based on special or supernatural revelation.

Viewed in one of its important aspects, deism might be classed as a distinct religion, a rival of other religions. It might also be regarded as a rationalistic school of theology. In another aspect, it appears as a system of philosophy. Since its tendency was to discard rites and mysteries and to make religion almost exclusively a matter of ethics, it might well be regarded as a school of ethical thought. The fact is that deism lies along the rather hazy boundary lines that separate the domains of religion, theology, philosophy,

ethics, and science. Some deists wrote with a theological
slant, others with a scientific. Toland could probably be
most accurately placed as a philosopher while another deist,
Shaftesbury, is more correctly classified as a writer in the
field of ethics.

Deism, as a distinct and well-developed system of thought,
first appeared among the English people. But many deistic
ideas and tendencies were manifest yet earlier in Italy and
France. Herbert of Cherbury published his *De Veritate* in
the year 1624 A.D. In the main, it can be said that this
work taught the doctrines and expressed the attitudes characteristic of deism and earned for Lord Herbert the title,
"Father of Deism." Yet it would be a mistake to infer from
this title that deism was a system of thought originated by
the fertile brain of one man. "Fathers" or "founders" of
systems of thought are often but children of their own age
who faithfully represent the spirit and skillfully present
and formulate the ideas current all about them. Deism had
a long ancestral line. It was a product resulting from the
coming together in one period of many lines of influence.

Similar influences to those which led Lord Herbert of
Cherbury to entertain the principles which he published
were operating upon others to produce thoughts of like kind.
That conception of history which looks upon events in the
realms of both thought and action as being only the products of original personalities of great genius contains an
element of truth but leads to serious error when it causes
the overlooking of the fact that outstanding men are to a
very large degree children of the age in which they live,
products of the "zeitgeist" of their times. Had Lord Herbert
never lived or written his books, a deistic movement very
like the one of history would probably have occurred, and
would have occurred about the same time.

Deism as an organized, active thought movement belongs
chiefly to the eighteenth century. Although it began early
in the seventeenth century with the publication of Herbert's
De Veritate in 1624, the development of deism was slow. It
was fully fifty years before the works of Charles Blount,
which ushered in the active period of English deism, began
to appear. The only important English deist who wrote
during this period was Thomas Hobbes, and he was not a
typical deist. David Hume's writings began to appear in
1739. Henry Dodwell published his *Christianity Not Founded on Argument* in 1742. Though these two writers had
much in common with the deists, their fundamental philoso-

phy of religion naturally led to skepticism or agnosticism and was as unfavorable to the main position of the deists as it was to that of their orthodox opponents. Some important English deistic works appeared after 1742, but the movement was rapidly waning and soon practically came to its close in England. It developed somewhat later in France, Germany and America, but had practically come to an end with the end of the eighteenth century. It was in the main an eighteenth century thought movement.

Before taking up the study of English deism, consideration will be given to its roots in the thought of the past and to those things which produced in the seventeenth and eighteenth centuries an intellectual atmosphere favorable to its growth. It would not be wise for one to assert dogmatically that he had found an exhaustive list of such influences or to claim ability to estimate nicely and exactly the relative weight of each favoring influence. The expert cook might much more easily state the exact importance of each ingredient in his cake, though that were a sufficiently difficult task. Yet, by a genetic study of deism and by a close scrutiny of the writings of the important deists, it is possible to discover the main influences that had to do with the development of deism and to give a worth while estimate of the importance of each line of influence named. This will be attempted in the following pages.

The lines of influence that helped to produce and shape eighteenth century English deism may be conveniently examined under the following heads: (*a*) historical events, including some important discoveries and inventions; (*b*) advancement in science; (*c*) certain controversial theological writings; (*d*) certain philosophical writings, including some works usually classed as literature rather than as philosophy. These lines of influence are not to be regarded as isolated from each other but rather as related and interdependent and as supplementing each other.

After studying in Part I the influences that produced and moulded early English deism, the reader will be asked in Part II to study the history of English deism itself. This will include an examination of its slow rise, of its flourishing period and of its rapid decline. In Part III, after a study of the spreading of deism from England to France, Germany and America, an effort will be made to indicate the evidence of the influence of English deism as this is found in several recent schools of theological and philosophical thought.

CHAPTER II

INFLUENCES THAT PRODUCED AND MOULDED
EARLY ENGLISH DEISM

DEISM as one of the thought movements of the modern age has some sources in common with most other schools of modern thought. Were one seeking to trace the sources of and the influences that had moulded almost any system of more recent thought, he would find among those sources and influences such important factors as the rise and spread of Mohammedanism, the Renaissance, the Reformation, the great geographic discoveries, the invention of the printing press and the great advance of Science and the use of scientific method. It cannot be claimed that deism had any exclusive monopoly on the influences that came from these sources. Nevertheless these things did greatly influence the rise of deism, in some cases in a general way as they influenced other modern thought movements and in other cases in ways peculiar to deism alone. Often a fruitful thinker or an important event may have great influence upon the development of quite different schools of thought. Thus the Megaric, the Cyrenaic and the Cynic schools of ethical thought are all greatly obligated to the influence of Socrates,[1] though Socrates himself belonged to none of them. Thus also the Reformation was a potent influence in the rise of such diverse things as deism and the various modern protestant churches.

A. HISTORICAL EVENTS LEADING TO THE RISE OF DEISM.

1. THE RISE AND SPREAD OF MOHAMMEDANISM.

The rise of Mohammedanism in Arabia in the seventh century and its subsequent spread into southeastern and southwestern Europe were events that deeply affected the thought life of the European world. The Crusades brought peoples of the West into contact with the real advances made in mathematics and astronomy by the Arabs. This stimulated the development of science in the West. The

---

[1] ROOP, HERVIN U., *Christian Ethics or the Science of Christian Living.* New York, Chicago, London, and Edinburgh. Fleming H. Revell Company; 1926. p. 15.

advance of the armies of Islam in the seventh century and still more their advance which culminated in the fall of Constantinople in 1453 drove into western Europe classical scholars who carried with them their treasures of ancient Greek and Latin and Hebrew writings.[2] A revival of interest in the old writings took place. The interest in the classical works of Greece and Rome gave the Renaissance. The interest in the Bible and the works of the Church Fathers helped to bring on the Reformation. As will be noticed later, both these movements greatly influenced deism. Extensive use of ancient authors characterized the works of the deists. But for the effects of the Mohammedan invasions this would hardly have been true.

The contact of Mohammedanism with Christianity brought about a crude development of the science of comparative religions. The deists made use of this infant science. No comparison of religions was more frequent with them than that between Mohammedanism and Christianity. The spectacle of these rival religions, each with its sacred book and each claiming to be from God, naturally suggested the doubts and disbeliefs characteristic of deism.

The direct thought influence of Mohammedan writers upon the English deists was probably not very great. Averroes' ideas were undoubtedly known through his great influence with Italian Renaissance writers.[3]

2. The Protestant Reformation.

The Protestant Reformation and the consequent division of Christianity into many sects which warred against each other had a marked influence upon the rise of deism. A brief consideration of a number of ways in which the Reformation affected the deistic movement follows.

a. *The Reformation Gave a Less Important Place to Orders, Ordinances and Rituals.* The dominant church of western Europe before the Reformation made much of the hierarchy, and magnified the importance and power and authority of the clergy. The reformers were opposed to this and magnified the right of private judgment on the part of laymen. The pre-Reformation church had many sacraments, many special days and many and elaborate rituals. It also made the observing of these to constitute a very large

2) D'AUBIGNÉ, J. H. M., *History of the Reformation in the Sixteenth Century.* New York, Wm. L. Allison; 1882. p. 25.

3) OWEN, JOHN, *The Skeptics of the Italian Renaissance.* London, Swan Sonnenschein & Co.; New York, Macmillan & Co.; 1893. Second edition. pp. 23, 70–71.

and essential part of religious duty. Most of the reformers reduced the sacraments to two, did away with the observance of most of the special days and greatly simplified the rituals of religion. Though they did not deny the need and value of some sacraments and rituals, yet they gave them a much less important place as compared with the importance they gave to the ethical side of religion.

The deists moved much farther in this same direction. They made no provision for any order of clergy in their religious scheme. They also made no provision for sacraments or special days or rituals.[4] They made the reason of the individual sovereign. They made religion almost entirely ethical, leaving little or no place for institutions, ordinances, or rituals. It therefore appears that in these features deism was a farther movement in the same direction in which the reformers had gone.

b. *The Reformers Lessened the Miraculous Content of Religion.* The protestant reformers usually regarded as spurious the many miracles claimed by the Romanists, such as those claimed in connection with relics, shrines and saints. But the reformers generally retained belief in Bible miracles. A few of the deists, such as Conyers Middleton, also made their attacks upon the church miracles without saying much about Bible miracles. But most deists rejected miracles as such and many of them, such as Woolston, violently attacked Bible miracles. In this respect also deism was a move farther in the direction taken by the reformers. The protestant rejection of the miracle of transubstantiation was just an outstanding illustration of the general tendency to keep to a minimum the mysterious element in religion rather than to magnify it as Romanism did. But the deists went much farther than protestants in rejecting the mysterious in religion. Their attitude appears in such books as Toland's *Christianity Not Mysterious.*

c. *The Reformers Gave an Increased Importance to the Use of the Reason in Religion.* The Roman church had not taught people to reason about the problems of religion or of Bible teachings. It had called for implicit acceptance and obedience to its teachings on the part of laymen. Protestantism encouraged men to read the Bible and to think for themselves. They were to use their own reason in interpreting Scripture. However, this did not mean putting

---

[4] Thomas Hobbes may be regarded as an exception to this. But he was not, in many respects, a typical deist.

reason above Scripture as an authority. The Bible was the authority for the reformers as the church was for Romanists. Protestantism gave the reason a larger field in which to function and gave it authority as against the church but not authority as against or above the Bible. Deism went further and placed reason on the throne above either church or Bible. At this point also deism was a protestant trend carried farther.

d. *In the Reformation, Charges of Corruption Were Often Made against the Clergy.* Before the Reformation proper had begun there was an insistent demand in the church for reform in head and members. Charges of unworthy living were often made against priests and monks. Wycliffe and Huss voiced it. Erasmus the humanist who remained in the Roman church wrote a work entitled the *Praise of Folly,* which went through seven editions in a few months, to expose and ridicule the corruption and immorality of many Romanist clergy and monks. Later, the protestant reformers pushed these charges. They also charged fraudulent claims of miracles to awe the people into submission. In the heat of the controversies that developed, Romanists hurled counter-accusations against protestant preachers. And, when protestantism divided into sects, ministers of one such sect often said uncomplimentary things about ministers of the other. This hurling of charges against the clergy tended to produce distrust of the clergy. It also provided abundant ammunition to anyone who wished to discredit the clergy. The deists soon used this ammunition in their guns which were directed against all clergy. One of the most characteristic features of eighteenth century deism was a bitter anti-clericalism that laid the blame for the alleged corruption of natural religion at the door of a fraudulent, self-seeking priesthood. The connection between the Reformation with its bitter counter-accusations and this element in deism is apparent.

e. *The Reformation Greatly Multiplied the Number of Rival Sects Each of Which Claimed to Have the True Religion.* If the contact of Christian Europe with the Mohammedan world had tended to unsettle the faith of men in the claims of either of the rival religions that it was a true revelation from God, much more did the division of Christendom into many sects tend to unsettle faith in the claims of any or all of them. This division made the way of the unbeliever easy and provided the deistic enemy of historical Christianity with weapons for his attack.

f. *The Evils of the Religious Wars That Followed the Reformation Tended to Produce the Bitter Anti-Christianity That Was Characteristic of Many Deists.* There developed from the great reformation movement a series of wars that were semi-religious and semi-political. Men who would probably have been rather indifferent to the claims and the disputes of various Christian sects had these claims and disputes been carried on peaceably were embittered against the various churches and against Christianity itself, which they did not always distinguish from the churches, by the evils that they had to suffer from the religious wars.

g. *The Hardships Suffered by Nearly All Men as a Result of a Policy of Religious Intolerance Helped to Bring About the Strong Advocacy of Toleration by the Deists.* Most deists did argue for religious toleration. Writers of nearly every religious sect could be named who did the same, but usually when their own particular sect was the victim of persecution. Writers of the sect in power were usually either silent on the subject of toleration or argued in favor of a policy of intolerance. It seemed to matter whose ox was being gored. However, the frequent and rapid changes in the political position of various sects made most of them to taste the bitter experience of being persecuted and thus helped them to appreciate the arguments for toleration. This was especially true in England just before and at the time of the rise of deism. The rapid and frequent changes of the established religion during the reigns of Henry VIII, Edward VI, Mary, Elizabeth, the Stuarts and during the rule of Cromwell, gave Roman Catholics, Episcopalians and Puritans the experience of being in power and also the experience of being the persecuted party. This enabled most Englishmen to see reasons for toleration and gave deists some of their best arguments on this subject. Since deists were never in power in England, perhaps they should not be given too much credit for their advocacy of toleration. It was nothing exceptional for any persecuted group to advocate toleration. In France, when deism did come to power in the period of the French Revolution, it did not show itself notably tolerant either in religion or politics.

Yet it should be noted that deism, being a religious philosophy which magnified the reason and gave little place to authority, would naturally be expected to champion religious toleration. For it is not in the nature of reason to function well under compulsion. Probably this natural affinity of their system of thought for toleration worked with

the effect of their own sufferings from a policy of intolerance to make them champions of toleration. Certainly the
common sufferings through intolerance in the century following the Reformation gave them abundant material out
of which to construct appealing arguments.

3. THE GREAT GEOGRAPHIC DISCOVERIES OF THE EARLY
MODERN ERA.

The great geographic discoveries that followed the invent-
ing of the mariners' compass certainly had an important
bearing upon the rise of deism. Before the compass was
invented, mariners had hugged the shores of known lands.
Now they ventured far. Columbus discovered America.
Magellan's ship went around the world. These and other
great voyages of discovery that followed affected the rise
and the content of deism in several ways.

a. *These Discoveries Tended to Discredit the Church and
the Scriptures as These Had Been Interpreted by the Church.*
The church had taught and had claimed that the Scriptures
taught that the earth is flat. The world was now proved to
be a sphere. With many this greatly weakened the credit
of both church and Scriptures. It tended to produce just
the attitude manifested by many deists toward the church
and the Bible. Deists made use of these discoveries in their
attacks on church and Bible.

b. *The Discovery of Many New Races Gave Added Force
to Objections against Making Salvation Depend upon a
Book That Was Unknown to So Many.* The old problem of
the justice of making salvation depend upon the knowledge
of a book unknown to many became more acute with the
discovery of many new lands and races that did not have
the Bible. Most deists raised this objection to a book
religion.

c. *The Discovery of Hitherto Unknown Religions Added
to the Embryo Science of Comparative Religions from
Which the Deists Developed Arguments.* The deists claimed
to find evidence of the corruption of a primitive pure natural religion known to all men in their study of many newly
discovered religions. They also claimed to find in all particular religions certain sound principles common to all out
of which they would formulate their religion of nature. In
the light of later and fuller knowledge, it may be doubted
that they so much gathered these principles out of various
religions as that they read them into those religions out of
their theory. At any rate, numerous references to the

religions of recently discovered peoples entered into the deistic writings. This suggests the influence of these new discoveries upon deism.

4. THE INVENTION OF THE PRINTING PRESS.

All thought movements subsequent to it were greatly affected by the invention of the printing press. Deism was no exception to this rule. The invention furnished an illustration of what human reason could accomplish and thus encouraged that boastful confidence in the power of the human mind which characterized deistic rationalism. In this way it did do something toward the emergence of the spirit if not of the idea of deism. But its main effect upon deism was not this. Few of the deists would probably have ever read the older works from which they gleaned seed-ideas of deism had not the printing press made such books readily accessible. Certainly the deists could not have spread their own views so rapidly had not the printing press made the widespread dissemination of their works in cheap popular form possible. Between the setting up by Gutenberg of his first press about 1450 and the rise of deism, a great reading public had been developed. Though toleration lagged, it was much more difficult to suppress proscribed views after the invention of printing. By stimulating confidence in the powers of the human mind, by giving access to old writings that tended to give rise to deism and by making it easy for deists to circulate their views, the printing press exercised its influence upon the deistic movement.

B. THE RISE OF MODERN SCIENCE.

The rise and development of modern science undoubtedly had some influence upon the coming into existence of the deistic movement and still more influence upon its later development and content. The French deism which arose later than English deism was probably more influenced by science than was English deism. The English deists would certainly not have claimed or admitted that their natural religion, or religion of reason, was in any way a product of modern science. They claimed that it was the original universal religion which had been corrupted through the ages by crafty, self-seeking priests and princes. They regarded miracles, prophecy and all other supernaturalistic elements in the Bible, as well as most of the institutions, ordinances, rites and theological dogmas of the historical Christian churches as constituting corruptions. What they did seem

to claim for modern science was that it had made these
things, particularly the supernaturalistic elements in the
Bible and historical Christianity, appear as corruptions
which men instructed in modern science could no longer
hold.[5] They thought science had discredited the authority
of the church and the Bible by its disproving of theories
taught by the church and by the Bible as interpreted by the
church.[6] The uniformity of nature was a presupposition
upon which the new science builded. The advance of
science also gave extensive illustrations of the fact of uniformity. The deists regarded this uniformity as discrediting
the supernaturalism of the Bible and of historical Christianity.[7] Medieval thought not only gave the earth a central
place in astronomy but it also gave man a prominent place
in relation to the rest of the universe. The modern scientific
thought that was developing contemporaneously with deism
was heliocentric and not geocentric in its astronomy and
was nature-centered rather than man-centered in its
science.[8] The influence of modern science in both these
respects was evident in the works of the deists.[9]

A quite important influence that the successes of modern
science during the earlier period of its development had
upon the rise of deism and upon the attitude of the deists
was that they tended to produce great confidence in the
powers of the human mind if that mind were left untrammeled by authority. The important scientific achievements
of Copernicus (1473-1543), Brahe (1546-1601), Kepler (1571-
1630), Galileo (1564-1642), Francis Bacon (1561-1626), Descartes (1596-1650), Harvey (1578-1657), Huygens (1629-
1695), Newton (1642-1727), and others, were adding to the
prestige of the modern age in contrast to the barrenness and
futility of the authority-dominated thought of the Schoolmen. A new intellectual atmosphere was being produced
that was favorable to the development of a system of
thought like deism which was against authority and thoroughly rationalistic. The discoveries and triumphs of the

   [5] Bolingbroke, Henry St. John, Viscount, *The Works of Lord
Bolingbroke*. Philadelphia, Carey & Hart; 1841. vol. 2, p. 495.
Shaftesbury, Anthony Earl of, *Characteristics of Men, Manners,
Opinions, Times*, etc. London, Grant Richards; 1900. vol. 2, pp. 93–94.
   [6] Bolingbroke, *Works*, vol. 2, p. 495.
   [7] Shaftesbury, *Characteristics*, vol. 2, p. 94.
   [8] Burtt, Edwin Arthur, *The Metaphysical Foundations of Modern
Physical Science*. New York, Harcourt, Brace & Co., Inc. London,
Kegan Paul, Trench, Trubner & Co., Ltd.; 1927. p. 4.
   [9] Blount, Chas., *Miscellaneous Works;* 1695. *Orac. of Reason,*
pp. 53, 55.

new age were producing a new attitude toward the past.
Hitherto men had greatly reverenced the past and such
things as were hoary with age. Old systems of thought, old
achievements, old authorities, had been held in highest
esteem and nothing modern had been thought worthy of
comparison with things that were ancient. But now men
had discovered that the ancients were guilty of gross errors.
Now men had shown skill and wisdom in invention beyond
the achievements of the ancients. This was leading men to
think highly of new things and to despise such things and
theories as were old. This reversal of attitude was evident
in the deists and was very favorable to the development of
deism. Unbounded confidence in the ability of the human
reason to accomplish anything, if but left free from the
trammels of authority, was the very spirit of deism.

With the possible exception of the demonstration that the
earth is a sphere, no scientific achievement did more to
lessen men's esteem for things old, to discredit the church
and the Bible, as the Bible had hitherto been interpreted,
and to make men boastfully confident of the powers of
human reason than the revolutionary advance in astronomy
that began with the publication in 1543 of Copernicus' book
On the Revolutions of the Celestial Orbs. The author was
excommunicated by the pope for championing such novel
views as that the sun and not the earth is the center of the
solar system. Galileo, after adding to astronomical knowledge by the use of the telescope which Janson had invented
and Galileo himself improved, championed the Copernican
view. The inquisition forced him, against his real convic-
tions, to abjure the theory. Gradually the force of accumu-
lating scientific evidence brought about a rather general
acceptance of the Copernican position. As a result, the
church which had stubbornly championed the old astronomy
and the Bible which the church had long interpreted as
teaching the older view, lost much in standing. This undoubtedly helped to produce such attitudes toward the
church and Bible as characterized the deistic movement
and provided deists with material for their attack.

Deists, more especially the later deists, naturally liked
to think and claim that their deism had its main root in this
uptodate scientific world view. Many of the later historians
of philosophy have, in their brief treatments of eighteenth
century deism, assumed the correctness of this claim. The
writer, however, is convinced by his examination of the
writings of the deists and by chronological considerations

that this view is incorrect. He recognizes, as indicated above, that the rise of modern science was one of the influences that tended to bring about the appearance and development of deism, that it tended to produce the attitudes toward authority, toward the supernatural and toward reason that were characteristic of deism and that it provided deism with some of its arguments. He also recognizes that it provided an intellectual climate very favorable to the rise and spread of such a thought movement as deism. But all this is not saying that the rise of modern science was the main root of deism.

The great scientists of the age were not deists nor were the deists great scientists. Few, if any, of the deists could claim any rank at all as scientists. Were science the main root of deism, one would naturally expect to find the greater scientists among the first champions of deism. The general character of the works of the leading deists is not that of works of science. The writings of most of the deists were philosophical or theological in character and not scientific. And the tone and method of reasoning in them has much more in common with medieval philosophy and theology than with modern scientific philosophy. Their reasoning is mostly of the old deductive type. Their numerous quotations from ancient authors is characteristic of Renaissance works rather than of modern scientific writings. Though they do repudiate the authority accepted in medieval works and do occasionally refer with praise to some achievement of the new age of science that was opening, the reader feels that in most respects these writings have more in common with the works of the medieval age than with works of modern science. They have the character and tone of a transitional period. But there is more of the flavor of the old than of the new in them.

The date at which deism appeared is not consistent with the view that regards modern science as its main root. Herbert of Cherbury's *De Veritate* which appeared in 1624 contained a rather complete presentation of the deistic position. Few of the works of the great early leaders of modern science, except in the realm of astronomy, had appeared at that time. Evidence of any influence of these astronomers upon Herbert is indeed scant. But, though Herbert is the first prominent English deist, deism in France goes back to an earlier date. Pierre Charron (d. 1603), and Jean Bodin (d. 1596), were deists and, as noted above,[10] Viret wrote as

---

[10] Above, p. 13.

early as 1563 of men who called themselves deists whose
views were the characteristic ones of later deism. Ueberweg would classify the views of Pomponatius, the Italian
writer who died in 1525, as deistic in character.[11]   At that
time, modern science was but in its early infancy. Of course
no exact date can be fixed as the beginning of modern
science. One can see an embryonic development of modern
science even as early as Roger Bacon (d. 1294). But embryonic deism, as will appear when the theological and philosophical roots of deism are considered, antedate even Bacon.
These time considerations indicate that modern science
could hardly be the main root of deism though it might well
be an important factor[12] in its development since modern
science and deism developed contemporaneously.

C.   CERTAIN   CONTROVERSIAL   THEOLOGICAL
WRITINGS.

Although the historical events and the scientific achievements just considered certainly did tend to produce the
thought system of deism and certainly did influence the
development and spread of that movement by providing a
favorable intellectual climate and by furnishing deistic
writers with many of their arguments, the more important
seeds of deistic thought are to be discovered in the fields of
theology and philosophy. The boundary line between the
fields of theology and philosophy has not always been sharply drawn and many writers, like Augustine and Aquinas,
have been both theologians and philosophers. For conveni-
ence of investigation, the two fields are separated in this
work and the sources of deism are first sought in the theological and then in the philosophical fields.

I. DIFFERENT TYPES OF TEACHING WITHIN THE BIBLE ITSELF.

The more radical among the later deists openly and
entirely rejected the Bible. They would have none of priest

---

11) UEBERWEG, FRIEDRICH, *Grundriss der Geschichte der Philosophie.*
Dritter Theil. *Die Neuzeit.* Berlin, Ernst Siegfried Mittler und Sohn;
1883.   Sechste Auflage, s. 5.
12) A few of the more important channels through which scientific influences reached the earlier deists and a few of the clearer evidences of
the influence of science upon later deists are here added. Hobbes was
personally acquainted with the important early modern scientists Galileo
and Francis Bacon.   Vid. below, p. 70.   Locke, who was not himself a
deist but had much influence with later deists, was also influenced by
Francis Bacon and was himself a scientist trained in medicine. Vid.
p. 83.   For evidence of a scientific influence in Blount, vid. below p. 113.
Bolingbroke also gave evidence of his being acquainted with the work of
several scientists and of having his views influenced by them.   Vid.
below, p. 156.

or prophet, nor of apostles or Christ himself. But the earlier and most of the less radical deists, while rejecting parts of the Bible and discarding the commonly held orthodox view of its inspiration and authority, held that it did contain many excellent religious teachings and that it told of the lives and precepts of some of the world's best moral and religious instructors. These deists who were less radical in their treatment of the Scriptures were accustomed to claim that different and inconsistent types of teaching could be distinguished within the Bible itself. In their interpretation of the Old Testament, these deists, like adherents of some modern schools of theology, set the prophets against the priests, making the former represent ethical religion and the latter a religion of ceremonies and mysteries. These deists would have themselves considered as successors of the prophets in this struggle for ethical as against ceremonial religion. Turning to the New Testament, these deists claimed that Jesus taught ethical religion as against the legalism and ceremonialism of the pharisees. Thus they claimed Jesus to be of their party. It was with this idea in mind that Chubb claimed Jesus as a deist. They also set Paul against Peter and James and took note of Paul's controversy with the Judaizers. In references to such controversies, the deists assumed that they were but carrying on upon the side of Paul when they opposed ritualistic religion in favor of ethical religion. But when arguing against doctrinal religion in favor of ethical, they drew a distinction between Paul and Christ, claiming Paul had corrupted Christianity by giving it a doctrinal cast. At this point these deists would claim to be of the party of Jesus as against Paul. Whether or not this setting of some of the great religious teachers of the Bible against others as was done by the deists is justified is a question at issue today between conservative and liberal schools of theological thought. That question cannot be discussed here. However, it is to be noted here that, on the assumption of the deist's own viewpoint, the dispute in the Old Testament between prophetic and priestly views was the first theological controversy that provided a root of deism. This claim would make the prophetic type of Old Testament religion the oldest theological root of deism and it would also make the teachings of Jesus and Paul to be among the sources of deism.

2. WRITINGS OF THE GNOSTICS.

The gnostic heresy of the early Christian era provided the next theological root of deism. Though deism was at the very opposite pole from gnostic mysticism and superstition, it had some things in common with gnosticism and derived ideas and material from gnostic sources.

The deist shared the gnostic pride of intellect. The gnostic, as the name implies, claimed to know. He held in contempt those who lived by faith. In like spirit the deist boasted of his reason and despised those who put faith in authority of church or Bible.

Marcion, the most critical and rationalistic of the gnostics, was the gnostic writer who probably exercised the greatest influence upon the deists and who was most like the deists himself. Marcion was hostile to the Old Testament[13] and to everything Jewish. He was fond of contrasting the God of the New Testament with the God of the Old Testament to the discredit of the latter.[14] Marcion attacked the commonly accepted canon of Scripture[15] and substituted a canon of his own. Several of the deists also made attacks upon the accepted canon of Scripture and, in doing so, took note of the difference between the church and the Marcionite canons.[16] Deists[17] also were anti-Jewish, anti-Old Testament and inclined to draw a contrast between the Old and New Testaments and their conceptions of God.

Was the unquestionable similarity at a number of points between the teachings of Marcion and those of the deists

[13] The works of Marcion are only partially extant. References to and extensive quotations from them are found in the writings of the early Fathers of the Christian Church. It was likely from these references and the quotations in the Fathers that the deists gained their acquaintance with Marcion rather than from his own separate works. For the teachings of Marcion, vid. *The Ante-Nicene Fathers*. Buffalo, The Christian Literature Company; 1885–1886, especially vols. 1 and 3. On Marcion's hostility to the Jews and the Old Testament, vid. *op. cit.*, vol. 1, p. 352.

[14] Tertullian made this plain in his extensive work against Marcion as did also Irenæus in his work against heresies. vid. *The Ante-Nicene Fathers*, vol. 1, p. 352; vol. 3, pp. 286, 297 ff., 429 ff.

[15] *op cit.*, vol. 3, pp. 347, 350, 262, 423 ff., 431, 460, 653.

[16] Hobbes, Toland and Collins were important deists who dealt with the canon of Scripture.

HOBBES, THOMAS, *The English Work of Thomas Hobbes of Malmesbury*. London, John Bonn; 1839. vol. 3. *Leviathan*, chap. 33.

TOLAND, JOHN, *Amyntor: or a Defense of Milton's Life*. London, John Darby; 1699. Part II.

COLLINS, ANTHONY, *Ground and Reason of the Christian Religion*. (Published anonymously without place of pub., publisher or date being given.) p. 14.

[17] A good illustration of this is supplied by Thomas Morgan in his *Moral Philosopher*.

merely an accidental coincidence or was there a direct influence of Marcion's works upon the deists? Two facts point strongly toward a direct connection and influence. The first of these is that the writings of the deists are filled with numerous references to and quotations from ancient writers including the church Fathers and their adversaries.[18] Though deism was a bitterly hostile reaction against medieval theology and philosophy, the deists followed the practice of medieval writers in quoting much from the works of the ancients. Evidently works were not then regarded as quite scholarly unless full of such quotations. This fact is impressed upon the reader who compares the works of the deists with their many quotations from the ancients with works on similar themes by twentieth century writers who but seldom quote the ancients. The second and more conclusive fact that proves connection between the deists and Marcion is that they make direct references[19] to him and his work. It is probable their information concerning him and his views was derived from early church opponents of Marcion rather than from his own separate works. The fact that the deists were familiar with the ancient writings in which Marcion's views are set forth, taken together with their direct references to him and the striking similarity of their views to his, sufficiently justifies the inference of a connection and influence.

3. The Allegorical Method of Bible Interpretation Used by Origen and Others.

Seventeenth and eighteenth century advocates of historic Christianity and a supernatural Bible having made much of arguments based on Bible miracles and Bible prophecies and their fulfillment, the deists made heavy attacks upon the miraculous and prophetic elements of the Bible. A number of the early church Fathers had made extensive use of an allegorical method of Bible interpretation, but not with any purpose of eliminating the miraculous or supernatural from the Scriptures. Origen was probably most noted among the Fathers for this method of Bible interpretation. Deists could not admit that Bible miracles as literally stated in the Bible occurred or that Bible prophecies literally interpreted were literally fulfilled. To so

---

18) vid. the writings of Collins and Tindal.
19) Tindal, Matthew, *Christianity as Old as the Creation; or The Gospel a Republication of the Rel. of Nature.* London; 1730, p. 130.
Annet, Peter, *The History and Character of St. Paul Examined.* London, F. Page (date not given). pp. 3–5.

admit would be to give up the fundamental position of deism
and would logically force acceptance of the Bible as the
divinely inspired and authoritative word of God. But miracles and prophecies interpreted in an allegorical way would
not require this. Several prominent eighteenth century
deists accordingly insisted that Bible miracles and prophecies were not to be taken literally but allegorically. They
defended their use of allegorical interpretation by pointing
to the example of the Fathers, notably of Origen. Anthony
Collins did this in his treatment of Bible prophecies.[20]
Thomas Woolston applied the same method of interpretation to Bible miracles,[21] but was not so clever in its use as
Collins. Thus the deists made use of a method of Bible
interpretation suggested by the early church Fathers.

4. THE TRINITARIAN AND CHRISTOLOGICAL CONTROVERSIES.

Some of the roots of deism go back into the series of bitter
doctrinal controversies that raged in the early Christian
church. The first and perhaps the greatest of these was the
controversy over the doctrine of the Trinity. Trinitarianism,
ably championed by Athanasius, won a difficult victory over
Arianism and was embodied in the Nicene and Athanasian
creeds. But the defeated followers of Arius carried on the
controversy in the protracted disputes that arose over the
person and nature, or natures, of Christ. Through the Middle Ages there was an occasional outbreaking of debate on
these doctrines. But no widespread reviving of the old
conflict came until the Reformation. Laelius and Faustus
Socinus started the antitrinitarian movement known as
Socinianism which spread widely and became especially
strong in Poland. It resulted in seventeenth century England in a revival of the controversy over the doctrine of the
Trinity. Many unitarians were not deists. But all deists
had a unitarian conception of God and were sympathetic
with the unitarians as against the trinitarians.[22] Deism's
spiritual ancestry leads back through unitarianism to
Socinianism and on back to Arianism.

---

[20] COLLINS, *Ground and Reason of the Christian Religion*, p. 173 f.

[21] WOOLSTON, THOMAS, *The Works of Thomas Woolston*. London.
Printed for J. Roberts, 1733; vol. 1, pp. 3–57.

[22] BLOUNT, CHARLES, *Miscellaneous Works of Charles Blount, Esq.*
(Place of publication and publisher not given.) 1695. p. 97 f.

COLLINS, ANTHONY, *A Discourse of Free-Thinking, Occasion'd by the
Growth of a sect call'd Free-Thinkers*. London. (Published anonymously and without name of publisher.) 1713. pp. 62–64.

TINDAL, MATTHEW, *Christianity as Old as the Creation*, p. 75.

5. The Pelagian and Arminian Controversies.

Before the bitter controversies over the doctrines of the Trinity and the person of Christ had subsided in the early church, another series of controversies arose over such doctrines as Grace, Freedom of the Will, Original Sin, Fore-ordination, and that whole group of related doctrines. Pelagius and Augustine were the leading antagonists in the early stage of this series of controversies. As Athanasius had defeated Arius, so now Augustine defeated Pelagius. But as a modified Arianism kept reappearing in later centuries, so did a modified Pelagianism known as semi-Pelagianism. This type of doctrinal controversy also revived in the period of the Reformation. Calvin of Geneva championed the Augustinian views while Arminius, a Dutch theologian, championed semi-Pelagian doctrines. In this controversy, during its later stages, the deists were spiritually affiliated with the Arminian, semi-Pelagian type of thought. They vigorously championed Free-Will and satirically attacked such doctrines as Predestination.[23] Here is another theological root of deism.

It is to be borne in mind that deism not only took up and developed certain types of theological thought of earlier dates, but that it resulted to some degree from disgust with endless theological disputing that seemed fruitful only of persecution and strife. As the new empirical philosophy of Bacon and Locke represented a turning away in disgust from the fruitless argumentation of Scholasticism to a type of philosophic thought and procedure that promised advance and practical utility, so, to a considerable degree, was deism a turning away in disgust from what seemed to the deist a similarly endless and valueless type of theological dispute. However, neither in philosophy nor theology, can a thinker entirely break with the past. In the deists, an illustration is provided of men making use of some of the theological ideas that came from the past while at the same time they are inclined to despise the old theology and its methods as fruitless.

Consideration will next be given to the roots of deism that are to be found in the philosophic thought that preceded the rise of deism. Some of these influences in the

[23] Herbert of Cherbury, Edward Lord, *The Antient Religion of the Gentiles, and Causes of their Errors Considered.* London, John Nutt; 1705. p. 259. This work was first published by Isaac Vossius at Amsterdam in 1663.

Tindal, *Christianity as Old as the Creation*, p. 340.

philosophy of the past that helped to produce eighteenth century deism are found in the works of well-known and famous philosophers. Others are found in the writings of men now almost forgotten. Still others are found in the works of writers more often thought of as literary men than as philosophers but whose works had a philosophic cast. It is likely that this literature with a philosophic vein was often, just because of its literary merit and its wider circle of readers, more influential than more technical works of philosophy.

D. CERTAIN PHILOSOPHICAL WRITINGS.

Though large sections of the works of many of the deists would be more accurately called theology than philosophy, yet deism in its fundamental tenet was a philosophy rather than a theology. Therefore it might be thought that its main source in the past would be found in philosophy rather than in theology. And this is so. Its taproot is in the philosophy of preceding ages. Some elements in it can be traced back to the ancient Greek philosophers Socrates and Plato, Democritus and Leucippus. Deism also drew inspiration and support from the works of a group of literary philosophers, including Cicero, Plutarch and Seneca, who flourished near the beginning of the Christian era. But a more important source of deistic ideas is to be found in the works of a group of writers who sought to perpetuate pagan culture and religion against rapidly spreading Christianity. Of this group, Celsus and Porphyry had probably the greatest influence upon deism and the deists. Had not the Renaissance brought a revival of interest in ancient literature, philosophy and religion, the influence of the more ancient writers might never have reached the deists of the eighteenth century. The Renaissance also helped to supply deists with methods and modes of criticism. Scholasticism, though in many respects at the opposite pole from deism, nevertheless supplied one of the most important philosophical influences that entered into the development of that movement. It had both a negative and a positive influence upon deism which must be examined. Just preceding the rise of English deism, a group of writers arose in France, some of whom should probably be regarded as skeptics and others as deists, who certainly had a great influence upon the beginning of English deism. Finally, there were some English writers who preceded the deists and had considerable influence upon them. These different groups of philosophical writers call for special attention in this study of the influences that produced and moulded English deism.

I. ROOTS IN PRE-CHRISTIAN PHILOSOPHY.

a. *Socrates and Plato.* The English deists went back to Socrates and Plato to find illustration and support for their claims that man, without the help of any supernatural revelation, both could and does know of one supreme God and could attain knowledge of worthy moral principles and ideals. They thus sought to prove that supernatural revelation is unneeded.[24] Collins classed Socrates as one of his free-thinkers.[25] They drew arguments for toleration,[26] one of their favorite themes, from Socrates' reasoning on that subject as recorded by Plato in the *Apology.*

b. *Democritus, Leucippus and Epicurus.* These men were the remote source of arguments advanced by such deists as were materialists. Hobbes was the father of materialism in England.[27] Hobbes was no doubt influenced in favor of materialism by his contact with Gassendi who had reviewed the materialism of Democritus and Leucippus.

c. *Cicero and Plutarch.* The deists often referred to and quoted these two writers and the somewhat later writer Seneca who were all in good favor with them. The deists almost seemed to regard these ancient writers as deists like themselves. They made use of these ancient writers when seeking to construct the positive ethical code which deists called the religion of nature[28] and also when making attacks upon what they called "priestcraft" and "superstition."[29]

2. ROOTS IN ANTI-CHRISTIAN WRITINGS OF THE SECOND, THIRD AND FOURTH CENTURIES.

Most of the arguments advanced against Christianity by deists and others in modern times were anticipated in the

[24] COLLINS, *A Discourse of Free Thinking,* pp. 124–127.
[25] *Ibid.*
[26] *Ibid.*
[27] FARRAR, A. S., *A Critical History of Free Thought in Reference to the Christian Religion.* New York, D. Appleton & Co.; 1882. pp. 118–119.
BOLINGBROKE, *Works,* vol. 3, pp. 72–73, 173 ff.
[28] COLLINS, *A Discourse of Free-Thinking,* p. 148.
HERBERT OF CHERBURY, *The Antient Religion of the Gentiles,* p. 299.
[29] COLLINS, *A Discourse of Free-Thinking,* pp. 111, 131, 135–137, 147–148.
HERBERT OF CHERBURY, *The Antient Religion of the Gentiles,* pp. 297, 299.
Blount and Bolingbroke also showed familiarity with these three ancient authors.

writings of a number of philosophers of the Neo-Platonic
and Epicurean schools who, in the second, third and fourth
centuries of the Christian era, sought to revive and perpetuate pagan culture and philosophy and to stop the spread of
the Christian religion which was rapidly gaining ascendancy
in the Roman world. Among the more famous of the early
philosopher opponents of Christianity were Celsus, Lucian,
Porphyry, Julian, Philostratus and Jamblichus. The fame
of these men in the history of thought rests chiefly upon
their attacks upon Christianity and their efforts to perpetuate paganism. Celsus and Porphyry have been generally
regarded as the most able of these early literary opponents
of Christianity. As will appear later, the deists made more
use of them and of Philostratus than of the others named
above.

If any connection is discovered between this group of
ancient pagan writers on the one hand and the eighteenth
century deists on the other hand, it will be between the
negative element in the work of the ancients and the negative element in the work of the deists. The deists were not
interested in the positive arguments in favor of pre-
Christian Graeco-Roman religion. They were not seeking
the re-establishment of that religion. What they were seeking to establish was a monotheistic religion of nature or of
reason. Nor had the ancients been seeking to establish such
a religion as that the deists were advocating. One must
look elsewhere for the roots of deism as a positive system of
thought. These ancient champions of pagan civilization
made extensive and varied attacks upon the Bible. They
attacked its miracles and prophecies. They attacked its
moral teachings. They attempted to set one part of the
Bible against another part. They were especially hostile to
the Jews and to the Old Testament. They set Christ against
the apostles to the discrediting of the latter. They claimed
Israel's ordinances and institutions were borrowed from
Egypt and were not of divine origin. They sought to weak-
en the evidential value of the miracles of the Bible and
especially of Christ by claiming parallels to them among
non-Christians. They ridiculed the zeal of the early Christians. They made extensive use of the weapons of ridicule
and mockery. Everyone of these modes of attack was used
by the eighteenth century English deists in the negative,
critical part of their works which constituted a very large
part of their writings. Here, if at all, must be found the

evidence of an influence exercised by the group of ancient philosophers now under consideration upon the deists.

Is there evidence that the deists were actually influenced by these ancient writers? Were there only a few points of general similarity between the works of any group of ancient authors and those of some group of modern authors and were there no references in the works of the modern group to indicate acquaintance with the ancient writers, the few points of general similarity might be regarded as accidental. But were the points of similarity much more numerous and much more exact and specific, then, even though references showing direct acquaintance were wanting, a presumption would arise that the later writers were influenced by the earlier ones. This presumption would be weakened if the facts of the situation considered by both the ancient and modern groups of writers were such as to naturally and logically suggest the methods and conclusions in which the similarity appears. But if the facts did not justify either the methods or conclusions of either the ancient or modern groups of writers, then the presumption of influence would be strengthened.[30] The nature of the similarities between the ancient writings of Celsus and Porphyry and the others of that group of writers and the writings of the deists suggest influence even when no direct references are taken into consideration. But the evidence that the deists were influenced by such ancient writers as Porphyry and Celsus is stronger than the above discussion would suggest for there are not only many marked similarities between the criticisms of the Bible and of Christianity made by the ancient writers and those made by the deists but there are also many references[31] in the works of the deists to the older philosophers who made these criticisms. These references indicate acquaintance with the earlier writers and their views, though it is probable that some of them were only known through quotations made by Church

[30] It is easy for the historian to allow a subjective element to influence his reasoning at this point. If he is in agreement with the criticisms of Christianity made by both the deists and the ancient writers he is likely to regard the evidence of influence as weak.

[31] HERBERT OF CHERBURY, *The Antient Religion of the Gentiles*, etc., pp. 69, 299.
COLLINS, *A Discourse of Free-Thinking*, p. 118.
TINDAL, *Christianity as Old as the Creation*, p. 42.
BOLINGBROKE, *Works*, vol. 3, pp. 244, 287, 362, 462.
BLOUNT, *Misc. Works. Great Is Diana of the Ephesians*, p. 37.
BLOUNT, CHARLES, *The Two First Books of Philostratus, Concerning the Life of Apollonius Tyaneus*. London, Nathaniel Thompson; 1680. The entire work.

Fathers who were replying to the criticisms of Christianity that had been advanced. Celsus, Lucian, Porphyry, Julian, Philostratus and Jamblichus are all referred to by one or another of the deists and some of them are often mentioned.[32] Of course the mere fact that an earlier writer is mentioned or quoted by a later one does not in itself prove the latter under any debt to the influence of the former. Such references might be merely casual or even for purposes of criticism and disagreement. However, the references do prove acquaintance with the earlier writer. This fact of acquaintance having been established, if the ideas, attitudes and methods of the author making the quotations or references are much like those of the author quoted or referred to, the inference of influence is justified. This was the case with the deists in relation to the group of philosophers who wrote in opposition to Christianity in the early centuries of the Christian era. The fact that these ancient writers were not the great outstanding names in ancient thought and the additional fact that their chief claim to fame was just the fight which they made against the Bible and Christianity while they were seeking to perpetuate pagan culture tend to strengthen the inference of influence that is drawn from the references to them by the deists.

When making arguments against the Bible and historic Christianity which were restatements of arguments used many centuries earlier by Celsus and Porphyry, the deists usually made no reference to the earlier writers. Their reason for not doing so may have been fear that the mention of these names, long notorious as enemies of the Christian faith, would prejudice readers against the arguments themselves or it may have been a desire to present these arguments as their own clever thought, brought forth because of the brilliant new light of the modern age.

The writings of the deists show more connection with the works of Celsus, Porphyry and Philostratus than with those of Lucian, Julian and Jamblichus, although some reference

---

[32] Herbert of Cherbury, Blount, Collins, Tindal, Woolston, and Annet refer to Celsus, vid. pp. 42–43.

Blount refers to Lucian. vid. *Life of Appollonius Tyaneus*, p. 228. Bolingbroke had much in common with Lucian.

Herbert of Cherbury, Blount, Collins, Bolingbroke, and Annet all make references to Porphyry. vid. p. 44.

Blount translated the work of Philostratus.

Bolingbroke makes reference to Jamblichus. vid. *Works*, vol. 3, p. 462. Herbert of Cherbury and Shaftesbury both refer to Julian. vid. Herbert of Cherbury's *Ancient Religion of the Gentiles*, p. 69. vid. Shaftesbury's *Characteristics*, vol. 2, pp. 210, 212.

is made to all of these. Lucian was a clever mocker and may have influenced the deists to use that style. Jamblichus made use of much the same arguments as Celsus and Porphyry. Deists make but few references to him. Church historians have usually fastened the title "the Apostate" upon the emperor Julian whom they describe as a rather weak and ignoble character.[33] But the deist Shaftesbury thought him worthy of praise.[34] His arguments against Christianity were also much like those of Celsus and Porphyry. Because Celsus and Porphyry were the more important of the ancient group of writers against Christianity and because they were more often referred to by the deists than were Lucian, Julian and Jamblichus, special consideration will be given to their teachings and their connection with deism. Although Philostratus could hardly be ranked as one of the greater enemies of Christianity, his work was an illustration of one of the important methods of opposing Christianity which was used by the ancients and deists alike. The deists also made extensive use of him. Therefore he also calls for special consideration.

a. *Celsus.* Celsus (cir. 150 A. D.) made a many-sided attack upon Christianity. Though his writings themselves have been lost, extensive quotations from them in Origen's refutation of Celsus[35] and some quotations by other church Fathers have made his views fairly well known to interested scholars. He was decidedly anti-Jewish[36] and sought to show that not only the ordinance of circumcision[37] but also that articles of both Hebrew[38] and Christian[39] faith were Egyptian in origin. A common characteristic of the English deists was their anti-Jewish attitude.[40] Likewise, beginning with Herbert of Cherbury, a number of them claimed that those corrupting additions to and modifications of natural religion which are found in the religions of the Old and New

---

[33] SCHAFF, PHILIP, *History of the Christian Church.* New York, Charles Scribner's Sons; 1905. Eighth Edition, vol. 3, p. 43.

[34] *Characteristics*, vol. 2, p. 212.

[35] The views of Celsus are drawn from Origen's extensive quotations from Celsus in his work *Against Celsus*, which is found in vol. 4, pp. 395–669 of the American reprint of the Edinburgh edition of *The Ante-Nicene Fathers*, edited by A. Roberts and J. Donaldson. The American reprint was published in 1885 by The Christian Literature Publishing Company, Buffalo.

[36] *op. cit.*, p. 402.

[37] *op. cit.*, p. 405.

[38] *op. cit.*, p. 467.

[39] *op. cit.*, p. 470.

[40] This was notably true of Blount, Tindal, and Morgan.

Testaments largely originated in Egypt.[41]   Celsus assailed
the book of Genesis, particularly its story of creation and
its account of the fall of man into sin.[42]   Several of the
deists made similar attacks.[43]   He made vigorous attacks
upon both Bible prophecies and miracles.[44]   He spoke particularly against those prophecies usually regarded as referring to Christ.[45]   He scoffed at the story of the virgin
birth of Jesus[46] and opposed the doctrine of the incarnation.[47]   He also gave unfriendly attention to the Bible story
of the resurrection of Jesus, criticising the account of the
rolling away of the stone at the tomb.[48]   Jesus himself was
not exempted from attack.   Celsus called him a "God-hated
sorcerer"[49] and likened his miracles to the tricks of
jugglers.[50]   Celsus criticised the ways of human kind by
writing about bees and their wars.[51]   All of these features
are found in the writings of the seventeenth and eighteenth
century deists.   Collins dealt most with the prophecies.[52]
Nearly all deists made criticisms of Bible miracles.   Thomas
Woolston's extensive writings[53] against particular Bible
miracles attracted wide attention.   Like Celsus, Collins[54]
and Woolston[55] and Peter Annet[56] made special attacks
upon those Bible miracles associated with the birth and
resurrection of Christ.   In Mandeville's *Fable of the Bees*,[57]

41) HERBERT OF CHERBURY, *The Antient Religion of the Gentiles*, p. 13,
BLOUNT, *Miscel. Works*, p. 134. TINDAL, *Christianity as Old as the
Creation*, chaps. 8, 9.
42) *Ante-Nicene Fathers*, vol. 4. *Origen Against Celsus*, pp. 404, 511,
515.
43) BLOUNT, CHARLES, *Miscel. Works*. *Great is Diana of the Ephesians*, pp. 25, 53. BOLINGBROKE, *Works*, vol. 3, p. 20.
44) *Ante-Nicene Fathers*. Origen *Against Celsus*, vol. 4, pp. 566,
611 ff.
45) *loc. cit.*
46) *op. cit.*, p. 413, pp. 499–502.
47) *loc. cit.*
48) *op. cit.*, p. 566.
49) *op. cit.*, p. 428.
50) *op. cit.*, p. 427.
51) *op. cit.*, p. 533.
52) COLLINS, *Ground and Reason of the Christian Religion*, p. 27 ff.
53) WOOLSTON, THOMAS, *The Works of Thomas Woolston*. London.
Printed for J. Roberts; 1733. 5 vols. Vols. 1 and 2 are mostly on miracles.
54) COLLINS, *Ground and Reason of the Christian Religion*, p. 130 ff.
55) WOOLSTON, *op. cit.*, vol. 1.
56) ANNET, PETER, *The Resurrection of Jesus Considered; In Answer
to the Tryal of the Witnesses*. London. Printed for the Author (Anonymous) ; 1744.
57) MANDEVILLE, BERNARD DE, *The Fable of the Bees; or, Private Vices
Public Benefits*. London, Allen & West. Edinburgh, J. Mundell & Co.,
1795. *The Grumbling Hive, or Knaves Turned Honest*, which constitutes the most important part of this work, was written about 1706.

there is a revival of Celsus' use of bee-life in criticising human religion and morals. This usage of bee-fable can hardly be thought an accidental coincidence. Unlike Celsus, most of the deists spoke highly of Jesus and blamed apostles and later priests for corrupting his teachings. But some deists, such as Annet,[58] Woolston[59] and Bolingbroke,[60] were like Celsus in that they spoke ill of Jesus himself.

Though, in the absence of specific references to Celsus in the discussions by the deists of some of these points of likeness, it cannot be proved beyond question that the deists were influenced by Celsus, yet the fact of the number of such similarities together with the ample evidence that the deists were acquainted with Celsus and that they were familiar with the works of the Church Fathers in whose works Celsus is extensively quoted,[61] make the likelihood that they were influenced by the ancient writer great. Herbert of Cherbury,[62] Charles Blount,[63] Anthony Collins,[64] Matthew Tindal,[65] Thomas Woolston[66] and Peter Annet[67] refer to Celsus. Woolston specifically refers, while arguing against the resurrection of Jesus, to Celsus arguments on the same subjects. He maintains that Celsus' arguments have never been answered.[68] This specific reference adds to the evidence of influence shown by general likeness of arguments.

b. *Porphyry*. Porphyry (233-304) was evidently regarded by ancient Christians as one of the most prominent and dangerous of the enemies of Christianity for Apollinarius, Eusebius and Methodius sought at length to refute him.[69] Modern church historians have the same opinion of him. One such historian writes of Porphyry's work that it was "the most important weapon devised by the ancients against

[58] *The Resurrection of Jesus*, p. 15.
[59] *Works*, vol. 1. *Sixth Disc. on Miracles*, p. 6.
[60] *Works*, vol. 3, p. 381.
[61] It is to be borne in mind that it was in the works of the oft-quoted Church Fathers that the deists had access to Celsus.
[62] *The Antient Religion of the Gentiles*, p. 279.
[63] *Life of Apollonius Tyaneus*, p. 5.
[64] *Ground and Reason of the Christian Religion*, pp. ILV, 27.
[65] *Christianity as Old as the Creation*, pp. 42, 331.
[66] *Works*, vol. 1. *Sixth Disc. on Miracles*, p. 24.
[67] *The Resurrection of Jesus*, p. 8.
[68] *Works*, vol. 1. *Sixth Disc. on Miracles*, p. 24.
[69] *Nicene and Post-Nicene Fathers of the Christian Church*. New York, The Christian Literature Company; 1890. Second Edition, vol. 3, pp. 378, 381.

Christianity."[70]   Ancients and Moderns agree in regarding
Porphyry as one of the ablest of those who have opposed
Christianity. Though he made use of many of the same
lines of argument as Celsus, he presented them more skillfully.

As in the case of Celsus, so also in the case of Porphyry,
the inference that the deists were influenced by him is based
on the evidence that they were familiar with him because
of their references to him and the fact that they used arguments similar to those used by him.

Although Porphyry's large fifteen volume work in which
he attacked Christianity was destroyed by a zealous emper-
or, many of its arguments and many extensive quotations
from it survive in the writings of the fathers. It was from
these and from later quotations from them that the deists
gained their acquaintance with Porphyry's ideas.

The main method of attack used by Porphyry was to set
one part of the Scriptures against another part and one Bible
character against another Bible character. Thus he set the
New Testament against the Old to the discredit of the latter.
He sought to discredit the authority of both Peter and Paul
by setting them against each other.[71]   Peter, he accused of
lies and fraud. He sought to draw a distinction between the
teachings of Jesus and the apostles to the discredit of the
latter. He usually pictured Jesus as a good man, but merely a man, and one guilty of inconsistency.[72]

The deists made extensive use of just this method of
attack upon the Scriptures and historic Christianity, and
there is reason to believe that Porphyry influenced them to
do so. References to Porphyry in the writings of leading
deists are numerous. Among the deists who made direct
reference to Porphyry were[73] Herbert of Cherbury, Charles
Blount, Anthony Collins, Lord Bolingbroke and Peter Annet.

d. *Philostratus.* An extensive effort to discover and to
present parallels from heathen story and mythology to Bible
stories and especially to events in the life of Christ was one
of the common methods used by the early opponents of

---

[70] DUCHESNE, MONSIGNOR LOUIS, *Early History of the Christian
Church.* New York, Longman Green & Company; 1909. Translation
of Fourth Edition, vol. 1, p. 402; cf. p. 403.
[71] *Nicene and Post-Nicene Fathers,* etc., vol. 6, p. 497.
[72] HARNACK, ADOLF, *Die Mission u. Ausbreitung des Christentums in
den ersten Drei Jahrhunderten.* Leipzig, J. C. Hinrichs'sche Buchhandlung; 1902. s. 352.
[73] CHERBURY, *The Antient Rel.,* etc., p. 69. BLOUNT, *Life of Apollonius,* p. 5. COLLINS, *Ground and Reason,* etc., pp. 173–174. BOLING-
BROKE, *Works,* vol. 3, p. 462. ANNET, *The Res. of Jesus Considered,* p. 8.

Christianity in opposing the claims of that faith. One of the most famous of these parallels of which they made use was the story of Apollonius of Tyana. Julia Domna, wife of Septimius Severus and a zealous opponent of Christianity, requested the rhetorician Philostratus (217 A. D.) to write a life of the Pythagorean Apollonius.[74] This he did. Though Philostratus did not mention Christ in his story, the many parallels to events in the life of Christ which are found in his story of the semi-legendary Apollonius together with the circumstances of the writing of the book, caused the belief that the author intended his work to be a check to the spreading faith in Christ. It is certain that later opponents of Christianity took this story of Apollonius and used it against Christianity.[75]

Charles Blount, one of the early English deists, translated two books of Philostratus' life of Apollonius into English and added copious deistic notes of his own.[76] Other deists whether getting their material directly from the ancient author or, which is more likely, from Blount, made use of this story in arguing against commonly accepted historical Christianity.[77]

3. ROOTS IN ITALIAN AND FRENCH WRITINGS OF THE PERIOD OF THE RENAISSANCE AND REFORMATION.

For nine centuries after the death of Julian and the triumph of Christianity over paganism in the Roman empire there is little evidence of the existence of any philosophical thought that could be regarded as a root of deism. Such thought of this period as had any kinship with deism was theological, of the Arian and Semi-Pelagian types, rather than philosophical. The Renaissance, with its revival of classical studies, brought also a revival of interest in ancient philosophy. It brought also a partial revival of paganism and led some gifted writers to take a free-thinking attitude in matters of religion.

Through Averroes, a modified Aristotelianism came from Moorish Spain into Italy and became influential at the universities of Bologna and Padua. As O'Leary has pointed

---

[74] UHLHORN, G., *The Conflict of Christianity with Heathenism.* New York, Charles Scribner's Sons; 1879. pp. 278, 279. Translated, with the author's sanction, from the 3rd German Edition by E. C. Smyth and C. J. H. Roper.

[75] SCHAFF, PHILIP, *op. cit.*, vol. 2, pp. 99, 100, 103.

[76] cf. below, p. 110.   !

[77] TINDAL, *Christianity as Old*, etc., p. 170. BOLINGBROKE, *Works*, vol. 3, p. 382. WOOLSTON, THOMAS, *Works*, vol. 1, p. 51.

out,[78] this was a precursor of the rationalism and anti-church feeling of the Renaissance. Dante, who was himself not unfamiliar with this type of thought, complained, in the tenth canto of his Inferno, that already as early as his day many did not believe in a future life.

The Renaissance began about the beginning of the four-teenth century and continued into the period of the Refor-mation. Since it developed somewhat earlier in Italy than in France, fewer of the Italian Renaissance writers were in-fluenced by the bitter controversies of the Reformation than was the case among the French writers. The French writers showed less enthusiasm for the ancient classical culture and less of a tendency to revive pagan religion than did the Italians. On the other hand, the French showed more of a tendency to skepticism. This skeptical[79] trend is seen in the works of such men as Montaigne (1533-1592), Sanchez (1552-1632) and Le Vayer (1588-1672). Some of the later French writers such as Jean Bodin (1530-1596) and Pierre Charron (1541-1603) were deistic in their viewpoints. Bona-venture Des Perriers used the weapon of mockery[80] against Christianity and the Bible in his book *Cymbalum Mundi*[81] which was published in 1537. In doing this he anticipated Shaftesbury and Voltaire. Instead of the tendency noted above on the part of early Italian Renaissance writers to revert to the religion of classical Greece and Rome, the later French Renaissance writers manifested an inclination to set up a religion of nature or reason. John Owen puts Sanchez among those who emphasized the place of reason rather than of revelation in religion.[82] Lechler and Noack show that Jean Bodin went still further toward rejecting revela-tion and setting up a religion of nature.[83] Pierre Charron

78) O'Leary, De Lacy, *Arabic Thought and Its Place in History.* Lon-don, Kegan Paul, Trench, Trubner & Co., Ltd.; 1922. New York, E. P. Dutton & Co.; 1922. pp. 290–291.
79) Flint, Robert, *Agnosticism.* New York, Charles Scribner's Sons, 1903. pp. 119–122, 125–129.
80) Earlier writers such as Petrarch (1304–1374), Boccaccio (1317–1375), Pulci (1432–1484), and Rabelais (1495–1553), had used wit and mockery against what they considered the unworthy element in the clergy and in the Roman Catholic Religion of their day.
81) Perriers, Bonaventure Des, *Cymbalum Mundi, ou Dialogues Sa-tyriques Sur differens Sujects.* Amsterdam, Prosper Marchaud; 1537. pp. 77, 125 ff.
82) Owen, John, *The Skeptics of the French Renaissance.* London, Swan Sonnenschein & Co. New York, Macmillan Co.; 1893. p. 639.
83) Noack, Lucius, *Die Freidenker in der Religion, oder die Repraesenten der religioesen Aufklaerung in England, Frankreich un Deutsch-land.* Bern, Jent u. Reinert; 1853–1855. 3 Baende, bd. 2, s. 7 ff. Cf. Lechler, G. V., *Geschichte Des Englischen Deismus.* Stuttgart u. Tue-bingen, J. G. Cotta'scher Verlag; 1841. s. 31.

rejected the authority of revelation and held to natural religion.[84) Thus the drift toward deism manifested itself.

A revival of interest in and acquaintance with ancient philosophers and classical writers, the development of free-thinking tendencies in matters of religion, the growth of an attitude unfriendly toward church and clergy and, to a less degree, toward the Bible, a growing emphasis upon the function of reason in religion with a lessening emphasis upon revelation, and the development of a method of attacking with wit and satire and raillery, were general features of the philosophical writings of the Renaissance and Reformation periods. Each of these features of the Renaissance had a marked influence upon the rise or character of deism. The English deists were very fond of quoting such ancient writers as Plutarch, Cicero and Seneca. Cicero was a favorite of Petrarch. Montaigne, who was often quoted by the English deists, was himself fond of quoting Plutarch, Cicero and Seneca.[85) Thus the thought and influence of the ancients was brought to bear upon the deists through the medium of Renaissance writers. Though this did not in itself constitute a thought-contribution to deism on the part of Renaissance writers, it did mediate such a contribution. The use of raillery and mockery by these older writers also did not constitute a thought-contribution but only a suggestion as to method, a suggestion acted upon by such English deists as Shaftesbury and Bolingbroke and finding its highest development in the French deist Voltaire who was supreme master of the art of mockery. Shaftesbury almost created a philosophy of ridicule, making the ability to stand ridicule one of the highest tests of truth.[86) While doing this he indicated his acquaintance with the Italian users of this weapon by saying that Italians are the greatest buffoons because under the greatest slavery.[87) The growing trend toward free-thinking, the giving of increasing value to natural religion and to reason and of lessening value to revealed religion and to revelation and the development of an increasingly hostile attitude toward the church and

---

[84) CHARRON, PIERRE, *Of Wisdome.* (Place and pub. not given.) Trans. by Sampson Lennard; 1601.
[85) MONTAIGNE, MICHEL DE, *The Essays of Montaigne.* New York, A. L. Burt Co. (date not given). Trans. by Charles Cotton. Edited by W. Carew Hazlitt. Two vols.; vol. 2, pp. 627, 642, 645. Cf. BLOUNT, *Miscel. Works,* p. 41. Cf. also BLOUNT, *Life of Apollonius,* pp. 20, 128.
[86) Shaftesbury published an *Essay on the Freedom of Wit and Humor* in 1709 which was translated into French before 1713. Cf. *Characteristics,* vol. 1, p. 44.
[87) *Characteristics,* vol. 1, p. 51.

clergy, had a more direct connection with the thought-content of deism.

In addition to these influences that came from the Renaissance writings in general, there were specific influences from particular writers of the period under consideration that call for some notice. Petrarch fought the superstition and dogma and philosophy of medievalism. Boccaccio, in his story of the *Three Rings*,[88] hinted strongly that Judaism, Christianity and Mohammedanism had an equal claim to be from God, if indeed any of them had a just claim to be so. This line of argument was used by several deists and then the story of the *Three Rings* itself was used by the German deist Lessing as the basis for his famous story, *Nathan der Weise.* Pomponazzi (1462-1525) sought to explain away miracles and denied the immortality of the soul. The English deist Charles Blount directly referred to Pomponazzi's teaching about the soul.[89] An effort to get rid of the miraculous was characteristic of the writings of nearly all deists while the so-called "mortal deists" rejected the doctrine of the immortality of the soul. Machiavelli (1469-1527), in his famous work in political philosophy, *The Prince,* put religion on a low plane by making it primarily a political tool to be used by princes.[90] With the exception of Hobbes whose teaching about religion and its use by sovereigns[91] was very like that of Machiavelli, most English deists would reject this political conception of religion and would condemn the use of it as a tool for rulers. But they generally held that it had often been so used in the past and had been developed into its corrupted state by such usage.[92] La Mothe Le Vayer (1586-1672) wrote on *The Virtue of the Heathen.* He was an advocate of religious toleration and a champion of moral as against ecclesiastical and ritualistic Christianity. Each of these ideas had a prominent place in deism. By finding evidence of virtue among the heathen in such men as Socrates, deists sought to show that no need for revelation existed. All of them with the exception of Hobbes, advocated toleration. A characteristic feature of deism was the repudiation of ritualistic Christianity and an

88) BOCCACCIO, GIOVANNI, *The Decameron or Ten Days' Entertainment of Boccaccio.* New York, Albert and Charles Boni; 1925. Fine Paper Edition, pp. 16–18.
89) BLOUNT, *Miscel. Works. The Oracles of Reason,* p. 127.
90) MACHIAVELLI, NICOLO, *The Prince.* London, George Routledge & Sons, Ltd. New York, E. P. Dutton & Co.; 1883. pp. 110–112.
91) HOBBES, *Works,* vol. 3, *Leviathan,* p. 99.
92) BLOUNT, *Miscel. Works. Oracles of Reason,* Preface. cf. BLOUNT, *Miscel. Works. Great Is Diana of the Ephesians,* p. 7.

advocating of ethical religion in its stead. L. Vanini (1585-1619), an Italian who labored and was martyred in Toulouse, France, was the champion of a naturalistic conception of religion not greatly different from that of deism. G. Bruno (1548-1600), the more famous and influential philosopher who died a martyr to his philosophic faith, was more a pantheist than a deist. He was under the influence of the early scientific movement, being one of those who accepted the Copernican Theory. In theology, he rejected the doctrine of the Incarnation,[93] as did the deists of later date.

Pierre Charron was the most prominent French writer of the period who can be classed without hesitation as a deist. Others like Montaigne often differed from the deists in some important respect, so that, though they had much in common with deism and helped to shape and develop some thought elements in that movement, they could not be classed as deists. Jean Bodin advocated natural religion and, in a work entitled *Seven Addresses on the Things of Hidden Mystery*, strongly hinted doubt of the truth of any particular religion because there are so many particular religions the priests of each of which speak ill of the priests of other religions. But, though Bodin is no doubt correctly classed as one of the early French deists, there is not much evidence of direct influence being exerted by him upon English deists. Early English deists such as Herbert of Cherbury and Thomas Hobbes spent some time in France and it is likely they were influenced by such a writer as Bodin even though direct quotations are lacking to establish such influence. It is known from the Swiss theologian Viret's *Instruction Chretienne*, which was published in 1563, that at that early date there were already in the French speaking world many who called themselves "deists." Viret's description of the teachings and attitudes of these men makes it plain that they were truly "deists." They claim to believe in God but have no regard to Jesus Christ. They consider the doctrines of the apostles and evangelists to be fables and dreams. They laugh at religion. They say God does not concern himself in the government of human affairs. They are zealous in propagating their views. Such descriptive terms might well have been used of many eighteenth century English deists. Bodin evidently belonged to French thinkers of this type. Charron's book, *De la Sagasse,* or *Of Wisdom,* published in 1601, leaves no doubt that he is to be classed as a deist. The many ref-

---

93) vid. UEBERWEG, *Geschichte der Philosophie,* 3 bd., s. 35 ff.

erences to him and quotations from him in the works of the
English deists[94] give ample evidence of his influence with
them. He made morality more fundamental than religion
and not derived from it.[95] His disbelief in the great historical religions, Judaism, Christianity and Mohammedanism, is
indicated in his making all of them a product of the climate
of Arabia,[96] in his criticism of their conception of God as too
despotic and in his statement that all of them,[97] to gain credit
for themselves, claimed prophets, miracles, revelations and
mysteries.[98] In the way these teachings are put Charron
leaves the impression that, though he believes in God, he regards these claims and the religions that made them as im-
postures.[99] Elsewhere, he directly asserted his own belief
in God.[100] Like later deists, he rejected the doctrine of
sacrifice.[101]

The similarity of Charron's views to those of the English
deists, together with their frequent references[102] to him, indicates the very considerable influence he had upon the development of English deism. His criticism of the God of the
particular religions as being too despotic, his opposition to
sacrifice, miracles and a religion with rites and ceremonies,
his emphasis upon the ethical as against the ritual side of
religion and his sharp distinction between superstition and
religion and his insinuation that much of historical Christianity was the former, are all elements in his work that ally
him with the English deists who wrote about a century later.

Thus the philosophical thought that began with the mild
free-thinking tendency of the earlier Renaissance writers
gradually changed under the influence of revived classical
writings, of Reformation disputes and wars and of the early
advances in modern science which had opened up a new geographic world and was beginning to open up a new world of

---

94) Tindal, *Christianity as Old as the Creation*, pp. 53–54. Bolingbroke, *Works*, vol. 3, p. 396.
95) Charron, *Of Wisdom*, Preface. cf. Owen, *Skeptics of the French
Renaissance*, pp. 562–598. Bury, J. B., *A History of Freedom of
Thought.* New York, H. Holt & Co.; 1913. p. 75.
96) Charron, *Of Wisdom*, p. 258.
97) *loc. cit.*
98) *loc. cit.*
99) *loc. cit.*
100) This was in a lesser work entitled *Trois Verites contre tous athees,
idolatres, juifs, mahometans, heretiques et schismatiques.* Cf. Owen,
Skeptics of the French Renaissance, p. 571.
101) Charron, *Of Wisdom*, p. 259.
102) Tindal, *Christianity as Old as the Creation*, pp. 53–54.
Bolingbroke, *Works*, vol. 3, p. 396.

thought. At the end of the sixteenth century there had developed a decided trend toward skepticism and deism in religious thought.

4. ROOTS IN SCHOLASTICISM.

An important root of deism, strange though it may seem in the light of the dislike of deists for both the ideas and the methods of the schoolmen, leads back into the Scholastic philosophy of the medieval period. The deists disliked the way in which the schoolmen made reason and philosophy subservient to theology. They disliked the decidedly speculative, impractical and other-worldly character of much of scholastic thought. A few of the schoolmen, of whom Abelard (1079-1142) was perhaps the most notable example, had free-thinking elements in their thinking. But the general disfavor in which the schoolmen were held by the deists probably caused even these to have little direct influence upon any of the deists. However, these more liberal schoolmen contributed to that general liberal type of thought of which deism was a particular form of expression. This was not, however, the main contribution of scholasticism to deism. The main contribution was the conception of God which scholastic speculations about God as the absolute had made the common possession of practically all thinkers. The deists seem to have accepted without question and without any consciousness that they had received it from the despised schoolmen the scholastic conception of God.

Assuming this conception of God as the Absolute, the omniscient, omnipotent, infinitely just and unchanging Creator, the deists reasoned to those conclusions that constituted the characteristic deistic position. Probably they modified the scholastic idea of God somewhat in the direction of thinking of him as a mechanic, the perfect maker of a machine. This modification undoubtedly came from the youthful modern scientific movement. With the conception of God handed down by scholasticism and slightly modified by scientific influences as the main premise of their reasoning deists reasoned somewhat as follows, although the steps were not always clearly supplied. If a poor mechanic were making a machine, let us say a watch, then he could only make one that would run a little time without interference in the way of winding or repair by the maker. If a much better mechanic were making the watch, he would make it so it would run much longer without needing any attention by its maker.

But if the maker were a perfect mechanic, he would make it
so that it would run permanently without interference or attention. The deists put the world in the place here given to
the watch and argued that God, being a perfect Creator infinite in wisdom and infinite in power, would not create a world
so imperfect that it would require any interference of its
Creator in the form of miracles, supernatural revelation or
any other form of interference. They thought that to suggest any need of supernaturalistic interference was in effect
to charge the Creator with lack of power or lack of wisdom
or lack of omniscience and thus was dishonoring to God.[103]
In like manner they reasoned that any modification or change
of the way of blessedness or salvation for men, such modification as they thought the Bible and current Christianity both
taught, would be inconsistent with the omniscience and unchanging nature of God.[104] Still more frequently they argued
against revelation and against the idea of a "chosen people"
as inconsistent with the perfect justice of God. To them the
idea of a "chosen people" implied a partiality that would be
incompatible with justice.[105] In the spirit of Pelagian theology, they insisted that before men could be judged and rewarded or punished justly they must know the way of salvation.[106] Since they did not deny that all men are judged, this
involved the claim that all men do know the way of salvation.
But no special revelation is or, in the nature of the case, can
be known to all men.[107] Therefore they concluded that revelation cannot be necessary to a knowledge of the way of
salvation.[108] Two ways appeared to them by which all men
might have the knowledge necessary to salvation. One would
be for every man to have an innate possession of those principles which, if followed, would lead to reward and happiness. This was the way chosen by Herbert of Cherbury.[109]
But Locke's attack on innate ideas caused later deists to give
up that way and to put in its stead the statement that God

---

103) HERBERT OF CHERBURY, *The Antient Religion of the Gentiles*, pp.
2, 261.
   CHUBB, THOMAS, *The Posthumus Works of Mr. Thomas Chubb.* London, R. Baldwin; 1748. Two Vols., vol. 1, p. 9.
   104) TINDAL, *Christianity as Old as the Creation*, pp. 1–4.
   105) *op. cit.*, p. 173. cf. p. 363.
   COLLINS, *A Discourse of Free-Thinking*, p. 38.
   106) HERBERT OF CHERBURY, *The Religion of the Gentiles*, pp. 5, 6.
cf. BLOUNT, *Miscel. Works. Oracles of Reason*, p. 198.
   107) BLOUNT, *loc. cit.*
   108) BLOUNT, *loc. cit.*
   109) HERBERT, EDUARD, BARON DE CHERBURY EN ANGLETERRE, *De la
Verité, etc.* (pub. and place not given). 3 Edit., 1639, pp. 11, 80.

had given every man reason and the ability by the use of that reason to know the things he should do if he would be acceptable to God.[110]   In both cases, the concept of the justice of God is at the basis of the reasoning.   Undoubtedly the acquaintance with such ancients as Socrates, Plutarch, Cicero and Seneca which the deists had been brought to know through the influence of the Renaissance and the knowledge of the existence of many races which had not had the Scriptures, races of which the deists had learned as a result of the new modern knowledge of geography, had made more acute this problem of the justice of making salvation depend upon having the Bible.   Thus at this point the scholastic conception of God and the influence of the Renaissance and of modern exploration and discoveries worked together to produce the deistic type of reasoning.   It was also arguments derived from their conception of God that the deists used to justify their repudiation of particular elements in the Bible.   Thus Tindal argued against some Scriptures because they seemed to present God as cruel[111] others because they seemed to imply God to be changeable,[112] others because not as clear as a message from God would naturally be expected to be.[113]   Indeed it was by arguments based on their conception of God that deists ruled out all need for revelation[114] and made it appear that anything given in any claimed special revelation that was not simply a republication of the principles of that natural religion given at the creation was both unnecessary[115] and an imposture.[116]   A main line of argument used by deists against ritualistic and ceremonical religion, against revelation, miracles, prophecies and against the doctrine of salvation through Christ, was that these are inconsistent with their conception of God.   Matthew Tindal was the writer among the deists who made most extensive use of this type of argument from the nature of God and his book was known as "the bible of deism."   But the same line of reasoning crops out openly or is implied in the writings of all the deists.[117]   It will appear more fully in the detailed study of

[110] TINDAL, *Christianity as Old as the Creation*, p. 7.
[111] *Christianity as Old as the Creation*, pp. 237–245, 363.
[112] *op. cit.*, pp. 27, 51, 59, 115.
[113] *op. cit.*, pp. 23, 92.
[114] *op. cit.*, pp. 17, 49–54.
[115] *op. cit.*, pp. 49–54, 59.
[116] *op. cit.*, pp. 115, 123.
[117] COLLINS, *A Discourse of Free-Thinking*, pp. 37, 38.
CHUBB, *Posthumus Works*, vol. 1, pp. 98, 99.
BLOUNT, *Miscel. Works. Oracles of Reason*, p. 88 ff.

each of the deists. Here notice is simply taken of the fact
that the starting point of this line of reasoning was in the
conception of God supplied by the schoolmen. Thus scholasticism, in spite of the fact that deists were hostile to its general spirit and aim, furnished the main root of the doctrine
which was the distinctive characteristic of deism and the
idea of God which was the basis on which rested many of the
negative arguments of deism as well.

5. ROOTS IN ENGLISH THOUGHT PRIOR TO THE RISE OF
DEISM IN ENGLAND.

Naturally English deism roots back into earlier English
thought. English thinking has always had a leaning toward
the practical, toward the empirical and also toward an agnostic or skeptical attitude. These tendencies were apparent
even back in the days of scholasticism. William of Occam
had little in common with later deists except an anti-clerical
attitude. Roger Bacon opposed appealing to authority and
favored more empirical and scientific methods.[118] This
tended to prepare the way for these attitudes among the
deists. Wycliffe, though by no means a deist, favored less of
mystery and more of reason, less of the speculative and more
of the practical, than was found in the current religion and
theology of his day. These attitudes in more extreme form
reappeared in the deists. Nearer to the time of the deists and
undoubtedly having greater influence with them was the
famous statesman, philosopher and scientist, Francis Bacon
(1561-1626).

Bacon, both in his *Essays* and in his *Novum Organum,*
gave marked evidence of the three characteristic trends of
English thought. His attitude was strongly unfriendly to deductive logic and the spirit and methods of the schoolmen.
He was opposed to traditionalism and authority. He urged
scientific method, though the details of method he suggested
were too cumbersome to become the methods actually used
by later scientists. His insistence on the separation of theology from philosophy prepared the way for the complaints of
the deists against earlier theologians that they mixed too
much philosophy with their theology.[119] Bacon's study of
the common forms of error in human reasoning, errors
which he named "idols," and the examples which he gave of

---

118) BACON, ROGER, *Opus Major*. London, S. Jebb (Editor), 1733.
119) TOLAND, JOHN, *Christianity Not Mysterious*, etc. London, (publisher not given), 1702. p. 154.

them, served the deists in their attacks upon orthodox leaders. Collins claimed Bacon as one of his "Free-Thinkers."[120]   But Collins is notorious for claiming all original thinkers as "free-thinkers" and then shrewdly using that term to denote a particular brand of deistic liberalism on the subject of religion.[121]   There is no evidence that Bacon was a deist or other than a fairly orthodox Christian. But at all the points noted above he influenced the deists. He had a considerable influence upon Hobbes, who was a deist, though not a typical one, and upon Locke, who was not a deist but a writer who had very great influence with the deists. His greatest influence upon deism was probably that mediated through these two later writers.

Reginald Peacock, a somewhat earlier writer (cir. 1450), asserted the authority of reason against that of the Bible and so was a forerunner of the deist position on the question of authority. Robertson and Lechler probably ascribe too much importance and influence to Peacock[122] as the deists give little evidence of having read or of having been influenced by him.

Conclusion.

In the above study of the things that operated to produce and mould eighteenth century English deism, it has been made evident that the influences that helped to produce and shape that thought-movement were many and reached far back into the past. Without any of these main lines of influence, deism would not have arisen in just the form it did take. Ancient philosophy, ancient arguments against Christianity, direct and indirect Mohammedan influences, the influence of the Renaissance, the conception of God handed down by the schoolmen, the influence of the new discoveries and inventions, the early development of modern science, the theological controversies and wars, all were at work to produce the deistic movement. In-so-far as deism was a negative destructive criticism of the Bible and of historic Christianity it was evidently greatly influenced by such ancient writers as Celsus, Porphyry and Philostratus. In-so-far as it was a hostile movement against contemporary forms of Christianity it

120) COLLINS, *A Discourse of Free-Thinking*, p. 169.
121) BENTLEY, RICHARD, "Phileleutherus Lipsiensis," *Remarks upon Late Discourse of Free-Thinking*, London, (pub. not given), 1737. pp. 67, 71.
122) ROBERTSON, *A Short History of Freethought Ancient and Modern*, p. 238.
LECHLER, *Geschichte Des Englischen Deismus*, s. 15.

was undoubtedly influenced by and developed as a reaction
against actual abuses that were evident in the religion of the
day such as over-emphasis upon the doctrinal and ritualistic
as against the practical and ethical elements of religion. As
a thought movement opposed to supernaturalism, deism was
probably most influenced by the conception of God which had
largely come to the deists from Scholasticism but which had
been modified in the direction of making God a master mechanic by the influence of the new scientific movement. Most
deists did not seem to doubt or question a supernatural creation of the world by God. But they argued from the various attributes of the Creator against any supernaturalistic interference with the laws given at the creation. The new
scientific movement was beginning to make men more deeply
impressed with the idea of the uniformity of nature. This
strengthened the attitude of opposition to any supernaturalistic interference with the operation of the laws of nature. It
would probably be correct to say that the chief root of the
doctrine that formed the main and distinctive characteristic
of deism came from the deists' conception of God and that
their conception of God was derived partly from historical
Christianity, partly from the teachings of the new scientific
movement, but chiefly from scholastic theological philosophy.

PART II

ENGLISH DEISM

CHAPTER III

THE RISE OF ENGLISH DEISM
(1624-1695)

IT has been sufficiently shown that deism did not appear
in seventeenth century England as an entirely new
system of thought with no roots in the past. Many deistic
ideas, attitudes and methods had a history leading back into
the remote past. It has been found that it had affinity with
some teachings as early as the philosophers of ancient
Greece. Much of its negative element was a restatement of
the anti-Christian arguments of Celsus and Porphyry. In
important respects it had a close relation to the Arian and
Pelagian doctrines, especially in their late Reformation
forms as Socinianism, antitrinitarianism and Arminianism.
Several of its principles and something of its method can be
discovered in the Renaissance authors of Italy and France.
In a negative way, the disputes, schisms and wars of the
Reformation prepared for its appearance. The counter-
accusations of clergy of different sects provided ammunition
for its anti-clerical campaign. The Reformation itself, by
its rejection of much of the formalism, ritualism and mystery of the Roman Catholic Church, by its teaching that, in
matters of religion, each individual should use his own
reason and by its putting greater stress on the ethical element in religion, was a movement in the same direction as
deism although it did not go so far. The new inventions
and discoveries and the new advance in science tended to
discredit the old authority and to produce a spirit of theological rationalism. This rationalism expressed itself in
varying degrees of theological liberalism and in such attitudes as are denoted by the terms "skepticism," "deism"
and "atheism." Deism, which Viret has shown[1] to have
existed as early as 1563, grew to be an important element in
the thought of the seventeenth century and the dominant
form of theological liberalism in England during the first
half of the eighteenth century.

While there were a few writers before Herbert of Cherbury, such as Bodin and Charron in France and Peacock in
England, who sufficiently combined both the positive and
negative ideas characteristic of deism to deserve the name
"deists," most of the early evidence of deistic tendencies has

---

[1] above, p. 13.

to do with its negative aspects only. Anti-clericalism and anti-supernaturalism were common enough. The setting forth of a positive natural religion was more rare. Though Herbert of Cherbury was not the first to hold many of the opinions characteristic of deism, yet, because he combined so many of the characteristic ideas, attitudes and methods of deism in his writings and because he exercised so great an influence upon the later and greater development of the movement, he well deserved the title[2] "Father of English deism" which was early given and generally conceded to him.

The history of English deism can be advantageously divided for study into three periods: (*a*) the rise of English deism; (*b*) the flourishing period of English deism; (*c*) the decline of English deism.

The first period, which is the subject of this chapter, may be regarded as having begun with the publication in 1624 of Lord Herbert of Cherbury's famous book, *De Veritate*. Though written in Latin and first published in Paris, France, this book, which was the first important deistic book written by an Englishman and the most important deistic book by any author that had yet appeared, had great influence upon the later deism of England. The period may be regarded as closing with the publication in the year 1695 of the completed works of Charles Blount. Herbert and Blount were the two writers of the period whose classification as deists is unquestioned. Thomas Hobbes, whose *Leviathan* appeared in 1651, should probably also be classed as a deist, though the correctness of such classification is subject to dispute. Thomas Browne, Archbishop John Tillotson and John Locke were three other English writers of the period whose works contained deistic elements and had an important influence upon the development of deism although these men were not themselves deists. Their dates require that they be given consideration in this chapter although their influence was undoubtedly greater upon the writers of the second period of the English deistic movement. So great was the influence of Locke upon the whole movement, in spite of the fact that he himself was not a deist, that deism might with much justfiication be divided into Pre-Lockian and Post-Lockian deism. Such a division would practically coincide with the point of division between the first and second periods as here given. The whole period can best be studied by examining the works and in-

---

[2] LELAND, *A View of the Principal Deistical Writers*, vol. 1, p. 3.

fluence of Herbert of Cherbury, Thomas Browne, John Tillotson, Thomas Hobbes, John Locke and Charles Blount.

A. HERBERT OF CHERBURY

Edward Lord Herbert of Cherbury (1583-1648) famous as "The Father of English Deism," assumed during the course of his life history several very different roles. As a soldier adventurer upon the continent, he was involved in many escapades characteristic of that type of life.[3] As a diplomat representing England at the French Court, he was knighted for able service.[4] As a philosopher, he gained a very considerable reputation and influence.[5] He wrote an *Autobiography* which reveals that he combined naïve superstition with his theological rationalism. In it, he gives some facts concerning his life which would otherwise be unknown, throws light upon the development of his own thinking and gives some information concerning the writing of his chief work, *De Veritate*.

The deistic works of Herbert of Cherbury include, in addition to the *Autobiography* and *De Veritate* which have been mentioned, two other works bearing the titles *De Religione Laici* and *De Religione Gentilium*. The last two works named contain a restatement of the positive principles of the deistic religion as first set forth by the author in the *De Veritate* but they are chiefly devoted to his theory of the history of religions. This had also been given, but in briefer form, in the more important work.[6]

The history of the *De Veritate* during its author's lifetime was interesting and suggestive of the importance of the book. The *De Veritate* was mostly written in England but was first published in Paris. After having written the book, the author hesitated to publish it. But, he tells us in his *Autobiography*, having prayed about it, he heard a miraculous sound that convinced him he should give it to the public.[7] This is a strange story to come from the pen of a deist. The author had three Latin editions of the work pub-

---

3) CHERBURY, EDWARD LORD HERBERT OF, *The Autobiography of Edward Lord Herbert of Cherbury with Introduction, Notes, Appendices, and a Continuation of the Life by Sidney Lee*, London, Geo. Routledge & Sons Limited; New York, E. P. Dutton & Co., 1906. 2nd Edit., Revised. pp. xiv–xviii.

4) LECHLER, *Geschichte Des Englischen Deismus*, s. 29.

5) *loc. cit.*

6) CHERBURY, *Autobiography*, pp. 133–134.

7) Herbert's account says, "I had no sooner spoken these words, but a loud though yet gentle noise came from the heavens, for it was like nothing on earth," etc. This, he says, encouraged him to publish his book. *Autobiography*, pp. 133–134.

lished. The first and second of these were issued in France in the years 1624 and 1633, respectively, while the third was published in London in 1645. The author also prepared a French language edition bearing the title *De La Verité* which was published in France in 1639.

Most of the *De Veritate* consists of a presentation of the author's theory of knowledge and therefore the book is, like the chief works of Descartes, Locke, Hume and Kant, epistemological in character. The particular epistemological theory championed by Herbert is akin to that of Descartes. Thus, at its beginning, Herbert gave to the deistic movement an epistemological character which it retained to a large degree throughout its later development though it soon deserted the theory of Herbert in favor of that advocated by Locke. Herbert magnified the power of the human reason. Yet he distinguished between truth attainable by the reason reflecting upon experience and truths which he styled innate. The latter, he claimed, are common to all men and need no proof from outside since they carry the proof of their truth in themselves. No inquiry is to be made into their origin. Herbert took over two-thirds of his book in presenting and arguing his epistemological theory before coming to the application of his views to religion and the presenting of his deistic religious philosophy.

In the latter portion of the book, Herbert named five principles or notions of religion ("notitiae communes") which he claimed were common to all men, and gave their distinguishing marks. These, as they are stated by Herbert himself in his later English book, *The Antient Religion of the Gentiles, and Causes of their Errors Consider'd*, read as follows: "I That there is one Supreme God. II That he ought to be worshipped. III That Virtue and Piety are the chief parts of Divine Worship. IV That we ought to be sorry for our sins and repent of them. V That Divine goodness doth dispense rewards and punishments both in this life and after it."[8] Herbert maintained that these five

---

[8] CHERBURY, *The Antient Religion of the Gentiles*, etc., pp. 3–4. As given by their author in the French edition of his major work, the five principles read as follows: (1) "Qu'il y a Une puissance Souveraine." (2) "Que cetta puissance Souveraine doit estre adoree." (3) "Que la boune confirmation, ou disposition des facultez de l'homme, sait la principale ou la Meilleure partié do culte diuin, & que l'ou a tonjours creu cela." (4) "Que tous les vices & les crimez se doiuent expier & efacer par le repentir." (5) "Qu'il y a des recompenses & des chastiments apres cette Viè." CHERBURY, EDOUARD HERBERT BARON DE, *De la Verité Entant Qu'ell est distincte de la Revelation, du Vray-semblable, du Possible & du Faux.* (Place of publication and publisher not given. Probable place, Paris.) 1639. Troisieme Edition, pp. 271–284. See next page for the original Latin form of the five principles.

principles[9] are innate truths and that they are differenti-
ated from truths reached by means of reflection by six distinguishing features:[10] "Prioritas," "Independentia," "Uni-
versalitas," "Certitudo," "Necessitas," and "Modus Confor-
mationis."

Herbert had a very high opinion of his five innate principles. Referring to his discovery of them, he wrote: "I found
those five articles I have so often mentioned, and thought
myself far more happy than Archimedes."[11] He also made
it plain that he regarded them as quite sufficient. "Nor can
any man by the assistance of common and right reason, add
another to our five articles, which will render men more
sincere and pious, and more promote the public peace and
tranquillity."[12] These five articles constituted the positive
element in what might be called the creed of their author's
new deistic religion. Most later deists followed Herbert in
making these the articles of natural religion. Some slightly
increased the number of articles. But they did so by analy-
sis or division of some of the five articles rather than by
adding any essentially new idea. Others lessened the number of the articles of natural religion by omitting some of
Herbert's articles. The one most frequently omitted was
that stating belief in a future life. Because these five articles were so important in Herbert's own opinion and so fully
expressed the content of deistic religion, or the religion of
nature, as held by not only Herbert but also by most later
deists, they require careful examination here.

The first article asserts the existence of God. All deists
unhesitatingly made this assertion. It is this which sharply
distinguishes deism from atheism, skepticism and agnosticism. It is of one God and one only that Herbert and the
deists who followed him spoke. This distinguished deism
from all forms of polytheism. Like the great historic religions Judaism, Christianity and Mohammedanism, the
deistic religion of nature was monotheistic. When Herbert
and other deists spoke of God they meant God the Creator
whom they conceived as distinct from his creation. This

---

[9] The Latin version of the five articles as given by Locke read:
"1. Esse aliquod supremum numen. 2. Numen illud coli debere. 3. Vir-
tutem cum pietate conjunctam optiman esse rationem cultus divini.
4. Resipiscendum esse a peccatis. 5. Dari proemium vel poenam post
hanc vitam transactam." LOCKE, *Essay*. I:iii:15, 16. Cf. LECHLER, *Geschichte Des Englischen Deismus*, s. 42.

[10] LOCKE, Essay, I:iii:15. For French version vid. HERBERT, *De La
Verité*, p. 81.

[11] CHERBURY, HERBERT OF, *The Antient Rel. of the Gentiles*, p. 367.

[12] *op. cit.*, pp. 364–365.

distinguished deism from pantheism. One English deist,
John Toland, probably became a pantheist before his death,
but in so doing he ceased to be a deist. It is because Spinoza, the famous Jewish philosopher of Holland, differed
from the deists in his conception of God that he is not classed
as a deist.[13] Yet Spinoza had much in common with the
English deists, especially with Hobbes, and exercised a considerable influence upon the deism subsequent to his time.
By "God" the deists did not mean the all or the sum total of
reality as do pantheists. They meant God the Creator, distinct from his creation and possessing in infinite measure
and perfection those attributes such as omnipotence, omniscience, infinite goodness and justice, which scholastic
theology had discussed[14] and assigned to God.

Herbert's maintaining of this first article concerning the
existence of God required that he deny that there are any
atheists. This was especially true because he asserted that
this and the other four articles as well were all innate
ideas[15] one of whose distinguishing characteristics was uni-
versality.[16] Herbert did not hesitate to make the denial.[17]
But though he denied the existence of atheists, he did not
deny that many individuals and peoples had degraded and
unworthy conceptions of God. Indeed he claimed that the
high and true conception of God given in natural religion
had been corrupted in all the particular religions. The most
he concedes to Christianity is that in it the conception of
God is a bit less corrupted than in other religions. To prove
the universality of his five articles and to explain their corruption required of Herbert a study of various religions and
also a theory of the history of religion. This led to his making use of an embryo science of comparative religion. It
likewise led to his development of a theory of the corruption
of natural religion by a fraudulent self-seeking clergy or
priesthood.[18] The anticlerical note is prominent in the
writings of Herbert[19] as well as in those of later deists.[20]

---

13) Spinoza is usually classed as a pantheist. Some would class him
as a materialist. It is aside from the purpose of this work to argue the
point. His view was not that of the deists.
14) vid. above, p. 51.
15) CHERBURY, HERBERT OF, *De La Verité*, p. 81. cf. LOCKE, *Essay
Concerning Human Understanding*, I:iii:6.
16) CHERBURY, *De La Verité*, pp. 75, 81.
17) *op. cit.*, p. 81.
18) CHERBURY, *The Antient Religion*, etc., p. 3.
19) *op. cit.*, pp. 13, 41, 270, 281, 299, 293, 318, etc.
20) Anticlericalism is prominent in the writings of such deists as
Blount, Collins, Toland, Tindal, and Woolston. Blount's *Great Is Diana
of the Ephesians* consists chiefly in expressions of it.

Though this anticlericalism may be explained as partly due to prejudice or to known facts of clerical corruption or to the transmission from earlier writers of such an attitude, or to all of these combined, yet it evidently provided Herbert with an explanation which he needed to explain the fact that men have such corrupted ideas of God and religion in fact in spite of his theory of innate universal correct conceptions.

Herbert did not greatly labor on the second of his five articles as few indeed would deny the second article if they admitted the first. If there is such a God as the first article posits and he is man's creator, then it follows that man should worship him.

The third article, that virtue and piety are the chief parts of divine worship, was given fuller consideration by its author. It was in connection with his discussion of this article that Herbert stressed the ethical character of natural religion and opposed religion that makes use of forms and rites and sacraments in worship. But most religions are full of such rites and this called for explanation. In his explanation the author again brings in his anti-clericalism. Rites, he says, were invented by priests "that worship might not seem bare and naked."[21] Moreover the priests sought by means of them to eradicate the principles of natural religion and to establish their own power.[22] The making of religion essentially ethical, the rejection of rites and ordinances in religion and the claim that such rites and ordinances are inventions of crafty, self-seeking priests, manifested in Herbert's work features that became characteristic of deism.

The discussion of the fourth article, "that we ought to be sorry for our sins and to repent of them," gave Herbert an opportunity to express his views on repentance and sacrifice. He held repentance in high esteem and evidently regarded it as sufficient to put the sinner back into harmonious relationship with God. And he held a correspondingly low opinion of sacrifices and rejected them as unnecessary and as cunning priestly inventions. He wrote: "The heathens esteemed repentance the universal atonement or sacrament of nature. But now the priests began to obscure and involve it in multiplicity of dark rites and ceremonies; that they might make men believe they only had the power and

---

[21] CHERBURY, *The Antient Religion*, etc., p. 281.
[22] *op. cit.*, p. 318.

authority of divine mysteries."[23]   He also wrote: "But to
the great detriment of virtue and civil society, the priests
boasted that they could expiate the most notorious crimes;
which made sinners secure, and continually perpetrating
new villanies, depending on the assistance of the priest,
they set the vengeance of God at defiance."[24]   What Herbert added to this statement gives his opinion both of priests
and sacrifices.   "But nothing was ever so destructive to
virtue, and injurious to the true worship of the supreme
God, as this religious cheat of the priests.   For what is it
that a wicked wretch will not perpetrate, who can make
such an easy atonement for his sins."[25]   Herbert's attitudes
toward the doctrine of sacrifice and toward the clergy are
evidenced by his assertion that priests invented bloody
sacrifices[26] to terrify people and in order that the priests
might "feast themselves with the remainder."[27]   Herbert's
discussion of the subject of sacrifice is written as though
directed against that element in heathen religions.   But his
statements are of such an inclusive character as to evidently include in his condemnation the sacrifices of the Old
Testament and the widely held Christian doctrine of the
propitiary sacrifice of Christ.   Yet so guarded were his
statements that if he were attacked for them he could claim
to be simply opposing heathen doctrines and practices or
such abuses in the Christian church as Luther had criticized
when he protested against the selling of indulgences by
Tetzel.

The fifth and last article of Herbert's summation of
natural religion deals with rewards and punishments in this
life and in the life that the soul enters upon at death.   It
included several distinct ideas.   It involves the doctrine of
a future life.   It also asserts that God punishes and rewards
men according to their character and deeds.   It further
maintains that his punishing and rewarding takes place
both before and after death.   Herbert did not develop a
doctrine of heaven and hell though some such conceptions
are assumed in his position.   He did speak of "la beatitude
eternelle"[28] as among men's natural instincts.

This fifth article of Herbert's was the one that found less
general acceptance from later deists than the others.   Some

23) CHERBURY, *The Antient Religion of the Gentiles*, etc., p. 318.
24) *op. cit.*, pp. 318–319.
25) *ibid.*
26) CHERBURY, *The Antient Religion*, etc., p. 320.
27) *op. cit.*, p. 321.
28) CHERBURY, *De La Verité*, p. 84.

did accept it. Others accepted it but analyzed it and sub-divided it so as to give more than Herbert's five articles.[29] Others, among whom Bolingbroke was notable, rejected it in so far as it referred to a future life.[30] So much were deists divided among themselves on the question of the im-mortality of the soul that some authors have divided them into two groups[31] called, respectively, "Mortal Deists" and "Immortal Deists."

One of the distinguishing characteristics which Herbert claimed for his five articles was universality. He wrote of "consentement universel."[32] He generally based their uni-versality on the fact that they were innate ideas. It was this that led Locke to name Herbert's five articles in his famous attack upon the doctrine of innate ideas.[33] But on at least one occasion Herbert wrote as if he thought his articles de-pended upon a process of reasoning, but of reasoning upon such clear evidence that all men must reach the same con-clusion. He wrote: "Yet the five above-mentioned truths ever were, and always will be, of that divine nature, that like the sunbeams, which no weight can depress, nor any wind blow out, they have darted their glorious rays into the minds of men in all parts of the earth, where they did but exercise their natural use of reason."[34]

Notice must now be taken of the negative side of deism as represented in the works of Herbert. Herbert, like practi-cally all other deist writers, not only set forth a positive religion of nature which he championed but also made criti-cal attacks upon religions claiming supernaturalism. Her-bert lived at a time when there was no religious toleration whereas some of the later deists lived and wrote at a time when a large measure of religious toleration was granted. This fact probably explains why Herbert of Cherbury and most of the earlier deists rather carefully avoided direct attacks upon the Bible and Christianity and assumed the role of loyal Christians seeking to reform and purify that faith from its corruptions, whereas some of the later deists openly attacked the Bible and Christianity itself. Herbert's attacks were upon heathen religious books, heathen sacri-

---

[29] This view appears in Blount's correspondence. BLOUNT, *Miscel. Works. Oracles of Reason*, pp. 197–198, q. v.

[30] BOLINGBROKE, VISCOUNT HENRY ST. JOHN, *The Works of Lord Bo-lingbroke*, with a Life, Phihladelphia, Cary and Hart, 1841.

[31] Herbert and Blount were "immortal deists."

[32] CHERBURY, *De La Verité*, p. 75.

[33] LOCKE, *Essay*, I:iii:15.

[34] CHERBURY, *The Antient Religion*, etc., p. 357.

fices, heathen miracles and other features of heathen religions which he characterized as corruptions of the original and pure religion of nature.[35]   Yet the wording of these attacks was such as to make the reader feel that the author had the Bible and historic Christianity in mind.[36]

He made it plain that he regarded special or supernatural revelation as unnecessary. He said that those that would not allow that the five articles were sufficient for salvation seemed to him to pronounce a "bold, rash and severe sentence."[37] He did not think that anything was needed beyond his five articles for the promotion of piety or of public peace and tranquility.[38]   Out of them, he believed it possible to construct a universal religion.[39]

Herbert would excuse a man who did not believe anything that claimed to be a revelation. He wrote: "For it is not in him to repose an entire faith and assurance in the truth of traditions, especially when they are controverted."[40]

The way in which Herbert worded his conditions that any book claiming to be a revelation must meet ere it be accepted as what it claimed to be would suggest his disbelief that any book met these conditions.[41]   These conditions included proof that God was once accustomed to "speak with an articulate voice and deliver oracles," that he who heard was certainly assured that it was the supreme God that spoke to him and that in hearing he was not "delirious, or between sleep and awake at the same time," that a faithful record was promptly given to the people or put in writing by the recipient so that should anyone later introduce changes they could be corrected by its authority, and, finally, that it be apparent that the doctrine contained in it is absolutely necessary.

It seems probable that Herbert was indirectly casting doubt upon the inspiration of the Bible in what he records concerning a sacred book of the Egyptians. He wrote that "the Egyptians had a book written in red letters, which was in great veneration amongst them, which they report to have

---

35) CHERBURY, *The Antient Religion*, etc., pp. 13–15, 41, 269, 293, 363.

36) The writer recognizes that great caution is necessary in ascribing motives to any author. But the facts brought out on the next page, (q. v.), amply justify the statement made above concerning Herbert of Cherbury.

37) CHERBURY, *The Antient Religion*, etc., p. 364.

38) *op. cit.*, p. 365.

39) *op. cit.*, p. 386.

40) *op. cit.*, p. 354.

41) *op. cit.*, p. 366.

received from a hawk,"[42] etc. It will be borne in mind that those believing in the inspiration of the Bible ascribe such inspiration to the Holy Spirit who is, in the Bible itself, represented under the figure of a dove. Also it is to be remembered that Herbert had ascribed the corruption of natural religion to priests, and especially to Egyptian priests, and that he had not failed to emphasize the close contact of the Israelites with Egypt from the time of Abraham to the time of Moses.[43]

The whole tenor of Herbert's writings is to the effect that underneath the rubbish of all particular religions are the innate principles of natural religion which are quite sufficient and that therefore special revelations have neither been needed nor given.

In tracing its theological roots, it was pointed out that deism had affinity with Pelagian-Arminian as against Augustinian-Calvinistic theology.[44] Calvinism makes much of the Genesis story of the Fall of man into sin. Herbert rejected this story.[45] Calvinism both teaches and gives prominence to the doctrines of Original Sin and Predestination. Herbert rejected both of these.[46] Thus the characteristic theological affinity of deism is already evident in the works of Herbert.

Herbert's writings called forth a number of replies. Richard Baxter wrote *More Reasons for the Christian Religion and no reason against it*. Thomas Halyburton wrote *Natural Religion Insufficient*. Herbert built his scheme of natural religion on a doctrine of innate ideas. This attracted the attention of the famous philosopher John Locke, who singled out Herbert's five innate articles of natural religion as a clear example of the Cartesian theory of innate ideas which he wished to refute. Thus part[47] of Locke's *An Essay Concerning the Human Understanding* became an answer to part of Herbert's writings. There is little doubt that Locke had Herbert, as well as some who had followed Herbert, in mind when he wrote his vigorous argument for special revelation in *The Reasonableness of Christianity*.[48]

---

[42] CHERBURY, *The Antient Religion of the Gentiles*, etc., p. 363.

[43] *op. cit.*, pp. 13–15. cf. LECHLER, *Geschichte Des Englischen Deismus*, s. 45.

[44] above, p. 35.

[45] CHERBURY, *The Antient Religion of the Gentiles*, etc., p. 266.

[46] *ibid.* cf. *op. cit.*, pp. 5-6.

[47] LOCKE, *An Essay Concerning the Human Understanding*. I :iii: 15–19.

[48] LOCKE, JOHN, *The Works of John Locke*. London, printed for W. Olridge and Son, Leigh and Southey, et. al., 1812. Eleventh Edition, vol. 7, *The Reasonableness of Christianity*, pp. 135–149.

B. THOMAS HOBBES

Thomas Hobbes (1588-1679), who ranks as one of the most logical thinkers England has produced, is the next author after Herbert whose works require attention in a history of English deism. Though there is some disagreement among students of Hobbes on the question whether Hobbes should be classed as a Christian, a deist or an atheist in religion, there is no doubt that he had much in common with the deists and that he exercised a considerable influence upon the development of that movement.

Hobbes' life and social contacts undoubtedly exercised a considerable influence upon both his political and his religious philosophy. He took his bachelor of arts degree at Oxford. For a short time, he served Lord Francis Bacon as secretary and elicited praise for being an exceptionally intelligent secretary. Later he had the privilege of meeting Galileo. Hobbes' contact with these two men probably influenced him in the direction of empirical, scientific and mathematical types of thought. Soon after taking his degree at Oxford, Hobbes became a tutor in the Cavendish or Earl of Devonshire family. He was associated with this family through much of his long life. Connection with this aristocratic family undoubtedly strengthened Hobbes in his royalist sympathies. It certainly gave him opportunities of foreign travel and of contacts with important thinkers such as Galileo, Descartes, Gassendi and Herbert of Cherbury, who did help to direct Hobbes' thinking. Descartes was stimulating to Hobbes as to others and probably helped make Hobbes the close logical reasoner he became. Gassendi had revived a modified Epicurean materialism. Hobbes became the leading English materialistic philosopher of his day and the founder of a little school of English materialists. Undoubtedly Hobbes' contact with Gassendi had much to do with bringing this about. It is likely that his acquaintance with Herbert of Cherbury turned Hobbes' thought to religious questions and particularly to the deistic conception of religion. But the influence of these men upon Hobbes, though great, should not be exaggerated for it is to be remembered that Hobbes was an original thinker and that these men were just outstanding representatives of thought currents that were prevalent in the age in which Hobbes lived.

Though the literary activity of Hobbes was extensive and varied, his most famous and enduring work was in the fields of political and religious philosophy. However, his earlier

efforts were in the fields of classic literature and mathematics.
When political strife was bitter in England in the year 1640
A. D., Hobbes wrote a small pro-royalist political pamphlet,
which, though not published, was widely circulated and
brought its author both fame and danger. He found it expedient to retire for a time to France. There he elaborated
the ideas of his pamphlet. He later published them under the
title *De Cive*. After still further extensive elaboration, they
were again published, in England, in the year 1651 A. D., with
the title *Leviathan*. This was easily Hobbes' most famous
and influential work. Though primarily a work on the
philosophy of politics, it gave, in their ablest form, the
author's views on nature, ethics, religion and the Bible. Other
writings by Hobbes, most of which contain some of his ideas
on religion though in many cases these ideas are better expressed in the *Leviathan*, include *Behemoth*, *De Homine* or
Human Nature, *De Corpore Politico*, *Concerning Heresy*,
*Considerations upon the Reputation, Loyalty, Manners, and
Religion of Thomas Hobbes* and *The Questions concerning
Liberty, Necessity, and Chance*.

Hobbes and his *Leviathan* were not popular in his own
day. Both his religious and political doctrines got him into
controversy with the Presbyterian clergy. His bitter attacks
upon the Roman Catholic Church, which he called "The Kingdom of Darkness," [49] antagonized the numerous adherents of
that faith. His outspoken materialism aroused the opposition
of all non-materialistic philosophers. His views on law got
him into controversy with the adherents of Coke's theory of
common law. Hobbes' views on this subject are found in his
Behemoth. His unorthodox theology and his criticism of
the Bible aroused Christians in general and the protestant
clergy in particular against him. His doctrine of political
absolutism was hateful to all liberal-minded men. Even
royalty and the members of the royalist party, which he had
hoped to please with his *Leviathan*, frowned upon him because of his religious views and also because his doctrine
of sovereignty seemed to justify whatever party happened
to be in power. Most of the deists, though undoubtedly they
found much that pleased them in his criticisms of the Roman
Catholic Church, of the clergy, of revelation and of the Scriptures, were antagonized by the political aspect that he
gave religion and especially by his advocacy of intolerance.

---

[49] HOBBES, THOMAS, *The English Works of Thomas Hobbes of
Malmesbury*. London, John Bohn, 1839. vol. 3, *Leviathan*, p. 603 ff.

Therefore, though there was widespread recognition of Hobbes as a thinker to be reckoned with, there was equally widespread unpopularity for the gifted author.

This unpopularity lessened Hobbes' influence with the deists and lessened still more the number of their references to him. Just as they were proud to claim any agreement with their views on the part of the popular Tillotson and Locke, so they were ashamed to claim intellectual kinship with the unpopular Hobbes. As a consequence of this, a comparison of their ideas with those of Hobbes suggests that they owed more to Hobbes than the number of times he is named or directly quoted would indicate. When they did name him they usually added a protest against his political religion and his doctrine of intolerance.[50]

In his metaphysical views, Hobbes was frankly materialistic.[51] While admitting a distinction between more coarse and subtle kinds of materials, he argued that all reality is material.[52]

In his epistemological views, Hobbes was a sensationalist. Locke is usually credited with being the father of English sensationalistic philosophy. But before Locke's works were written Hobbes had said, "There is no conception in a man's mind, which hath not at first, totally, or by parts, been begotten upon the organs of sense." [53] It is true that Hobbes did not work out an argument against innate ideas nor elaborate the sensationalistic theory of knowledge as did Locke so that Locke's influence upon the development of this type of thinking was probably greater than that of Hobbes. Nevertheless Hobbes was first.

While it is easy to classify Hobbes as a materialist in metaphysics and a sensationalist in epistemology and a royalist in politics, it is not so easy to place him with regard to his views on religion. Was he a fairly orthodox trinitarian Christian theist, an atheist or a deist? Each of these opinions of him has had its champions.

The opinion that holds Hobbes was a Christian theist rests on the fact that he often wrote respectfully of the Christian religion, of Christ and of the Bible and that he made frequent professions of Christian faith. In one passage which frequently refers to Christ as "our Savior," he says, "The Scrip-

50) COLLINS, *A Discourse of Free Thinking*, pp. 170-171.
51) HOBBES, *Works*, vol. 3, *Leviathan*, pp. 381–383.
52) HOBBES, *Works*, vol. 3, *Leviathan*, pp. 381–383.
53) *op. cit.*, p. 1.

ture was written to show unto men the kingdom of God, and
to prepare their minds to become his obedient subjects; leaving
the world, and the philosophy thereof, to the disputation of
men, for the exercising of their natural reason." [54]   Again,
in words of rigid orthodoxy, Hobbes wrote of God being per-
sonated: "Secondly, by the son of man, his own Son, our
blessed Savior Jesus Christ, that came to reduce the Jews, and
induce all nations into the kingdom of his Father; not as of
himself, but as sent from his Father. And thirdly, by the
Holy Ghost, or Comforter, speaking, and working in the
apostles: which Holy Ghost, was a Comforter that came not
of himself; but was sent, and proceeded from them both." [55]
Hobbes also seemed to be proclaiming his belief in God, revelation and miracles when he wrote the following: "But God
declareth his laws three ways; by the dictates of natural reason, by revelation, and by the voice of some man, to whom
by the operation of miracles, he procureth credit with the
rest." [56]   Accepting such declarations at par, Blakey reached
the conclusion that there is nothing in Hobbes decidedly hostile to sound religion and that Hobbes was an orthodox
Christian.[57]

But there are weighty reasons for doubting this conclusion.
After speaking of supernatural revelation, Hobbes added:
"Nevertheless, we are not to renounce our senses, and experience; nor, that which is the undoubted word of God, our natural reason." [58]   That phrase, "the undoubted word of God,"
suggests an assurance that there is a God and that what natural reason gives is his undoubted word while what is not given
by natural reason may be of doubtful origin. Hobbes' tone
was unfavorable to supernatural revelation when he wrote:
"For it is with the mysteries of our religion, as with wholesome pills for the sick, which swallowed whole, have the virtue to cure; but chewed, are for the most part cast up again
without effect." [59]   Hobbes' disbelief in supernatural revelation becomes more apparent in what he wrote concerning
modes and proof of such revelation. "For if a man pretend
to me that God hath spoken to him supernaturally and immediately, and I make doubt of it, I cannot easily perceive

---

[54] HOBBES, *Works*, vol. 3, *Leviathan*, p. 68.
[55] *op. cit.*, pp. 150-151.
[56] *op. cit.*, p. 345.
[57] BLAKEY, R., *History of Moral Science.* London, James Duncan,
1833. pp. 75, 82.
[58] HOBBES, *Works.* vol. 3, *Leviathan*, p. 359.
[59] HOBBES, *Works.* vol. 3, *Leviathan*, p. 360.

what argument he can produce, to oblige me to believe it."[60]
Hobbes proceeds with his answers to a man supposed to be
claiming special revelation. "To say he hath spoken to him
in a dream, is no more than to say he dreamed that God
spake to him.—To say he hath seen a vision, or heard a
voice, is to say, that he hath dreamed between sleeping
and waking.—To say he speaks by supernatural inspiration, is to say he finds an ardent desire to speak, or some
strong opinion of himself, for which he can allege no
natural and sufficient reason."[61]   Hobbes concluded this
line of reasoning with the following suggestive words.   "So
that though God Almighty can speak to a man by dreams,
visions, voice, and inspiration; yet he obliges no man to
believe he hath so done to him that pretends it; who, being
a man, may err, and, which is more, may lie."[62] Had Hobbes
thus argued directly against the writers of the Bible, his
rejection of it would have been rather clearly established.
But Hobbes did not do this.   Instead he directed his arguments against later writers who might lay claim to inspiration.   However, enemies of the Bible were quick to make
use of these arguments against the claims of Bible writers
themselves.   In the light of Hobbes' later work in Bible
criticism and on the canon of Scripture, it is likely Hobbes
himself had the Bible in mind.   Such deists as did reject the
Scriptures sometimes pictured the Bible writers as self-
deceived enthusiasts but more often as fraudulent.   Hobbes'
words in the last given quotation,—"May err, and, which is
more, may lie,"[63]—suggest kinship with the deistic position.

Hobbes maintained that the things which the Bible itself
gives as the distinguishing marks between true and false
prophets are the working of miracles and conformity with
the teachings of established religion.   One of these marks
alone would not suffice.   Both must be present.[64]   But if
one asks how true and false miracles or wonders are to be
distinguished, Hobbes replies that those are to be accepted
as true which the sovereign commands to be accepted.[65]
This results in the making of the decision which are true
and which false prophets entirely a matter of decision by
sovereign authority.

[60] Hobbes' *Works*. vol. 3, *Leviathan*, p. 361.
[61] *op. cit.*, pp. 361–362.
[62] *op. cit.*, p. 362.
[63] *loc. cit.*
[64] *op. cit.*, pp. 362–365.
[65] *op. cit.*, pp. 427–437.

Hobbes discussed the Canon of Scripture quite extensively. In the course of this discussion, he took occasion to argue against the usually accepted authorship of a number of the books of the Bible.[66]   His conclusion is that such books as the sovereign commands to be accepted as canonical are canonical while such books as the sovereign rejects must be regarded as uncanonical.[67]

Hobbes, by making the distinction between true and false prophets, true and false miracles and canonical and uncanonical books to depend entirely upon the sovereign of each country, unmistakably leaves the impression that he regarded no prophets and miracles as true and no books as canonical in the usual acceptation of those terms. For he well enough knew that sovereigns of different countries and often successive sovereigns in the same country would render different decisions as to what must be accepted as true and canonical. He also knew that sovereigns were in no way specially qualified to know the absolute truth in such matters.

While discussing revelation, Hobbes made the remark that the transmission of these Scriptures had been in the hands of power-usurping clergy who were not averse to using fraud.[68]   Most deists made a similar observation and from it concluded that the text of Scripture is therefore probably utterly corrupted and untrustworthy. Hobbes, however, did not draw this conclusion. Instead, he says that probably the clergy did not actually corrupt the text for if they had been doing so they would have made their reading more favorable to the authority of clergy and less favorable to the authority of civil rulers.[69]

Since Hobbes was evidently a rationalist in his whole attitude toward religious questions and gave little or no weight to anything that claimed to be a supernatural revelation, the question whether he should be classed as a deist or as an atheist must be decided by determining whether he believed in God and in a religion of nature attainable through the use of reason. Hobbes' writings are so filled with references to God that the casual reader would form the opinion that he not only believed in God but that God occupied a large place in all his thinking.[70]   When dis-

---

66) HOBBES, *Works*. vol. 3, *Leviathan*, pp. 366–380.
67) *loc. cit.*
68) *op. cit.*, pp. 375–376.
69) *ibid.*
70) This is particularly true of the last half of the *Leviathan*.

cussing the origin of the idea of God and the origin of religion, Hobbes divides men into two groups one of which has the idea of many gods and the other of which has the idea of one eternal, omnipotent, infinite God.[71] He named four things that gave rise to the religious conceptions of the first group. "And in these four things, opinion of Ghosts, ignorance of second causes, devotion toward what men fear, and taking of things causal for prognostics, consisteth the natural seed of religion."[72] Most deists differed from this theory of Hobbes by making the polytheistic religions with their corruptions a product of the corrupting of pure and true natural religion by fraudulent and corrupt priests. Some tried to combine the two types of explanation. Hobbes gave a different theory for the origin of monotheistic religion. He derived it from a search after the first cause or mover.[73] "Curiosity, or the love of the knowledge of causes, draws a man from the consideration of the effect, to seek the cause; and again, the cause of that cause; till of necessity he must come to this thought at last, that there is some cause whereof there is no former cause, but is eternal; which is it men call God."[74] Commenting further on this Hobbes says: "So that it is impossible to make any profound inquiry into natural causes, without being inclined thereby to believe there is one God eternal; though they cannot have any idea of him in their mind, answerable to his nature."[75] In his work on human nature, Hobbes gave practically the same line of reasoning. "The effects we acknowledge naturally, do include a power of their producing, before they were produced; and that power presupposeth something existent that hath such power: and the thing so existing with power to produce, if it were not eternal, must needs have been produced by somewhat before it, and that again by something else before that, till we come to an eternal, that is to say, the first power of all powers, and first cause of all causes: and this is it which all men conceive by the name of God, implying eternity, incomprehensibility, and omnipotence."[76] By this process of reasoning, Hobbes says, "All that will consider, may know that God is, though not what he is."[77] Anthony Collins quotes Hobbes

---

[71] HOBBES, *Works.* vol. 3, *Leviathan,* p. 95.
[72] *op. cit.,* pp. 95, 98.
[73] *op. cit.,* p. 95 ff.
[74] HOBBES, *Works.* vol. 3, *Leviathan,* p. 92. cf. p. 96.
[75] *loc. cit.*
[76] HOBBES, *Works.* vol. 4, pp. 59–60.
[77] *op. cit.,* p. 60.

as saying that "They who are capable of inspecting the vessels of generation and nutrition, and not think them made for their several ends by an understanding being ought to be esteemed destitute of understanding themselves."[78] Lord Derry, in his *Catching of the Leviathan,* accused Hobbes of atheism. Hobbes in replying said, "It is agreed between us, that right reason dictates, there is a God."[79] These statements require the conclusion that Hobbes did believe in a God whose existence man could certainly infer by the use of his natural power of reasoning. Therefore, in spite of the fact that Hobbes was often accused of atheism and was regarded by some as the outstanding philosopher of atheism, and in spite of the further fact that his theories making the sovereign final authority in questions of religion and making religion a mere tool in the hand of politicians raise doubts about his having any serious belief in God or religion, he must be classed as a deist.

Though Hobbes reasoned to the conclusion that there is a God, he maintained an agnostic position on the question of man's ability to know what God is.[80] However, in spite of this he managed to make quite a number of assertions about God.[81] He maintained that He is eternal, omnipotent, incomprehensible, understanding, creator, providential ruler, and that He is material in substance. The explanation he offered of the fact that so many persons think of God as immaterial was that this teaching arose from a desire to honor God by making him remote from gross bodies.[82]

Hobbes was not only with the deists in discarding supernatural revelation and claiming that the one supreme God is knowable by reason alone but also in that he set forth a scheme of natural religion whose content was to be known in the same manner. This natural religion he set forth under the name of "The Kingdom of God by Nature" and he made all belong to it, who, "by the natural dictates of right reason" acknowledge the providence of God.[83]

There was some similarity but marked difference between the contents of natural religion as set forth by Herbert and most deists on the one hand and as set forth by Hobbes on the other hand. Both made the first two and main articles

---

78) COLLINS, *A Discourse of Free Thinking,* pp. 104–105.
79) HOBBES, *Works.* vol. 4, p. 293. cf. pp. 306, 313.
80) *op. cit.,* p. 60.
81) *op. cit.,* pp. 59–60. Cf. *Leviathan,* Part II, chap. 31. Also cf. COLLINS, *A Discourse of Free Thinking,* pp. 104–105.
82) HOBBES, *Works.* vol. 3, *Leviathan,* p. 97.
83) HOBBES, *Works.* vol. 3, *Leviathan,* Part II, chap. 31.

of such religion to be belief that there is one supreme God[84]
and that He should be worshipped.[85]   But Hobbes differed
in a characteristic way on both articles. Instead of making
God's rights as king of this natural kingdom depend upon
either his ethical character or his position as Creator, as the
others would have done, Hobbes made them to rest on God's
irresistible power alone.[86] The other elements of natural religion are just the natural obligations to such an all-power-
ful one.   Instead of making worship almost exclusively
private and ethical, as did Herbert and most other deists,
Hobbes made it to consist in sacrifices and rituals and insisted that it must be public and uniform within the
nation.[87]   Hobbes gave little or no place to repentance or
belief in a future life. The natural religion he set forth was
more scant in content than that of Herbert although it allowed a larger place for ritual.

Hobbes was a deist,[88] but a deist who differed so sharply
at several points from most other deists that he was not
popular with them and had less influence than he would
have had were it not for these differences. They were especially repelled by his making religion political, by his favoring intolerance and by his presenting religion as more ritualistic than ethical.   Such deists[89] as later asserted materialism and denied or doubted the immortality of the soul
were the ones who show Hobbes' influence most. Few if
any English deists followed Hobbes in his shifting of the
question from "What is the true religion?" to "What is the
legal religion?"[90]   The most important writer who seemed
ready to follow this feature of Hobbes' thought was the
continental philosopher Spinoza.

Yet Hobbes' influence upon later deism was important in
spite of his unpopularity. His sheer intellectual ability
gave great encouragement to the religious rationalism of
his day, a rationalism of which deism was a prominent
manifestation.   He encouraged the anti-clerical spirit
which had already been manifested by deism. He sup-

---

[84] *Leviathan,* pp. 353–355.
[85] *ibid.*
[86] *op. cit.,* p. 345.
[87] *op. cit.,* pp. 353–355.
[88] Such terms as "atheist" have too often been used loosely or as a
kind of argumentum ad hominem. The term was probably applied to
Hobbes by orthodox writers partly because it seemed to them his political
religion logically suggested atheism and partly because atheists made so
much use of Hobbes.
[89] Such as Bolingbroke, Chubb and Annet.
[90] HOBBES, *Works.* vol. 3, *Leviathan,* pp. 45, 93.

plied later deists with some suggested explanations of the origin of religions. But Hobbes' most important contribution to deistic thought was in his Bible criticism and his teachings concerning the canon of Scripture, inspiration and miracles. After Hobbes, Bible criticism occupied a more important place in the works of the deists than was previously the case. Spinoza,[91] the famous philosopher of Rotterdam, was much influenced by Hobbes. This influence is apparent in both his religious and political philosophy and, perhaps most of all, in his work in Biblical criticism. Spinoza's indebtedness to Hobbes is best realized by comparing the former's *Tractatus Theologico-Politicus* with the latter's *Leviathan*. It is probable that Hobbes' influence upon later thought through the medium of his influence upon Spinoza was greater than his direct influence.

That Hobbes had a considerable influence directly upon the English deists who wrote after the publication of his works is apparent not only from the few direct references[92] they make to him but also in the unacknowledged incorporation of ideas and trends of thought to which Hobbes had first given expression. The number of attacks made upon Hobbes constituted a tacit acknowledgment of his importance. Warburton, who himself was no friend of the views of Hobbes, says: "The philosopher of Malmesbury was the terror of the last age, as Tindal and Collins are of this. The press sweats with controversy: and every young churchman militant would try his arms in thundering on Hobbes' steel cap."[93]

C. BROWNE, TILLOTSON AND LOCKE

After Hobbes, the next important deistic works to appear were the writings of Charles Blount. But between Hobbes and Blount there appeared the works of three important writers, who, although not themselves deists, were inclined to rationalism in theology and exercised a considerable influence upon the development of the deistic movement. These were the physician-author Sir Thomas Browne, the prominent churchman Archbishop John Til-

---

[91] Though having much in common with the deists, Spinoza is not to be classed as himself a deist. His fundamental metaphysical conception forbids such classification.

[92] BLOUNT, *Philostratus' Life of Apollonius Tyaneus*, p. 28.
COLLINS, *Discourse of Free-Thinking*, pp. 104, 170–171.
COLLINS, *Ground and Reason of the Christian Religion*, p. 112.

[93] BLAKEY, R., *History of Moral Science*. London, James Duncan, 1833. p. 50. (Quoting from WARBURTON'S *Divine Legation of Moses*.)

lotson and the justly famous philosopher John Locke. Because of their influence upon the development of deism all of these, and especially John Locke, call for consideration at this point.

1. Sir Thomas Browne

Browne (1605-1682) was a writer with a quaint style who wrote on out-of-the-way subjects[49] and who was unfriendly to anything of the nature of mystery in religion. He has sometimes been classed as a deist. But he himself claimed to be an Anglican Christian.[95] Gosse, a modern writer on Browne, thinks he should be classed among the skeptics.[96] An attitude unfavorable to mystery in religion was already apparent in the works of Herbert of Cherbury. Mystery was still more openly disfavored by Browne as illustrated by the following passage from his chief work, *Religio Medici*. "As for those wingy mysteries in divinity and airy subtleties in religion, which have unhinged the brains of better heads, they never stretched the pia mater of mine."[97] In the works of later deists such as John Toland, who wrote *Christianity Not Mysterious*, the attitude toward mystery in religion is openly hostile. Browne represents the transition from the milder to the more open hostility to the mysterious in religion. No doubt his influence tended to develop the trend of sentiment against the mysterious.

Browne had much in common with the deists and yet in some respects was quite unlike them. Like them, he denied the existence of atheists[98] and regarded faith and reason as at war with each other.[99] But he differed from the deists in that he did not discard faith for reason but instead sought to retain both by keeping them, as it were in separate compartments.[100] His writings differ from those of most deists in that they are peculiarly free from any evidence of a bitter controversial spirit. One who reads Browne's writings is likely to reach the conclusion that he

94) George, Edward Augustus, *Seventeenth Century Men of Latitude Fore-runners of the New Theology*. New York, Charles Scribner's Sons, 1908. p. 156.
95) Browne, Sir Thomas, *The Works of Sir Thomas Browne*. London, Faber and Groyer Limited; New York, W. E. Rudge, 1928. 6 vols., vol. 1, pp. 5–8.
96) Gosse, Edmund, *Sir Thomas Browne*. London, Macmillan & Co., Limited, 1905. p. 25.
97) Browne, *Works*. vol. 1, *Religio Medici*, p. 13.
98) Browne, Sir Thomas, *Religio Medici, Letter to a Friend*, etc., and *Christian Morals*. London, Macmillan & Co., 1885. p. 35.
99) *op. cit.*, p. 18.
100) Gosse, *Sir Thomas Browne*, pp. 65–66.

is studying the works of an author who at heart did not believe in miracles, revelation or in a religion that included much more than ethical principles. Yet it is not possible to cite passages that prove these to have been the author's views. In fact he declares his belief in both[101] miracles and witchcraft. Without at any time openly indicating his disbelief in them, Browne makes naïve references to many of those passages of Scripture which later deists openly rejected and ridiculed. Among such passages were the story of creation,[102] the making of Eve from the rib of Adam,[103] the Bible story of the fall of man into sin,[104] including the references to forbidden fruit and to the serpent being sentenced to a crawling posture, the miracle of the manna,[105] the finding of the account of Moses death in writings usually ascribed to Moses' authorship[106] the story of the sun standing still for Joshua,[107] the story of the fire coming down from heaven for Elijah on Mt. Carmel,[108] and many more of the peculiar and miraculous Scripture stories. Because Browne carefully avoided any direct statement of disbelief in these stories, the deists could not cite him against these stories when they themselves were rejecting them. But they could, and probably did have their attention directed to these parts of Scripture by Browne's writings. Browne was too good-natured a writer to show the bitter anti-clerical spirit in evidence in the works of many deists. Yet, like the deists, he did blame the clergy for corrupting religion.[109] He was like the deists also in condemning credulity, dependence upon authority and adherence to antiquity. He called the last of these the "mortallest enemy"[110] to knowledge.

2. ARCHBISHOP JOHN TILLOTSON

John Tillotson (1630-1694), Archbishop of Canterbury, was a liberal-minded churchman who emphasized the importance of the use of the reason and of common sense in religion. He advocated religious toleration before that was the policy of his church. People who were suffering from a

---

101) BROWNE, *Religio Medici*, pp. 46–47, 50.
102) BROWNE, *Religio Medici*, p. 58.
103) *op. cit.*, p. 38.
104) *op. cit.*, p. 19.
105) *op. cit.*, p. 35.
106) *op. cit.*, p. 49.
107) *ibid.*
108) *op. cit.*, p. 35.
109) BROWNE, *Works.* vol. 1, p. 6.
110) BROWNE, *Works.* vol. 2, pp. 38–42.

policy of intolerance on the part of the national church were usually strong advocates of toleration. The deists, being in that position, were vigorous advocates of religious toleration. Naturally they were glad to be able to quote in support of their arguments for toleration the writings of a man so highly placed in the national church itself as was Tillotson. Tillotson was vigorously protestant. He attacked the Roman Catholic clergy energetically and accused them of promulgating certain practices and doctrines for selfish ends.[111] Deists made use of such material in their attacks upon both Roman Catholic and Protestant clergy. Tillotson also rejected some Roman Catholic doctrines on the ground of "absurdity."[112] This type of attack was pleasing to the deists, who applied it to some Protestant as well as to Romanist doctrines. While Tillotson was even less of a deist than Browne and did not reject all the supernatural and all mystery in religion as did the deists, he did put the emphasis upon the natural and common-sense elements in religion. For this reason the deists felt that they had in him somewhat of a kindred spirit. They were glad to be able to cite so high a churchman as holding views at least somewhat like their own.

Because Tillotson did put the emphasis upon the ethical and the rational in religion and because he pleaded for toleration and because he brought charges against the clergy of at least a large part of the church similar to those the deists wished to bring against clergy in general, the deists were fond of quoting him and almost tried to claim him as one of themselves.[113] Anthony Collins called him "that religious and free-thinking prelate"[114] and "the most pious and rational of all priests.[115] He also referred to Tillotson as the man "whom all English free-thinkers own as their head."[116] Tillotson, though not himself a deist, had high standing with the deists and considerable influence upon the movement.

However, the influence of both Browne and Tillotson upon the development of English deism was very small compared with that of John Locke to whose works attention must now be given.

---

111) "Wycliffe," *The People's Right Defended*, to which is added *A Discourse on Transsubstantiation*, by Archbishop John Tillotson. Philadelphia, W. F. Geddes, 1831, p. 199.
112) *op. cit.*, p. 210.
113) COLLINS, *A Discourse of Free Thinking*, pp. 69, 171.
114) *op. cit.*, p. 51.
115) *op. cit.*, p. 69.
116) *op. cit.*, p. 171.

3. JOHN LOCKE

John Locke (1632-1704), perhaps the greatest and most influential of all English philosophers, was a man of varied experience and marked versatility. He was a younger contemporary of Hobbes and lived into the opening years of the most active period of the deistic controversy. While yet a student at Oxford he manifested a marked hostility toward the medieval type of intellectualism and a decided leaning toward empiricism and scientific method. He studied medicine and became skilled in the profession although he never became a practicing physician. Soon after leaving Oxford he became a tutor in the family of the Earl of Shaftesbury and remained in connection with this family during much of his life. Locke shared to a considerable degree in the vicissitudes of fortune of the Shaftesbury family during a period when revolution was in the air. When he found it wise to retire to the continent for a few years, he spent much of the time in Holland which was then a haven of refuge for both political and religious refugees from various lands. In Holland, Locke had stimulating intellectual contact with such liberal thinkers as Bayle and Le Clerc.

Locke's extensive writings include works on such subjects as coinage, education, colonial constitutions, toleration, the Bible, religion, as well as his famous work in the field of empirical philosophy. He holds an honorable place in the history of education, in the history of political science and in the history of economics as well as in the field of philosophy. However, his greatest fame and influence were in philosophy. His *Essay Concerning the Human Understanding* ranks as one of the greatest of philosophical works. Only those events in Locke's life and only those parts of his writings which concern his relation to the deists and the deistic movement can be given consideration here. The most important of these writings are his *Essay Concerning the Human Understanding, The Reasonableness of Christianity* and his first *Letter Concerning Toleration.* The later letters on toleration, the Bible paraphrases, the replies to the Bishop of Worcester and some of the correspondence of Locke also throw some light on his religious philosophy and his influence upon deism.

Locke's most far-reaching influence upon deism was that he gave to it a decidedly empirical character. Herbert of Cherbury had presented his five articles of natural religion as innate ideas. Therefore at its start deism was not on an

empirical basis. Hobbes was more of an empiricist. He
taught sensationalism. But because Hobbes' major interest
was in the field of political philosophy, he never greatly
elaborated his basic sensationalism. Locke, however, did
very thoroughly elaborate the doctrine of sensationalism.
Moreover Hobbes' strange, harsh political philosophy, his
crass materialism, his doctrine of intolerance, his unortho-
doxy and his ethical hedonism, estranged many and lessened his influence. Locke was relatively orthodox and his
spirit was in tune with the thought tendencies of his age.
These things, together with his great ability, gave him vast
influence. Though Locke was not the first empirical philosopher, yet he did so thorough and effective a piece of work
that scarcely any other than empirical philosophy has had
much standing in England since his day. After Locke's
works had been published long enough for their influence to
be felt, all deists built on the empirical basis laid by Locke
rather than on the basis provided by Herbert. They all presented the principles of their natural religion as the logical
conclusions of a process of empirical reasoning. Charles
Blount, the important deist whose works were published
posthumously in 1695 A. D., shows acquaintance with
Locke's work and also shows an attitude of hesitation
whether he would follow Herbert or Locke in the following
statement. "I know not whether the idea of a God be innate
or no, but I'm sure that it is very soon imprinted in the
minds of men."[117] But Blount was the last to hesitate between rationalism and empiricism. In a sense all deists
after him might be called Lockian.

Not all philosophical rationalists are orthodox Christian
believers nor are all philosophical empiricists skeptics in
philosophy and unorthodox in religion. But skepticism and
religious heterodoxy have seemed to affiliate more readily
with the empirical than with the rival type of thought.
Deism, when it adopted Lockian empiricism, spread more
rapidly and became more vigorous than it had been previously.

The first striking illustration of Locke's influence upon
deism came with the publication of John Toland's *Christianity Not Mysterious* which appeared in the year 1696 A. D.,
just one year after Locke's *The Reasonableness of Christianity* had been published. The similarity of the titles of the
two works caused some to think Toland had borrowed from

---

117) BLOUNT, *Miscel. Works*, p. 181.

Locke and so caused Locke to be accused of being an abbet-
tor of deism.[118]   It was thus that Locke first came under
suspicion of being friendly toward deism.   Toland was not
averse to being regarded as a friend of the already famous
Locke.   The evidence, however, seems to indicate that
Toland did not derive the title or suggestion of his book
from Locke's book on *The Reasonableness of Christianity*,
and was at work on his own book before Locke published
The Reasonableness of Christianity.[119]   But, on the other
hand, there is abundant evidence that Toland had read
Locke's *Essay Concerning the Human Understanding* and
that he built his doctrines on the Lockian epistemology contained therein.[120]   This master work by Locke had been
published in 1690 A. D.

Edward Stillingfleet, bishop of Worcester, believed that
he had discovered in Locke's *Essay* and other writings
some teachings inconsistent with orthodox Christianity
that gave encouragement to deists.   He therefore attacked
Locke's writings making these accusations.   A famous controversy ensued.   A number of Locke's works were replies
to the bishop.   The latter, though no match for Locke in
debate, had succeeded in detecting some points in Locke's
teachings that were not quite consistent with orthodoxy
and that probably did give encouragement to the deists.
Leslie Stephen's verdict on this debate is essentially correct.   "The bishop's instincts were better than his reasoning powers.   Locke, the unitarians, Toland, form a genuine
series in which Christianity is being gradually transmuted
by larger infusions of rationalism."[121]

While Locke was residing at Oates during the last years
of his life, he was visited by Anthony Collins.   Locke later
wrote some letters to Collins[122] in which he spoke favorably
of Collins as a "philosopher" and "Christian" and declared
no other had shown so good an understanding of his *Essay*.
However, to make use of these complimentary words written

---

[118] LOCKE, JOHN, *The Works of John Locke*.   London, printed for W.
Otridge & Son, et. al., 1812.   Eleventh Edition.   vol. 4, pp. 114, 116–117.
[119] Zscharnack is his "Einleitung" to the German edition of Toland's
book, quotes a letter of a friend to Toland that indicates Toland was
already at work on his book before Locke published *The Reasonableness
of Christianity*.
[120] TOLAND, *Christianity Not Mysterious*, p. 9 ff.
[121] STEPHEN, LESLIE, *History of English Thought in the Eighteenth
Century*.   New York, G. P. Putnam's Sons; London, Smith, Elder & Co.,
1902.   Third Edition.   vol. 1, p. 111.
[122] LOCKE, *Works*.   vol. 10, pp. 261–265.   A series of letters dated
1703.

concerning Collins by Locke as a proof that Locke was favorable to Collins' deistic views would be unjust to Locke. For Collins' deistic works did not appear until after Locke's death. Had Locke seen them, he might not have spoken so favorably of Collins. The writings of Collins contain frequent references to Locke.[123] The connection between Collins and Locke was one of the things on which the effort to connect Locke with deism was built.

Locke's association, his controversies and the high favor he generally received from deists[124] indicate that he was probably inclined to liberalism in matters of religion although he was a member of the Anglican Church. But a study of his views as ably expressed in his own works is the best way to discover his relation to deism. Locke's philosophy of religion can best be examined by asking what were his teachings concerning God, revelation, miracles, toleration and the nature and content of religion.

a. *Locke's Doctrine Concerning God Stated and Compared with That of the Deists.* Locke denied that men have any innate ideas of God.[125] He did this in connection with his rejection of the whole doctrine of innate ideas. Admitting that if any ideas were innate the idea of God would be most likely to be so,[126] he made an especially extensive argument against belief in an innate idea of God. He argued[127] that the existence in China and Siam and Brazil of whole tribes of atheists and the existence of individual atheists elsewhere disproved the teaching that the idea of God is innate. But Locke further argued that even were there no atheists that would not prove the idea of God innate for the idea might be derived from observation and reflection as are the universally known ideas of fire and the sun.[128] The fact that children have just such idea of God as they have been taught and that the ideas held by different people are different, proves such ideas of God as they do have not to be innate.[129] What ideas men have of God is determined by their instruction and by their powers of application and reasoning.[130] Some have a materialistic

---

[123] COLLINS, *A Discoure of Free Thinking*, pp. 85, 177.
[124] Nearly all the deists sounded Locke's praises. Voltaire sounded his praises in France. A good illustration of the attitude of deists to Locke is furnished by Bolingbroke in his *Works*, vol. 3, p. 84. q. v.
[125] LOCKE, *Essay*, I:iv:8–16.
[126] *op. cit.*, I:iv:8, 13, 17.
[127] *op. cit.*, I:iv:8.
[128] LOCKE, *Essay*, I:iv:9, 11.
[129] LOCKE, *Essay*, I:iv:13, 14, 15.
[130] LOCKE, *Essay*, I:iv:15. cf. *Essay*, IV:xvii:2.

idea of God, thinking of him as an old man sitting in
heaven, while others, through the use of reason, are certain
of the immateriality of God.[131]) The wise of all nations
have an idea of the unity and infinity of the deity which
they have acquired by thought and meditation and a right
use of their faculties.[132]) Herbert had reasoned that since
men were required to know God, justice would require
that God should have made provision for all men to have
an idea of God. And from this he had argued for an innate
idea of God.[133]) Locke's reply to this line of argument for a
doctrine of an innate idea of God was as follows. The goodness of God no more requires him to give all men an innate
idea of himself than it does that he build them bridges and
houses though he has provided reason, hands, and
materials.[134])

The relation of Locke's teaching about the idea of God,
as given in his argument against the belief that the idea of
God is innate, to the deist reasoning about the idea of God
is important. It resulted in their giving up the doctrine of
an innate idea of God and championing in its stead the
argument that the idea of God is so easy and natural an
idea to form if one observes and reasons at all that all men
have the idea by this reasoning method. Locke's admission
that the idea of God was one of the most reasonable and
natural for men to form and that the wise of all nations had,
by the use of natural faculties, attained an idea of the unity
and infinity of the deity, was readily taken by the deists as
support for their position. But they went farther than Locke
and asserted that not only the wise but all men had an idea
of the one supreme God and consequently they objected to
Locke's statement that there are atheist tribes.[135]) The
manner of Locke's answer to the plea that the goodness of
God requires him to give to men an innate idea of himself
seemed to imply on his part a belief, not only that man by
using observation and reason could attain knowledge of
God, but that he could attain to a satisfactory knowledge of
God in this natural way.

Locke maintained that the more complex ideas of God are

---

131) LOCKE, *Works*, vol. 4, *Second Reply to the Bishop of Worcester*,
p. 290.
132) LOCKE, *Essay*, I:iv:15. cf. IV:xvii:2.
133) HERBERT OF CHERBURY, *The Antient Religion of the Gentiles*, p. 6.
134) LOCKE, *Essay*, I:iv:12.
135) BLOUNT, *Miscel. Works. Oracles of Reason*, p. 181.
cf. LOCKE, *Essay*, I:iv:8.

derived from the more simple ideas of Him that are reached by reflection.[136]

Locke assigned very great importance to belief in the existence of God. He regarded such belief as absolutely essential to human society and as the foundation of morality.[137] It was because Locke thus regarded belief in God as at the very foundation of morality and of society itself that he, though one of the most vigorous, persistent and able of all the advocates of religious toleration, would not have the state tolerate atheists. It was also because he held belief in God's existence so important and because he recognized that arguments for the existence of God that appeal to one man do not always appeal to another, that Locke expressed disapproval of any attempt to show any argument for the existence of God, that appealed to anyone, to be weak.[138] He made the charge that those who argue for the existence of God from men having the idea of God in the mind have been guilty of doing this although their own argument is weak and inconclusive.[139]

Locke maintained that the existence of God can be demonstrated with mathematical certainty and that, though it is only attained by attention, thought and deduction,[140] it is the most obvious truth that reason discovers. He asserted that we are furnished with faculties to discover enough in the creatures to lead us to the knowledge of the Creator. For Locke, no truth seems clearer than that declared in the Scriptures which say that the invisible things of God are clearly seen from the creation of the world, "being understood by the things that are made, even his eternal power and Godhead." [141] By the following line of reasoning Locke demonstrated to his own satisfaction the existence of God. We know that we exist.[142] We also know that nothing cannot produce any real being. Something has therefore been from eternity. What had its beginning and being from another must have all its powers and properties from that other. Man finds power, knowledge and perception in himself. Things

---

136) Locke, *Essay*, II:xxiii:33.
137) Locke, *Works*, vol. 6. *A Letter Concerning Toleration*, p. 47.
138) Locke, *Works*, vol. 4. *Letter to the Bishop of Worcester*, p. 47. cf. *Essay*, IV:x:7.
139) Locke, *Works*, vol. 4. *A Letter to the Bishop of Worcester*, p. 52 ff. Locke is here a bit inconsistent, as the bishop pointed out, for he does what he says should not be done.
140) Locke, *Works*, vol. 4. *Second Reply to the Bishop of Worcester*, p. 289. cf. *Essay*, IV:ix:2.
141) Locke, *Essay*. IV:x:7. Cf. *Romans* 1:20.
142) Locke, *Essay*. IV:x:1.

void of knowledge and operating blindly could not produce a knowing being. It is repugnant to the idea of matter that it should put sense into itself. Matter and motion could not produce thought. The eternal being must be most knowing and the source of all knowledge. So from what we infallibly find in our own constitutions, reason leads to the knowledge of this certain and evident truth, that there is an eternal, most powerful and most knowing being, which, whether anyone will please to call God, it matters not.[143]

While Herbert made belief in the existence of God, as well as the other articles of the natural religion which he set forth, to rest on the foundation of innate ideas, post-Lockian deists followed Locke in making belief in the existence of God to be the result of a process of reasoning. They were pleased to find so strong a statement of the reasons for belief in God in Locke for it seemed to them that the more sure the reasoned belief in God could be shown to be and the more could be known about God through the reason, the less need there would be for any revelation. They made a good deal of the argument for the existence of God from universal consent. At this point Locke failed them somewhat as he denied universal consent and claimed there were some atheists. Locke however did not entirely discard that line of argument but weakened it, changing it from an argument from universal consent to an argument from general consent.[144] On the whole deists were pleased with Locke's arguments for a reasoned belief in God.

Locke did not claim man can know all about God. Rather he said we can have no notion at all of the substance of God.[145] But this does not signify much for Locke also maintained that we do not know the real essence of ourselves or of a fly or of a pebble. Yet he asserted that we can distinguish God from creatures, can know there is but one God and can demonstrate that he is not material but spiritual. He also taught that the order, harmony, and beauty of nature point to the conclusion that there is but one God, a conclusion that agrees with the teaching of the Scriptures.[146] He based his conclusion that God must be spiritual and not material on the fact that it is of the nature of matter, whether or not it

---

[143] LOCKE, *Essay*. IV:x:2–8, 10–11.
[144] LOCKE, *Works*. vol. 4, *Second Reply to the Bishop of Worcester*, p. 494.
[145] LOCKE, *Essay*. II:xxiii:35. cf. *Works*, vol. 9, p. 214.
[146] LOCKE, *Essay*. IV:x:10, 14.

be supposed eternal and cogitative, not to be a unit but to be made up of particles. A material God would therefore not be one eternal cogitative being such as the unity, harmony and order found in nature require but would be instead but an infinite number of finite cogitative beings.[147)] Locke also took note of the fact that the conclusion of reason that God is spiritual is in agreement with the teaching of the Scriptures.[148)] A few deists, such as Bolingbroke, followed the lead of Hobbes and regarded God as material, but most of them followed Locke and conceived of God as spiritual. The argument used by Locke in proving the spirituality of God shows that he regarded God as simple and uncompounded, even though our ideas of him must be complex.[149)]

Locke regarded the infinite attributes of God as but a projection upon an infinite scale of the finite attributes of men.[150)] This constituted a blow at the Cartesian form of the ontological argument for the existence of God.

Locke was a unitarian or Arian Christian rather than a trinitarian. When the Bishop of Worcester accused parts of Locke's *Essay* of being unfavorable to the trinitarian position, Locke denied that the passages attacked had any bearing on the question and refused to state his views concerning the doctrine of the trinity for the bishop's satisfaction. Instead he professed ignorance of the church doctrine and claimed the bishop's statement of it incomprehensible to him. He evidently desired to keep out of the raging trinitarian controversy. Another controversialist, named J. Edwards,[151)] sought to make Locke express his views on the doctrine of the Trinity, but without success. Trinitarians generally have held to the doctrine of two natures in one person in Christ. Locke denied that the Bible taught this.[152)] Trinitarians, holding to the doctrine of the deity of Christ, have generally interpreted the term "Son of God," when applied to Christ, as teaching his deity. In his *Reasonableness of Christianity*, and also in his paraphrases on St. Paul's Epistles, Locke puts an interpretation on the phrase that makes it not to teach deity.[153)]

---

147) Locke, *Essay*, IV:x:10, 14, 16, 17. cf. *Works*, vol. 4. *Second Reply to the Bishop of Worcester*, pp. 290–291.
148) Locke, *Works*, vol. 4, p. 291.
149) Locke, *Essay*, IV:x:5–17. cf. *Essay*, II:xxiii:33.
150) *op. cit.*, II:xvii:12, 17, and II:xxiii:33.
151) This is not the noted American Philosopher-Theologian Jonathan Edwards, but an English writer.
152) Locke, *Works*, 11th Edition. *Reply to the Bishop of Worcester*, vol. 4, p. 177. cf. *Second Reply. op. cit.*, vol. 4, p. 343.
153) Locke makes it denote merely Messiahship.

In his Latin letters to Limborch, Locke put a stress on the doctrine of the unity of God that is hardly consistent with the doctrine of the Trinity. Locke's unitarian friends made much of his writings and one of them translated his *Epistola de Tolerantia* into English. But the evidence for Locke's views and attitudes on this question of the Trinity is not confined to these hints. In his *Adversia Theologica,* which was not at first printed with Locke's other works but which was printed with King's *Life of John Locke,* he stated that Christ is not supreme God and is called Lord only by way of eminence and that he was not begotten by the supreme God but by the Holy Spirit who is represented as a created being. From these evidences it is manifest that the Bishop of Worcester was justified in suspecting Locke of anti-trinitarianism though unable to fully prove him such. But Locke's essentially Arian view of Christ and his denial of the Trinity did not spring from any desire to take from the glory of Christ but rather from his antipathy to mystery and incomprehensibility.[154]

In discussing the theological roots of deism, it was indicated that deism rooted back into Arian and antitrinitarian theology.[155] At this point Locke had much in common with the deists. Like them, too, he had a natural antipathy to the mysterious and incomprehensible. It is quite likely that this spirit in his works influenced such a deist as John Toland, who was a close student and admirer of Locke, to give out such views as that author expressed in his *Christianity Not Mysterious.*

b. *Locke's Doctrine Concerning Revelation Stated and Its Relation to the Deistic Teaching on the Same Subject Set Forth.* Locke, having denied that men have innate ideas or principles and having asserted that such ideas and principles as men do have are attained through sensation and reflection,[156] stated that knowledge is attainable in two ways, by reason and by revelation.[157] He defined knowledge as the perception of the connection and agreement, or disagreement and repugnancy of any of our ideas.[158] He distinguished reason from faith and derived the meaning he gave to the word revelation from his definition of faith. Reason is the dis-

---

[154] LOCKE, *Works*, 12th Edition. vol. 2, pp. 187–194. vol. 4, pp. 177, 343. (NOTE—Not found in 11th Edition of *Works*.)
[155] above, p. 34.
[156] LOCKE, Essay, I:ii-iv.
[157] *op. cit.*, IV:xix:4.
[158] *op. cit.*, IV:i:2.

covery of the certainty or probability of such propositions as
the mind arrives at by deduction from ideas gained by the
natural faculties of sensation and reflection.[159]   But "faith"
"is the assent to any proposition not thus made out by the
deductions of reason, but upon the credit of the proposer, as
coming from God, in some extraordinary way of communication." "This way of discovering truths to men, we call
revelation." [160]

Locke unhesitatingly asserted that revelation is possible. He
wrote: "For God, in giving us the light of reason has not
thereby tied up his own hands from affording us the light
of revelation."[161]   He warned that a traditional revelation
could not convey to men any new simple ideas.[162]   But God
might well use revelation to give to men either truths more
or less attainable by reason or truths not at all attainable by
reason.[163]

The deists did not usually make their attack upon revelation by denying its possibility.   But they certainly did not
affirm that possibility with the clear and vigorous affirma-
tion given by Locke.   They rather followed the doubting
attitude suggested by Hobbes who doubted that a man
could be sure he had a direct revelation and felt sure that
one thinking he had such direct revelation could never
prove the fact that he really had to another who might
doubt it.[164]

Locke asserted that there are some important items of
information for the gaining of which revelation is not
needed.   It is not needed to convey to men knowledge of
the existence and immateriality of God.[165]   It is not needed
to teach men that God is eternal, wise and powerful.[166]   Nor

---

159) LOCKE, *Essay*, IV:xviii:2.
160) *ibid.*   Locke, though well aware of the importance of the accurate
use of words, for he wrote much on that subject, gave to such words as
revelation, reason, faith, and knowledge different meanings in different
passages.   "Revelation," he made to sometimes mean a mode of com-
municating knowledge, and sometimes to mean the information so com-
municated.   A similar double use of "reason" is found in his works.
"Faith" may mean truth known by divine revelation, or any information
gained by testimony.   Or it may mean the attitude of trust.   "Knowledge" may mean truth gained by reason and not by revelation, or
truth that is certain however gained.   The context usually makes clear
the meaning to be attached to these words.
161) LOCKE, *Essay*, IV:xviii:8.
162) *op. cit.*, IV:xviii:3.
163) *op. cit.*, IV:xviii:7, 8.
164) above, pp. 73–74.   cf. TINDAL, *Christianity as Old as the Creation*, p. 163.
165) LOCKE, *Essay*, IV:x:3–6, 11, 13–17.
166) *ibid.*

is it needed to teach that it is man's duty to honor, fear and obey God, for he that has the idea of an intelligent but frail being, made by and dependent on another who is eternal, omnipotent and perfectly wise and good, will as certainly know that he is to honor, fear and obey God, as he will know that the sun shines when he sees it.[167]

Deists were naturally pleased to have Locke so clearly state that reason, without any need of revelation, could give the two first and chief articles of the religion of nature which they set forth. They, of course, went farther than Locke and stated in more or less restrained and guarded fashion the view that revelation is not needed at all.[168]

But Locke maintained that there are things for which revelation is needed. It is needed for the attaining of some truths not at all attainable by reason, such as the knowledge that there are other spiritual beings beside God and man, the knowledge of the fall of the angels and the knowledge of the future resurrection of the dead.[169] It is also needed for the more clear and authoritative giving of some truths that are attainable by reason such as truths concerning God, duty, right modes of worship and the sanctions of the moral law.[170] History reveals this need. For, though the works of nature sufficiently evidence a deity, yet the world made so poor use of reason even where God was easy to be found that it did not find him. Men were blinded by lust, indifference and fear and were kept by priests from learning of the existence of the true deity.[171] A few men like Socrates did attain such knowledge but most of them dared not proclaim it for fear of superstitious people and jealous priests. Socrates did declare it and they killed him.[172] History has proved that reason alone is not sufficient to overcome the indifference, superstition and greed of men and that the Christian revelation is needed. Wherever Christian revelation has gone, polytheism has died.[173]

---

[167] Locke, *Essay*, IV:xviii:3.

[168] The pre-Lockian Herbert expressed this view when he said nothing helpful to piety and public peace could be added to his five articles of natural religion. Herbert, *The Antient Religion of the Gentiles*, pp. 364–365. The post-Lockian Tindal expressed it even more emphatically, Tindal, *Christianity as Old as the Creation*, pp. 3, 4. cf. p. iii.

[169] Locke, *Essay*, IV:xviii:7 and IV:xi:12.

[170] Locke, *Works*, Eleventh edition, vol. 7. *The Reasonableness of Christianity*, p. 135 ff.

[171] Locke, *Works*, Eleventh Edition, vol. 7. *The Reasonableness of Christianity*, p. 135.

[172] *op. cit.*, p. 136.

[173] *op. cit.*, p. 137.

Revelation is also needed for the establishment of morality and virtue among the masses. Though a few earnest and learned seekers after truth might find the way of duty by the use of reason without revelation, the masses of mankind always have and always will lack the time, the education and the skill to do so.[174] The masses also lack desire to do so because lustrations and processions are easier than a clean conscience and a steady course of virtue and expiatory sacrifices that atone for the want of it are easier than a strict and holy life. Religion having been made easier than virtue, it became dangerous to distinguish them or to prefer virtue.[175]

Locke further maintained that though a few philosophers, isolated from each other in time and place, had fragmentary glimpses of important moral truth, yet only revelation could furnish a complete system of morality free from error and authoritative.[176] Solon and Socrates in Greece, Seneca in Italy, Confucius in China, had each discovered a fragment of moral truth but none had a complete system or knew some of the truths discovered by the others. The truths discovered by each one was mixed with errors. Only authoritative revelation could separate between the truth and the error and decide between disagreeing philosophers. For to send men to philosophers, were to send them to a wild wood of uncertainty, to an endless maze from which they could never get out and to send them to the religions of the world were still worse.[177]

Locke advanced the need for moral sanctions as another reason why revelation is necessary. As virtue is not always rewarded in this life men would be likely to excuse themselves from virtue were it not for the sanction of a future life of rewards and punishments.[178] And the only sure knowledge of such a future life comes by revelation. For the idea of a future life that men had without revelation was hopelessly mixed with fables. Christ brought life and immortality to light when he rose and proved his resurrection.[179] Virtue was thus made a substantial good and not a mere airy and useless ideal.[180]

---

174) LOCKE, *The Reasonableness of Christianity*, p. 139.
175) *ibid.*
176) LOCKE, *Works*, Eleventh Edition, vol. 7. *The Reasonableness of Christianity*, pp. 148–149.
177) *ibid.*
178) *op. cit.*, p. 150.
179) *ibid.*
180) *op. cit.*, p. 150 f.

Locke further regarded revelation as needed to give man encouragement in his moral struggles. Man is conscious of a need for strength. Revelation gives the knowledge of an almighty arm that assists and carries through.[181]

Finally, Locke claimed that revelation, and here he evidently had the New Testament, Christian revelation in mind, was needed to reform cumbersome modes of worship. Both gentile and jewish religion needed this reform. Christ brought this reform in his conversation with the woman of Samaria. Only enough ceremony is needed in religion to preserve order.[182]

Comparing Locke's teaching on the subject of the need for revelation with the attitude and teaching of the deists on the same subject, one notices some marked points of agreement and similarity and other equally marked differences. The meagreness and relative unimportance of the things Locke named as only to be known through revelation would tend to give encouragement to the deists who did not think revelation was needed to give any knowledge not attainable by reason. On the other hand the deists would not agree with Locke's reasoning concerning needs for revelation to supplement reason in the field of knowledge attainable by reason. In the main, they passed over this part of Locke's reasoning in silence. However, had they countered Locke's arguments directly they would probably have talked of the difficulty of knowing what is and what is not revelation, have pointed to the disagreements among the interpreters of what is claimed as revelation and perhaps even have said that what is claimed as revelation only makes things darker and more confused. Such modes of attack upon revelation are found in the writings of several deists,[183] although not as direct answers to Locke's arguments. Those "immortal" deists who taught the doctrine of immortality and future rewards and punishments as a part of natural religion were probably displeased with Locke's suggestion that revelation was needed to make this sanction of immortality more sure and clear. On the other hand, the "mortal" deists who were not ready to make immortality an article of natural religion undoubtedly felt that Locke's words about the need for revelation to make sure this doctrine of immortality, felt themselves strengthened against

---

[181] LOCKE, *Works*, 11th Edition, vol. 7. *The Reasonableness of Christianity*, p. 151.

[182] LOCKE, *Essay*, IV:xix:16, 5.

[183] COLLINS, *A Discourse of Free-Thinking*, pp. 52–53.
TINDAL, *Christianity as Old as the Creation*, pp. 27, 163. 23.

the "immortal" deists. Locke clearly advocated an ethical and non-liturgical or ceremonial religion. This was one of the positions of the deists and Locke certainly encouraged the deists who followed after him in arguing for an almost purely ethical religion and against a religion of ceremony. What Locke had to say about priests and their self-seeking and their misleading of the masses and of their substituting sacrifices for virtue, was undoubtedly written with the priests of gentile heathen religions in mind rather than with thought of Bible priests or Christian clergy. But the deists took these ideas and applied them to Bible, and to Roman Catholic and Protestant Christian clergy as well. Locke, allowing only enough of ceremony and ritual in religion for the preserving of order, was quite in line with the deistic opposition to ritualism in religion.

Locke, having accepted the fact of revelation and shown the need for it, proceeded to a brief discussion of the extent of revelation and then to a longer discussion of the proofs of it. How much revelation has been given? How much of revelation do we possess? Such were the questions he discussed. He warned that mere enlightenment or illumination by the Spirit must not be taken as revelation since it lacked the credential proofs. He admitted that there might be other revelation than the Bible but concluded that the only well-attested revelation is the Bible so that the Bible and revelation can be regarded as co-extensive.[184] In this he differed from the deists who more or less openly rejected all revelation. While writing of the value of the Bible revelation, Locke made the observation that men often think they have discovered by reason what in reality they owe to revelation and that consequently many are beholden to revelation who do not acknowledge their debt.[185] Naturally this idea was not pleasing to deists.

Locke represented miracles as a main proof of revelation and discussed them as such.[186] He would not accept mere strong belief or feeling as a proof. He illustrated the value of miracles as evidence for revelation by referring to Nicodemus' words: "Rabbi, we know that thou art a teacher come from God: for no man can do these miracles that thou doest, except God be with him."[187] Locke pointed out that

---

184) LOCKE, *Essay*, IV:xix:16.
185) LOCKE, *Works*, 11th Edition, vol. 7. *The Reasonableness of Christianity*, p. 145.
186) LOCKE, *Essay*, IV:xix:15. cf. *Works*, 11th Edition, vol. 9, *A Discourse of Miracles*, p. 256 ff.
187) *John* 3:2.

usually the more strange an event is the slower are men to admit it as a fact but also that the more evidently supernatural an event is the better it is suited to prove a thing from God who alone has the power to change nature. So the proper case for a miracle is the attestation of truths which need confirmation.[188] Locke defined a miracle as "a sensible operation, which, being above the comprehension of the spectator, and in his opinion contrary to the established course of nature, is taken by him to be divine."[189] Most definitions simply assert that a miracle is by divine power. But Locke argued for the more reserved and cautious form of his definition by saying that our ignorance of the laws of nature and of the limits of the powers of others than God forbid us from defining a miracle as a thing only wrought by divine power.[190] The Bible speaks of lying wonders. The Egyptian rivals of Moses wrought wonders. But when wonder is opposed to wonder the greater wonder is to be regarded as of God because one cannot suppose God would let his messenger be outdone. Thus Moses wrought greater wonders than his rivals.[191] Locke reasoned that nothing could be accepted as a miracle if it was a thing used to support a mission derogatory to God or to natural religion and morality, for God having given these through reason cannot be supposed to back the contrary. Were He to do so that would be to destroy the use of reason without which men could not distinguish divine revelation from diabolical imposture.[192] Miracles, according to Locke, were only given in support of matters of high concern. For God to have given them in matters of lighter importance would merely have been to encourage sloth. Only Moses and Christ came with revelations attested by miracles.[193]

Locke's giving of an unusual definition of miracles, his limiting of the number and occasions for them and his refusing to allow any that would be contrary to natural religion, together with his suggestion that their use for light occasions would be but to encourage sloth, were features in his discussion of miracles that later deists seized upon and used. But perhaps the main influence of Locke's writings

---

[188] Locke, *Essay*, LV:xvi:13. cf. *Works*, 11th Edition, vol. 9, *Discourse of Miracles*, pp. 257, 259–264.

[189] Locke, *Works*, 11th Edition, vol. 9. *Discourse of Miracles*, p. 256.

[190] *op. cit.*, pp. 261, 263–264.

[191] op. cit., pp. 260–261.

[192] Locke, *Works*, 11th Edition, vol. 9. *Discourse of Miracles*, pp. 261–262.

[193] Locke, *Essay*, IV:xix:15.

on miracles upon the deists who followed after him was
that he made miracles the main proof for revelation. They
directed their attacks against revelation very heavily against
miracles as the proof of revelation. Most deists had something to write against miracles. Some, such as Thomas
Woolston in his series of *Discourses on Miracles,* made that
the main attack. Most of the deists made their attacks
against particular miracles rather than against miracles as
such. But in Conyers Middleton and the famous skeptical
philosopher, David Hume, there is a return to a more philosophical discussion of miracles as such. After Locke, miracles had a more prominent place in the deistic controversy
than they had before Locke.

Locke gave revelation a high degree of credibility, but
scarcely as high as reason. He said the credibility of revelation could not exceed that of reason since reason must
determine what propositions are revelations.[194]   However,
revelation, coming from God, who cannot deceive, must be
accepted even when it differs from common experience.
Faith based on revelation is assent founded on the highest
reason and therefore its truth is not to be doubted.[195]   It
should overrule opinions, prejudices and interests.[196]   However, Locke added, for truths discoverable by it, the reason
is a surer means of attaining knowledge than revelation
since the evidence for a traditional revelation can never be
as sure as the knowledge we have from the clear and distinct perception of the agreement or disagreement of our
own ideas.[197]

Deists could find little in the first part of this statement
by Locke concerning the credibility of revelation that would
agree with or that could be used to support their own attitude toward revelation. But they could draw much support
from Locke's last statement which made reason surer than
revelation in truths discoverable by it. For Locke had
already made but very few, and those relatively unimpor-
tant, truths discoverable only by revelation.[198]   This statement by Locke also seemed to take away the force of his
statement elsewhere that revelation was needed for the
more clear and authoritative giving of truths attainable
by reason.[199]

---

194) LOCKE, *Essay,* IV:xviii:5.
195) *op. cit.,* IV:xvi:14.
196) *op. cit.,* IV:xviii:10.
197) *op. cit.,* IV:xviii:4.
198) above, p. 93.
199) *loc. cit.*

Locke retained the old distinction between things contrary to and things above reason and he held that nothing contrary to reason can be accepted as being truly revelation or true whereas things above reason might be accepted as being both revelation and true. Since he found the Bible fully evidenced by miracles and other means and containing nothing that he regarded as contrary to reason, though he did find it to contain things above reason, he declared it should be accepted as revelation and as true.[200]

Locke made a strong statement concerning his own acceptance of the Bible. He read the Scriptures with full assurance that all therein is true and yielded a submission to its inspired authors that he would give to no other writers.[201] He regarded the Bible as having God for its author, salvation for its end, and truth without any mixture of error for its matter. All other things heard about Christianity are to be judged by it.[202] The Bible is the constant guide of his assent, he declared. Then he added, "I wish I could say, there are no mysteries in it; I acknowledge there are to me, and I fear always will be. But where I want the evidence of things, there yet is ground enough for me to believe, because God has said it: and I shall presently condemn and quit any opinion of mine, as soon as I am shown that it is contrary to any revelation in the Holy Scriptures."[203]

This attitude of Locke toward revelation was certainly very different from that of all the deists and makes it very evident that Locke, however much he might have in common with deists and however much he might influence them, was not himself a deist.

In discussing the relation of reason to revelation, Locke made the first function of reason to decide what is and what is not revelation. It is the business of reason to guard against counterfeit revelations of enthusiasts and deceivers.[204] The longer the tradition in the case of a traditional revelation the more difficult is it to prove the revelation genuine. Copies of copies are not admitted in English court procedure. Those who think things gain

200) LOCKE, *Essay*, IV:xviii:10.
201) LOCKE, *Works*, 11th Edition, vol. 4. *Second Reply to the Bishop of Worcester*, p. 341.
202) This statement is in a letter by Locke to Rev. R. King, dated Aug. 25, 1703. *Works*, vol. 10, p. 306, q. v.
203) LOCKE, *Works*, 11th Edition, vol. 4. Postscript to *Letter to the Bishop of Worcester*, p. 96.
204) LOCKE, *Essay*, IV:xviii:11, and IV:xix:10.

force by aging are reversing the reasonable conclusion. Opinions do not gain force, as many mistakenly think, but lose force as they grow older and are often repeated.[205]

Deists got much in Locke's discussion of this first function of reason in relation to revelation. Of course theists and deists alike would agree that if there is any true revelation, reason must decide between the true and the counterfeit. Some deists, rejecting all revelation on various grounds, would probably say that the only function here left to reason would be to reject all claimed revelations and give reasons for so doing. Locke's mention of enthusiasts and deceivers seems to indicate that he believed, as did the deists who wrote[206] much about enthusiasm and enthusiasts and deceivers, especially among the clergy, that the history of religion was heavily loaded with those types of people. Few remarks by Locke were more greedily seized upon and made use of by the deists[207] than the one to the effect that the older a traditional revelation became the more difficult it became to prove it genuine.

Having discovered what is revelation, reason must also interpret it. This does not mean deciding on its truth or falsehood, for once accepted as revelation it must be regarded as true. But it does mean finding out the meaning of the words in which the traditional revelation is expressed. Reason must take note of the fact that words change their meanings with the passing years. Reason's task of interpretation is made more difficult when it is required to translate into a strange language of peoples with different customs from those followed by the people to whom the revelation was first given. The style of the human authors of part of revelation, particularly the style of Paul, adds difficulty to reason's task of interpretation. Paul was too full and forceful to be always clear. The variety of interpretations of the Scriptures that exist shows how difficult is reason's task.[208] While Locke admitted that the Holy Spirit is given to guide men in the interpreting of Scripture, yet he insisted that the Bible must be studied and its meaning determined very much like other books.[209]

---

[205] LOCKE, *Essay*, IV:xvi:10. Locke was not here speaking of the Bible, but deists quickly applied this mode of reasoning to the Bible.
[206] Bolingbroke and Shaftesbury are good illustrations of this feature of deism. BOLINGBROKE, *Works*, vol. 3, pp. 56, 59. SHAFTESBURY, *Characteristics*, vol. 2, pp. 337, 345.
[207] TINDAL, *Christianity as Old as the Creation*, p. 163.
[208] LOCKE, *Essay*, III:ix:22, 23.
[209] *op. cit.*, IV:xix:16. cf. *Works*, vol. 4, pp. 341–342.

Locke's enlargement upon the difficulties of the task of
reason in interpreting revelation because of changes of
language, changes of words, strangeness of customs and the
fact that the style of some such writers as Paul were not
always clear, was seized upon by the deists in their attacks
upon revelation.[210]   They insisted that if God were giving a
revelation it should surely be clear.[211]   Then, with the evident intent of making the difficulties of Bible interpretation
an argument against accepting it as revelation, they made
remarks to the effect that the inspired or illuminated books
are the darkest of all.[212]   In effect they insisted that instead
of revelation being needed, as Locke had said in presenting
the needs for revelation,[213] to settle points of dispute in
natural religion and to give a clear and authoritative message, what claimed to be revelation was itself so dark and
so open to disputed interpretations that reason had to decide
the points after all.[214]   Locke himself, when speaking about
natural religion instead of about the need for revelation,
seemed to practically contradict what he had said about
revelation being needed as the clear and authoritative arbi-
ter between the views of conflicting reasoners, for he wrote
that, since the precepts of natural religion are plain and
very intelligible to all mankind whereas the truths revealed
by books and languages are liable to the common and natural obscurities and difficulties incident to words, he thinks
men should give more heed to observing natural religion
and should be less magisterial, positive, and imperious, in
imposing their own interpretations of revealed religion.[215]
This found an echo in such deists as Tindal.[216]

c. *Locke's Doctrine Concerning Natural Religion and Its
Relation to the Deistic Natural Religion.* The statement by
Locke to which reference has just been made shows that he
not only recognized the existence of natural religion but
also held it to be of practical value and importance. The
content which Locke gave to natural religion was practically the same as that given at an earlier date by Herbert of
Cherbury. For though Locke refused to admit Herbert's
five articles of natural religion to be innate, yet he said that
they are all clear truths to which a rational creature could

210) TINDAL, *Christianity as Old as the Creation*, p. 23.
211) BOLINGBROKE, *Works*, vol. 2, pp. 429–430.
212) *ibid.* cf. TINDAL, *Christianity as Old as the Creation*, p. 23.
213) above, p. 93.
214) TINDAL, *loc. cit.*
215) LOCKE, *Essay*, III:ix:23.
216) TINDAL, *Christianity as Old as the Creation*, p. 2.

hardly avoid giving assent.[217]   He thought men ought to
magnify the goodness of God for giving men so sufficient a
light of reason that they to whom the light of the written
word never came could not fail to know God and their duty
of obedience to him if they but sought after truth.[218]   Since
post-Lockian deists practically all built their natural religion on the foundation of Locke's empiricism rather than
on Herbert's doctrine of innate ideas, it might seem that
Locke and these later deists were practically agreed on the
subject of natural religion.   However, Locke claimed natural religion to be weak and inadequate in some respects.
This deists did not admit.

Locke found some weaknesses in natural religion,[219] most
of which he attributed to ignorance, superstition and priestcraft.[220]   It does not provide a strong enough incentive to
make men bear the hardships which the good life involves.[221]   Its knowledge of a future life is too cloudy and
uncertain to be an effective sanction.[222]   It does not sufficiently recognize nor provide for human weakness and
sin.[223]   Its perfect moral law makes no provision for weakness and failure and therefore it is not a religion suited to
weak and sinful men.[224]   Yet natural religion as worked
out by the philosophers is better than the non-Christian
particular religions and these, in turn, are better than no
religion at all.[225]   But they have been so corrupted by the
selfish manipulations of rulers and priests that they have
become an abomination to God.[226]   Though perhaps it has
not yet been done, a true and adequate system of morality
could be wrought out without revelation.[227]

Closely related to the question concerning the adequacy
or inadequacy of natural religion is that concerning the fate
of those who have not known special revelation.   Locke

---

217) LOCKE, *Essay*, I:iii:15, 16.
218) *op. cit.*, III:ix:23.
219) LOCKE, *Works*, vol. 7.   *The Reas. of Christianity*, pp. 11–12; 156–
157.   cf. *Essay*, I:iii:8.
220) *ibid.*
221) LOCKE, *Works*, vol. 7.   *The Reas. of Christianity*, pp. 148–149.
222) *op. cit.*, pp. 149–151.
223) *op. cit.*, pp. 151, 139.
224) *op. cit.*, p. 157.
225) *op. cit.*, pp. 135–139.
226) *op. cit.*, pp. 135, 139, 144.
227) Although Locke gives the impression, when discussing the powers
of reason, that a complete system of morality could be worked out by
reason, yet he also implies it is unnecessary since we have the Christian
revelation.   But elsewhere he speaks as though the working out of a
system of morality without the aid of revelation would be a hopeless
task.   *Works*, vol. 7, *The Reasonableness of Christianity*, pp. 138–147.

says God, not men, must decide their fate.   But he adds that
those who come by the light of reason to repentance would
no doubt be forgiven and accepted by God.[228]   He inter-
prets Acts 4:12 to mean only that Jesus is Messiah and not
to mean that those without knowledge of him are lost.[229]

Locke's recognition of the five articles of natural religion,
his teaching that a true system of morality could be attained
and demonstrated by reason and his opinion that God
would accept repentance on the part of those without revelation, gave much encouragement[230] to the deists who held
these views also.   But though Locke had much in common
with the deists in views of natural religion, yet he held
natural religion inadequate and not well suited to sinful
men, a position deists would not accept.

Locke's discussion of the article concerning a future life
of rewards and punishments was very influential though he
wavered somewhat about this article.   He taught that natural religion includes knowledge of the fact of a future life.
But he seemed to regard its testimony concerning such
future life as not full or clear or sufficiently sure to serve as
a strong sanction for the good life.[231]   Herbert of Cherbury
had been perfectly sure that a future life with rewards and
punishments was part of the teaching of natural religion.
Hobbes had little to say on the question. Later deists divided
into two schools, one of which taught belief in immortality
as a part of natural religion while the other, represented by
such a deist as Bolingbroke, denied immortality.[232]   Locke's
hesitancy no doubt had influence on these views.   Locke
accepted immortality as revealed by Christ.[233]

d. *Locke's Doctrine Concerning the Soul and Its Influence
upon Deism.*   Locke regarded man as divided into two
parts, body and soul.   The body is material in substance,
having such qualities as extension.[234]   The soul, Locke said,
is probably immaterial.[235] His use of the word "probably" is

---

228) LOCKE, *Works*, vol. 7.   *The Reas. of Christianity*, pp. 126-134.
cf. *Essay*, IV:xx:23.
229) LOCKE, *Works*, vol. 7.   *The Reas. of Christianity*, pp. 133-134.
230) Among the deists, Tindal particularly enlarged upon the idea
that the goodness of God must lead to his acceptance of repentance as
sufficient.   Locke's idea that morality could be attained and demonstra-
tively proved by reason is expressed most clearly in a letter to Molyneux dated March 30, 1696.   *Works*, vol. 9.
231) above, p. 94.
232) BOLINGBROKE, *Works*, vol. 4, pp. 360-362.
233) LOCKE, *Works*, vol. 7.   *The Reas. of Christianity*, pp. 150-151.
234) LOCKE, *Essay*, II:xxiii:28-30.
235) LOCKE, *Works*, vol. 4.   *Letter to the Bishop of Worcester*, pp.
33-37.

significant. For he went on to ask if the soul might not be
material. How can we say that matter might not be given
the power to think, even though it is not of the nature of
matter itself to think? Could not God add a faculty of
thinking to matter as easily as to add another substance with
the faculty of thinking? Since God has given to matter such
a variety of characteristics as it shows in the peach, the rose
and the elephant, surely he might also have given it the
powers of thought, reason and volition.[236] Locke further
said that one who studies this question concerning the materiality or immateriality of the soul will find that each view
involves difficulties that tend to drive the investigator to the
opposite view.[237] Locke reached the conclusion that the
reason is scarcely able to determine for or against the materiality of the soul.[238] He denied, however, any intention
to undermine belief in the immateriality of the soul.[239] Yet
it was to Locke and his suggested lines of argument rather
than to Hobbes that the materialists among the deists
looked.

e. *Locke's Doctrine of Toleration and Its Relation to the
Thought of the Deists on That Subject.* Locke was an ardent
champion of toleration. In his four letters, or epistles, on
that subject he gave a remarkably full presentation of the
arguments in favor of toleration. Indeed, the first of these
letters, *De Tolerantia,* which first appeared in Latin but
soon appeared in English also, was probably the ablest and
most influential argument for toleration that was ever
penned.

With the exception of Hobbes, practically all the English
deists were champions of toleration. In so far as this was
due to the fact that they were victims of intolerance and
also in so far as their arguments for toleration were not a
part of their system of thought, neither the fact of their
advocating toleration nor their arguments for it are of
concern here. Nor are many of Locke's arguments for
toleration of interest from the standpoint of this study.
But in so far as toleration and the arguments for it were
essentially and logically a part of a deistic system of
thought, it does call for attention.[240] The deists were happy

236) LOCKE, *Works,* vol. 4. *Second Reply to the Bishop of Worcester,* pp. 460–476.
237) LOCKE, *Essay,* IV:iii:6. cf. Locke's Letter of Jan. 20, 1692, to
Molyneux. *Works,* 11th Edition, vol. 9.
238) *ibid.*
239) LOCKE, *Essay,* IV:iii:6.
240) CHUBB, THOMAS, *The Posthumous Works of Mr. Thomas Chubb,*
London, R. Baldwin, 1748. vol. 1, section 4.

to have Locke on their side in the toleration controversy and naturally made use of arguments which he ably developed.

Locke conceived of a church as a voluntary organization made up of people who joined it after reaching the age of discretion.[241] He also excluded control over the beliefs or religious actions of those not members of that particular church from the field of that church's jurisdiction.[242] Attempting such control was usurpation and not in harmony with the purposes for which the church was formed.[243] From these theories concerning the origin, nature and purpose of church organization, Locke argued against a policy of intolerance on the part of any church organization toward those outside its bounds.[244]

In the course of this line of argument for toleration, Locke had much to say in hostile criticism of the clergy of both the non-Christian[245] and the Christian[246] religions. The "holy tribe" were satisfied if people were strict about ceremonies.[247] They killed Socrates for teaching the people truth.[248] They were the corruptors and the oppressors of the people and the hinderers of all progress.[249] How unworthy were the Jewish priests was made evident by their treatment of Christ and the apostles.[250] The Christian clergy, with a few noble exceptions,[251] have done badly also. They have blocked the way to the conversion of non-Christians by their sectarianism.[252] They have been proud, ambitious and disputatious.[253] Their subtle disputes have only tended to make men conceited in ignorance and obstinate in error.[254] Their motives have not always been the best.[255] The pretence of religion has often been but a cloak for covetousness, rapine and ambition.[256] They have kept people ignorant to keep them obedient.[257] They have been

---

241) LOCKE, *Works*, vol. 6. *A Letter Concerning Toleration*, p. 13.
242) *op. cit.*, p. 18.
243) *op. cit.*, pp. 18, 19.
244) *ibid.*
245) *op. cit.*, pp. 21–23. cf. *Works*, vol. 7, pp. 135–139, 144.
246) LOCKE, *Works*, vol. 6. *A Let. Concerning Toleration*, p. 21 f.
247) LOCKE, *Works*, vol. 7. *The Reas. of Christianity*, pp. 138–139.
248) *loc. cit.*
249) *op. cit.*, p. 136.
250) LOCKE, *Works*, vol. 7. *The Reas. of Christianity*, pp. 72–73.
251) LOCKE, *Works*, vol. 6. *A Third Letter for Toleration*, p. 172 f. cf. *Essay*, IV:xvi:4.
252) LOCKE, *Works*, vol. 6. *A Third Let. for Toleration*, pp. 237–240.
253) LOCKE, *Essay*, III:ix:9, 12. Spoken of Scholastic Theologians.
254) *op. cit.*, III:xi:5.
255) *op. cit.*, IV:xx:17.
256) LOCKE, *Works*, vol. 6. *A Let. con. Toleration*, p. 53.
257) LOCKE, *Essay*, IV:xx:4.

after benefices rather than conversions.[258]   They have been
creatures of the court, ready to change their religion with
changes of sovereigns.[259]

It is evident from these charges by Locke that he shared
to a very considerable extent the anti-clericalism of the
deists, just as it is evident from their works that they made
more use of the anticlerical charges made by Locke in connection with his argument for toleration from the nature of
the church and the duties of its officers, than they made of
that argument itself.   Locke, however, recognized a place
for a church and for a clergy of the right sort,[260] whereas
deists had little or nothing to say that suggested any need
for any church or clergy of any kind.   They generally made
their charges against the clergy more sweepingly inclusive
than did Locke.

Locke found another argument for toleration in his speculations in the field of political philosophy.   His doctrine of
the origin of the state was like that of Hobbes. Both thought
that originally sovereign individuals delegated their sovereignty by entering into a compact in order to gain certain
important advantages.[261]   However, the original state of
men as conceived by Locke was less warlike than with
Hobbes and the delegation of authority was not so complete
giving a limited monarchy rather than Hobbes' absolute
monarchy.[262]   But Locke reasoned to the conclusion that
the sovereign state had no jurisdiction over the religious
opinions and practices of men except when such were prej-
udicial to the well-being of the state itself as in the case of
those who taught atheism or who taught that people of one
religious organization should not keep faith with those of a
different sect,[263] whereas Hobbes had reasoned to the conclusion that the state had full control in matters of religion
and should not tolerate any but the state religion.[264]   On
this point, all later English deists followed Locke rather
than Hobbes whose doctrines of state religion and state intolerance they detested.[265]

Locke argued that truth does not need the assistance of

---

[258] LOCKE, *Works*, vol. 6.   *A Third Let. for Toleration*, p. 234.
[259] LOCKE, *Works*, vol. 6.   *A Let. concerning Toleration*, p. 27 f.
[260] *ibid.*
[261] LOCKE, *Works*, vol. 6.   *A Third Letter for Toleration*, p. 212.
cf. LOCKE, *Works*, vol. 6, *A Let. Concerning Toleration*, p. 10.   cf. *Works*,
vol. 5, *Of Civil Government*, pp. 339–347.
[262] LOCKE, *Works*, vol. 5.   *Of Civil Government*, p. 339 ff.
[263] LOCKE, *Works*, vol. 6.   *A Let. Con. Toleration*, pp. 10, 45, 47.
[264] HOBBES, *Works*, vol. 3.   *Leviathan*, pp. 362–380.   cf. pp. 45, 93.
[265] COLLINS, *A Discourse of Free-Thinking*, pp. 170–171.

force and therefore religious intolerance is not needed. Truth would do well enough if left to shift for herself. She makes her way into the understanding by her own light and is but weaker for any borrowed force violence can add to her. Error, not truth, needs force to propagate and maintain itself. If it be a mark of the true religion that it will prevail by its own light and strength while false religions need force and foreign helps to support them, nothing can be more for the advantage of true religion than to take away compulsion everywhere.[266]

Locke further maintained that since the only possible reasonable excuse for use of force in religion would be thereby to promote the salvation of souls and since the effect of its use cannot be the salvation of souls, it should not be used. If salvation were by an outer conformity, force might compel men directly to such conformity and so save them. But salvation is not by such outer conformity. He who conforms to true religion without belief is not saved. A man cannot be saved by a religion he distrusts and a worship he abhors. To punish for honest disbelief would be to punish for honesty. The human understanding cannot submit blindly to the will of another.[267] Nor is the use of force suited to lead men indirectly to salvation by making them consider as it rather prejudices against the religion it is used to favor.[268] Moreover, one cannot rightly assume that the religion for which it will be used is truer than the one against which it is put in operation.[269]

In this part of his argument for toleration, Locke is tacitly assuming that religion is essentially a rational thing and that rites and ordinances are of relatively little importance as compared with reasoned beliefs. This of course was what the deists asserted in a more sweeping way than Locke would care to do. Since for them, even more than for Locke, true religion is a reasoned and a reasonable thing, the line of argument for toleration here developed by Locke from the nature of saving religion and of the human reason, appealed much to them[270] and was that part of their argument for toleration that made their advocacy of toleration a

---

266) LOCKE, *Works*, vol. 6. *A Let. Con. Tol.*, p. 40.

267) *op. cit.*, p. 11. cf. *A Second Let. Con. Tol.*, p. 67 ff.

268) LOCKE, *Works*, vol. 6. *A Second Let. Con. Tol.*, p. 71.

269) *op. cit.*, p. 77 f.

270) COLLINS, *A Discourse of Free-Thinking*, pp. 100–111.
COLLINS, *Ground and Reason of the Christian Religion*, preface, pp. v–xvii.

real part of their deistic system rather than a mere effort to escape the discomforts of the persecuted.

It must be concluded then that Locke was certainly not a deist but that he was sympathetic to many of their trends of thought without going to the same extremes as did they. He firmly believed in revelation and warmly defended it. They rejected it. He maintained the insufficiency of natural religion and the need for revelation. They maintained the sufficiency of natural religion and denied the need for revelation. He believed in miracles and accepted them as proofs of a special revelation. They rejected revelation and attacked and rejected the miracles advanced as proof of it. He maintained that there are atheists. They denied it, maintaining universal belief in one supreme God as the first article of natural religion. At these points he might be regarded as a defender of Christian theism against the deists. But on the other hand, Locke, as compared with the more orthodox Christian theists, magnified the office of reason in religion, gave a relatively large and important place to natural religion and a relatively small and less important place to revealed religion, minimized the mysterious and supernatural elements in the Christian religion, weakened the definition of the miracle,[271] and gave much weight to the ethical and little to the ritualistic side of Christianity. He rejected the trinitarian conception of God and the related doctrine of the deity of Christ. He manifested some of the anticlerical spirit common among the deists. From these facts it appears that Locke occupied a position about half-way between the deists and their orthodox opponents.

Locke's influence led the deists to build on an empirical foundation instead of upon the doctrine of innate ideas that Herbert of Cherbury had championed. Though not a materialist, Locke expressed the opinion that it would be difficult to prove the soul immaterial. This point was seized upon by such deists as favored materialism. Though a believer in a future state, he penned some expressions about the haziness and uncertainty of the sanctions for morality that come from what natural religion has to teach about a future life. This gave encouragement to the element among the deists who rejected the doctrine of the immortality of the soul.

Locke himself, of course, had no uncertainty about a future life but he based his clear certainty on revelation.

---

271) above, p. 97.

His remark to the effect that length of time weakened the evidence for a traditional revelation was greedily seized upon by the deists.[272] His charges against the clergy gave ammunition to the deists for their effort to prove that the Bible which had long been in the hands of clergy had been corrupted. His remark to the effect that men should give more heed to natural religion whose precepts are so plain and less to the difficult questions and disputes of revealed religion found a hearty welcome with the deists. As the views of individual deists are studied hereafter in the light of Locke's teachings as set forth in the preceding pages, the magnitude of Locke's influence with and upon the deists will become more evident. Here it must suffice to say that no other man exercised a greater influence upon the deistic movement than did Locke, though he was not a deist.

D. CHARLES BLOUNT

If Hobbes was indeed a deist, then Charles Blount (1654-1693), about whose classification there is no question, was the third influential deistic writer to arise in England. Blount, like most of the earlier but unlike several of the later deists, professed loyalty to Christianity.[273] But he very evidently sought to undermine that faith as it was understood and accepted by the more orthodox Christian groups.

Only a few words need be given to Blount's life. His father was of the lower order of the nobility and gave his son a good education. Blount made some claim to linguistic ability and quoted freely from Greek and Latin writers. Among the ancient writers whom he often quoted were Philostratus, Porphyry, Celsus, Lucian, Seneca and Cicero.[274] He also quoted such later writers as Averroes, Pomponatius, Erasmus, Montaigne, Spinoza, Francis Bacon, Hobbes and Locke. The names suggest where Blount prob-

---

272) TINDAL, *Christianity as Old as the Creation*, p. 163.

273) It is not necessary to decide here whether Blount was or was not sincere in his profession of Christianity. He may have thought that the religion he believed in should be called Christianity. Or he may have used the term with less worthy motive. At any rate he and the movement he represented came to have a reputation for duplicity among the more orthodox Christian groups.
Vid. BURY, J. B., *A History of Freedom of Thought*, New York, Henry Holt and Co.; London, Williams and Norgate, 1913. pp. 134, 139. cf. FARRAR, *A Critical History of Free Thought*, pp. 123–124.

274) There is no reason to doubt that Blount could or did read most of the writers named above in their own works. Of course, writers such as Celsus and Porphyry could only be read from quotations, since their own works were not extant.

ably gleaned many of his ideas for he was not noted as an original or creative thinker. His *Religio Laici* is so like the work of similar title by Herbert of Cherbury as to suggest heavy dependence upon it. However, though Blount failed to contribute much in the way of new ideas to deism, he did rather thoroughly gather up the deistic notions that were in the air and did show great zeal in making them known. His works revived the interest in deism which had seemed to decline somewhat after the first interest in Herbert of Cherbury's writings. Disappointed in an affair of the heart, Blount committed suicide in the year 1693.

A brief statement concerning the writings of Blount is in order. In 1680 he published a translation of *Philostratus' Life of Apollonius Tyaneus*. Hierocles and some other pagan opponents of early Christianity had tried to stop the spread of that faith by attempting to parallel the life and miracles of Christ in the life of the Pythagorean Apollonius. Julia Domna, consort of the Emperor Septimius Severus, gathered about her a group of learned men hostile to Christianity. "This circle produced the remarkable book of Philostratus, the biography of Apollonius of Tyana, in which characteristics drawn from the portrait of the despised Jesus are transferred to the heathen prophet."[275] Blount translated two books of this life of Apollonius from the Greek into English and added copious notes of his own which express his own deistic views. Blount's *Religio Laici* appeared in the year 1683. The main aim of this work, which borrowed so heavily from Herbert of Cherbury's book of like title, seems to have been to point out what the author considered good in the non-Christian faiths and bad in the Christian faith. Three short works by Blount bearing the titles *Oracles of Reason, Anima Mundi*, and *Great Is Diana of the Ephesians* were gathered into one volume by Blount's friend Gildon and published after the author's death under the title *Miscellaneous Works of Charles Blount*. This book appeared in the year 1695 A.D. The *Oracles of Reason* magnifies reason against revelation and states the positive content of deist or natural religion. The *Anima Mundi* discusses atheism, enthusiasm, prayer and heathenism. In it, the zealot is made out to be the greatest atheist and wisdom and industry are represented as prevailing more with heaven than does prayer. *Great Is Diana of the Ephesians*

---

[275] UHLHORN, G., *The Conflict of Christianity with Heathenism.* A translation from the Third German Edition. New York, Charles Scribner's Sons, 1879. pp. 278, 279.

was directed against the priests, the Bible and miracles. Blount in this work pointed to Egypt as the source of priestly corruption and did not fail to point out that Moses was learned in all the wisdom of the Egyptians.[276]

The positive element in Blount's writings set forth the deistic religion in seven articles. This was two more than Herbert of Cherbury had given, but the extra numbers came simply from a subdivision of some of Herbert's articles and not from the adding of any new content. Herbert had presented his articles as innate truths. Locke had accepted Herbert's articles but had asserted that they were conclusions of a reasoning process and not innate. Blount hesitated between these two positions, saying, "I know not whether the idea of a God be innate or no, but I'm sure that it is very soon imprinted in the minds of men."[277] Blount stated his belief in the immortality of the soul, making the belief rest on reason rather than on revelation.[278] As was usual with the deists he made religion to consist chiefly in morality and was unfavorable to mystery. Thus he wrote, "The morality in religion is above the mystery in it."[279] He argued for repentance as the way to divine favor, setting it over against sacrifice.[280]

The negative or critical aspect of deism was much more prominent in the writings of Blount than the positive. There was more of Bible criticism in his works than in those of Herbert. His quotations and references indicate that he was influenced in this direction by the works of Hobbes and of Spinoza, who had gone farther in this line than Hobbes and who was classed by Blount as an "ingenious" writer.[281] The following statements indicate the influence of Hobbes. "God appeared to him in a dream; that is, he dreamed that God appeared to him; for so the Malmesbury philosopher very ingeniously expounds it."[282] When comparing the stories of the birth of Christ and of Apollonius, he wrote: "For to believe any stories that are not approved by the public authority of our church, is superstition; whereas to

[276] BLOUNT, *Miscel. Works. Oracles of Reason*, p. 134.
[277] BLOUNT, *Miscel. Works. Oracles of Reason*, p. 181.
[278] *op. cit.*, p. 126.
[279] *op. cit.*, p. 91.
[280] *op. cit.*, p. 89.
[281] BLOUNT, CHARLES, *The First Two Books of Philostratus concerning the Life of Apollonius Tyaneus;* written originally in Greek and now published in English: Together with Philological notes by Charles Blount, Gent., London. Printed for Nathaniel Thompson, 1680. p. 99. cf. *Miscel. Works,* p. 72.
[282] BLOUNT, *Miscel. Works,* p. 28.

believe them that are, is religion."[283]   That Blount rejected
any miraculous element in the birth of Christ is evident
from the following statement. " 'Tis well known to all men
who have searched into the record of ancient time, how
necessary it hath ever been esteemed for heroes to have a
birth no less miraculous than their life."[284]   His attitude
toward a number of leading Bible characters was decidedly
unfriendly. He made Abraham and Moses to appear as
nothing but impostors who had learned the tricks of Egyptian priests.[285]   He poked fun at Elisha whom he called
"baldpate."[286]   After holding up David to contempt, he
sneeringly referred to him as "the man after God's own
heart."[287]   Saying that "Scripture stories exceed the poets'
fables,"[288] he ridiculed and rejected many of them including the story of paradise and the fall,[289] the story of the
flood and Noah's ark,[290] the stories of the shadow going
back on the sun-dial and of the sun standing still,[291] and the
story of the manna.[292]   He criticized both the Bible story of
creation and the homo-centric character of much human
thinking in the light of the Copernican astronomy.[293] While
criticizing the too great importance some give to man and
while writing against the Bible story of creation, Blount,
without indicating his own position on the question, says,
"Some authors are of an opinion, that man is nothing but
an ape cultivated."[294]

Blount brought to a close the first period of English deism
and prepared the way for its second or flourishing period.
He revived the interest in deism that had somewhat subsided since the time of Herbert of Cherbury. He marked
the transition on the part of deists from the rationalistic
basis of a doctrine of innate ideas to the empirical basis provided by Locke's philosophy. Blount himself hesitated be-

---

283) BLOUNT, *Life of Apollonius Tyaneus*, p. 13.   Based on Hobbes.
284) *loc. cit.,*
285) BLOUNT, *Miscel. Works. Great Is Diana of the Ephesians*, p. 134.
286) BLOUNT, *Life of Apollonius*, p. 37.
287) *op. cit.,* p. 6.
288) BLOUNT, *Miscel. Works. Oracles of Reason*, p. 3.
289) *op. cit.,* pp. 21, 22.   cf. *Great Is Diana*, etc., p. 25.
290) *op. cit., Oracles of Reason*, p. 5.
291) *op. cit.,* pp. 9–10.
292) *op. cit.,* p. 7.   In connection with the story of the manna, Blount
quoted a naturalistic explanation of that phenomenon from BROWNE'S
Religio Medici.
293) BLOUNT, *Miscel. Works. Great Is Diana of the Ephesians*, pp.
53, 55, 64.
294) BLOUNT, *Miscel. Works. Anima Mundi*, p. 45.   This reference to
a crude doctrine of evolution is of interest in the light of the date when
it was written.   It was published in 1695 and written a few years earlier.

tween the two schools of thought. Some Lockian influence appears in his works but not nearly as much as appears in the works of later deists. Blount seldom referred to Locke. In one reference he took occasion to sharply differ with Locke's teaching that there are atheists and atheistic tribes. He said: "I must beg Mr. Locke's pardon, if I very much question those authorities he quotes from the travels of some men, who affirm some nations to have no notions of a deity."[295]   Blount wrote more against the Bible and its characters and stories than Herbert of Cherbury had done. Later deists largely followed Blount in this.

Probably Blount's major contribution to the content and method of the developing deistic movement was his reviving of the method of opposing Christianity by attempting to parallel features of it from pagan history and legend. His bringing of the Copernican astronomy into the discussion was also of some significance.

Blount's writings called forth replies by a number of writers including Bradley, Nichols and Leslie.[296]   Blount was not equal to his opponents in theological and biblical learning. Gildon, the friend and admirer of Blount who published the latter's posthumus works, was himself converted away from deism by Charles Leslie's answer to Blount which bore the title, *A Short and Easy Method with the Deists.*[297]

---

[295] BLOUNT, *Miscel. Works. Letter to Dr. R. B.,* p. 181.
[296] LELAND, JOHN, *A View of the Principal Deistical Writers that have appeared in England in the last and present Century,* etc. London, T. C. Cadell, 1798. Fifth Edition, p. 48.
[297] SORLEY, W. R., *A History of English Philosophy.* Cambridge, Cambridge University Press, 1920. pp. 144–145. cf. LESLIE, CHARLES, *A Short and Easie Method with the Deists.* Wherein the Certainty of the Christian Religion is Demonstrated, by Infallible Proof from Four Rules, which are incompatible to any Imposture that ever yet has been, or that can possible be. London, J. Applebee, 1723. Eighth Edition. This short work was published anonymously at first.

CHAPTER IV

THE FLOURISHING PERIOD OF ENGLISH DEISM
(1696–1741)

THE various influences which had produced deism early in the seventeenth century were still potently active at the end of the century and there had been added to them the weight of liberal opinion and argument that had been published during the intervening period. This included the writings of such deists as Herbert of Cherbury, Hobbes and Blount. It also included the liberal element in the writings of such men as Tillotson, Browne and Locke. Such continental theological liberals as Spinoza, Bayle and Le Clerc were also exercising some influence upon English thought.

Toward the end of the century certain changes in the political situation and in the press laws of the English nation also affected deism. The restoration of the Stuarts had brought a reaction against both the strict morals and the strict theology of the puritans. This was favorable to deism. The growth of sentiment in favor of toleration had caused the modification in the year 1695 A. D. of the press law in the direction of greater freedom of the press.[1] Soon deistic books and pamphlets began to appear in rapid succession and most of them called forth several replies by anti-deists until the country was flooded with the controversial literature. No previous period in the history of Christianity had produced so extensive a literary attack upon that faith and its Scriptures and no other period produced a larger volume of apologetic literature than the first half of the eighteenth century. England became a debating society, and the subject of the debate was religion.

The deistic movement had developed to a considerable extent during the seventeenth century. Herbert of Cherbury had formulated the principles of natural religion, had declared their sufficiency, had ascribed departures from and corruptions of natural religion to self-seeking and fraudulent priestcraft, and had introduced the use of an embryo science of comparative religions as a means of attacking particular religions and of supporting a universal natural religion.

---

1) BURY, J. B., *A History of Freedom of Thought*, p. 139.

Hobbes had added an explanation of the origin or "seed" of religion, had made subtle and skillful attacks upon traditional revelation and upon inspiration, had introduced Bible criticism and had also introduced the question of the canon of Scripture into the discussion. Blount had revived the controversy and had introduced into it the method of the ancient pagans who sought to parallel Christian stories from heathen sources.[2] He had also brought developments in the science of astronomy to bear upon the religious discussion. He had given unfavorable criticism to many Bible characters and stories, thus directing the attention of later deists to them. He put in his *Miscel. Works* a line of argument frequently used by later deists to the effect that any "rule which is necessary to our future happiness, ought to be generally made known to all men," that no rule of revealed religion ever was or could be so revealed to all men, and that therefore "no revealed religion is necessary to future happiness." [3]   Locke, though not himself a deist, undoubtedly exercised a greater influence upon the deistic movement subsequent to his time than any other writer with the possible exception of Herbert of Cherbury. Later deists built upon his empirical sensationalistic philosophy. They found support for their advocacy of toleration in his able arguments on that subject. They found his definition of knowledge fitting in well with their opposition to the mysterious elements of religion.[4] His new definition[5] of a miracle was of help to them in their many arguments against the miracles of Scripture. They but carried his tendency to rationalize Christianity to a greater extreme. He ascribed to reason the power to discover nearly all the truths of religion while giving only a few truths such as are usually regarded of little importance as discoverable only by revelation.[6] The deists went just a little farther in the same direction, adding a little more to what reason could discover and making revelation altogether unnecessary. Locke was in line with the deists in making religion mostly ethical and rejecting rituals and forms. What he said about the weakness of traditional revelation[7] and about the importance of natural reli-

---

[2] above, p. 44.

[3] BLOUNT, *Miscel. Works. A Let. to Blount* by A. W., p. 198.

[4] Toland used Locke's definition of knowledge as his starting point in his *Christianity Not Mysterious*, q. v., pp. 11–12.

[5] LOCKE, *Works*, vol. 9, *Of Miracles*, p. 256.

[6] LOCKE, *Essay*, IV:x–xviii.

[7] *op. cit.*, IV:xviii:4, 6, and IV:xvi:10.

gion[8] suited them very well. His unitarian or Arian attitude
on the doctrines of the trinity and the deity of Christ showed
him to be[9] not far from the deistic position which regarded
Jesus as being a mere man, some deists holding him to be a
good man[10] and others regarding him as an imposter.[11] His
argument that the soul might be material[12] served as an encouragement to those more radical deists who favored materialism.

Locke's great influence is apparent in the work of the deistic
writer whose work opened the flourishing period of English
deism, John Toland. This writer's contribution to deism
must now be examined.

A. JOHN TOLAND

John Toland (1670–1722) was a man of varied experiences
and the author of a number of small deistic books. He was
the first of the deists in whose writings the influence of Locke
was an important factor. He began life as an Irish Roman
Catholic but became in succession a liberal protestant, a latitudinarian, a deist and a pantheist. After studying at several
British universities, he entered upon an ambitious career as a
writer. Bitter anti-clericalism characterized his early work,
The Tribe of Levi, which appeared in 1691. His fame as a
deist rests chiefly upon his *Christianity Not Mysterious*,
which Ueberweg has correctly classed as one of the important books of the deistic movement.[13] The first edition
of this work which was published in 1696 was burned by
order of the Irish parliament. It had appeared anonymously. Toland affixed his name and added an apology to the
second edition which he published in London in 1702. In
1698 he published a life of Milton under the name *Amyntor*.
The second part of this work contained an attack upon the
usually accepted canon of Scripture. Two works of less importance, *Letters to Serena* and *Adeisedaemon*, appeared in
1704 and 1709, respectively. The *Nazarenus*, published in
1718, attacks those features of the Christian religion which

---

8) LOCKE, *Essay*, III:ix:23.
9) LOCKE, *Works*, 12th Edition, vol. 2, pp. 187–194. Not in 11th Edit.
10) Among those deists who regarded Jesus as a good man and a great
reformer in religion, were John Toland, Thomas Morgan, and William
Wollaston.
11) Deists who more or less openly indicated that they regarded Jesus
as an impostor were Anthony Collins, Matthew Tindal, and Thomas
Woolston.
12) above, pp. 103–104.
13) UEBERWEG, *Geschichte der Philosophie*, Bd. 3, s. 122

distinguish it from natural religion.   Under the influence
of Bruno and Spinoza, Toland's views turned toward monistic pantheism.   This turn of thought shows itself in his
Tetradymus and *Pantheisticon* which were published in the
year 1720.

At the time of the publication of his most important book,
Christianity Not Mysterious, Toland claimed to be a Christian reformer and not an enemy of Christianity.   He called
"Christian" the "most glorious" of titles and claimed it for
himself.[14]   He said further: "I have no doubts concerning
the excellence, perfection, and divinity of the Christian religion in general as it is delivered in the Holy Scriptures,
and I willingly and heartily conform to the doctrine and
worship of the Church of England in particular."[15]   He said
concerning the Church of England that it had "at least as
few errors as any other church in the world."[16]   He frankly
rejected the authority of doctors, popes and councils.[17]   He
claimed that those who appealed to the Scriptures were
nearer right, provided Scriptures were rightly interpreted.[18]
He claimed that historic Christianity had been greatly corrupted from various sources.   First Jewish rabbis are accused of fathering their "heathen notions and mysteries" on
Moses.[19]   Next Jewish Christians are said to have brought
into Christianity their old loved forms.[20]   Then Christians
in their anxiety to gain converts are accused of having
"compounded the matter" with gentiles, allowing the latter
to bring in their secret mysteries with them into Christianity.[21]   But perhaps worst of all was the corruption by
selfish priests who sought to gain and keep power by making and keeping religion full of mysteries.[22]   Toland credited Christ with having for a time purged religion of the
mysteries and other unworthy elements that had gotten into
it.[23]   But when pagan priests and philosophers thought it
to their interest to become Christians at the time the Roman
Emperor did so, they again greatly corrupted Christianity
with mysteries in order to preserve their own power and in-

---

14) TOLAND, *Christianity Not Mysterious*, preface, p. xxviii.
15) TOLAND, JOHN, *Amyntor; or, A Defense of Milton's Life.* London,
(publisher not given), 1699. p. 106.
16) *op. cit., p.* 110.
17) TOLAND, *Christianity Not Mysterious*, p. 4.
18) *ibid.*
19) *op. cit.*, preface, p. xx.
20) *op. cit.*, pp. 151–152.
21) TOLAND, *Christianity Not Mysterious*, p. 152.
22) *op. cit.*, p. 169.
23) *op. cit.*, p. 151.

fluence.[24]   Genuine Christianity, according to Toland, is not only free from mystery but also from ceremony. He said, "There is nothing so naturally opposite as ceremony and Christianity."[25]   He claimed to be an opponent of both the "narrow and bigoted tenets" of the proponents of Christianity as commonly understood and of the "impious maxims" of the enemies of Christianity.[26] Toland, in his role of Christian reformer, also championed toleration.[27]

Most of Toland's work was negative in character, attacking things with which he disagreed. Yet he found some occasion to state positive articles of religious belief. He directly asserted his belief in God, in the immortality of the soul, and in the doctrine of future rewards and punishments.[28] These will be recognized as articles of the natural religion set forth by Herbert of Cherbury. Agreement with the other articles, such as that making religion essentially ethical, is implied in connection with Toland's opposition to ceremonies in religion.

Toland's treatment of the canon of Scripture, published with his *Amyntor,* was one of his most important contributions to the deistic movement. Hobbes had already done some work along this line. Toland gave a long list of books and writings which were attributed in early times by some people to Christ, the apostles and other prominent persons of the New Testament or of the early church.[29] The writing of a book on the history of the canon is suggested in connection with this list.[30] But what Toland did write toward the discrediting of the accepted canon of Scripture was put in the form of quotations from a writer named Dodwell. These remarks were to the effect that the books of the canon were not collected until the times of Trajan or Adrian, that no certain number of books was even then regarded as canonical and that no distinction was then made between canonical and apocryphal books.[31] Questioning the canonicity of books of the Scriptures was one of the features that characterized the works of many deists[32] and Toland made his contribution at this point.

---

24) TOLAND, *Christianity Not Mysterious,* p. 154.
25) *op. cit.,* p. 167.
26) *op. cit.,* preface, p. viii.
27) TOLAND, *Amyntor,* p. 112.
28) *op. cit.,* p. 106.
29) TOLAND, *Amyntor,* Part II.
30) *op. cit.,* p. 67.
31) *op. cit.,* pp. 69–71.
32) cf. above, p. 32.

However, Toland's main contribution to the development of deism consisted in his attack upon mystery in religion. He built this attack upon the foundation of the Lockian theory of knowledge. At first it was suspected from the date of his book, *Christianity Not Mysterious,* and from its similarity of title to Locke's *The Reasonableness of Christianity* that Toland had drawn his ideas from this book of Locke's. But even though that was not the case, it was very evident to every reader of Toland and Locke that the former had made heavy use of Locke's more famous *Essay.* The bishop of Worcester quickly connected Toland with Locke and accused Locke's theory of knowledge of leading to the to him very unacceptable conclusions reached by Toland. Thus developed the famous controversy between the bishop and Locke. Locke refused to assume any responsibility for Toland's conclusions but confined himself in his answers to a defense of his own theory.

The following is a brief statement of the mode in which Toland developed his argument against mystery from a theory of knowledge. Everyone experiences in himself a power of forming ideas and of affirming or denying as he sees these ideas to agree or disagree.[33] An idea is the immediate object of the mind when it thinks.[34] But receiving ideas is not reason as the mind is purely passive in receiving them.[35] "Ideas are the sole matter and foundation of all our reasoning."[36] "Knowledge is—the perception of the agreement of disagreement of our ideas.[37] When two ideas are perceived to agree or disagree without the use of intermediate ideas the truth is axiomatic or self-evident.[38] The reasoning process arises when one or more intermediate ideas are necessary.[39] Reason is "that faculty of the soul which discovers the certainty of anything dubious or obscure, by comparing it with something evidently known."[40] When a truth is not axiomatic and intermediate ideas fail, one cannot get beyond mere probability.[41] Experience and authority are the two means men have of gaining informa-

---

[33] TOLAND, *Christianity Not Mysterious,* p. 9.
[34] *op. cit.,* p. 11.
[35] *op. cit.,* pp. 9, 10.
[36] *op. cit.,* p. 12.
[37] *ibid.*
[38] *ibid.*
[39] *op. cit.,* p. 14.
[40] *ibid.*
[41] *op. cit.,* p. 15.

tion.[42] Experience may be internal or external.[43] Authority may be human or divine.[44] Men are very subject to deception and the only infallible protection against it is "evidence,"[45] i. e., "exact conformity of our ideas or thoughts with their objects, or the things we think upon."[46] Toland would accept nothing as true knowledge if it should be contrary to common notions, if its ideas should lack clearness or if the agreement or disagreement of its ideas could not be clearly perceived.[47] He asserted that "What is evidently repugnant to clear and distinct ideas, or to our common notions, is contrary to reason."[48] He demanded perspicuity of God and men.[49] This he regarded as equivalent to saying that nothing mysterious can be accepted as knowledge.

Certain features of this bit of reasoning by Toland are noteworthy. It is noticeable that he builds heavily upon Locke's doctrine of knowledge but stresses the necessity for clarity of ideas and for clearness of perception of the agreement or disagreement of ideas more than Locke did. It is noticeable also that he makes mystery practically equivalent to lack of clarity in ideas or their relations. In the writings of Toland's deistic predecessors, the reader easily detects an attitude unfavorable to mystery. John Locke also, whose influence is so evident in Toland's work, was inclined to disfavor such Christian doctrines as that of the Trinity largely because of the mystery involved in them. Locke frankly said that he did find some mysteries in Christianity though he wished there were not.[50] However, having accepted the divine authority of Christianity and the Scriptures, he felt compelled to accept some things in them that remained mysteries to him. But Toland went farther than his predecessors in attacking and rejecting all that appeared to him to be mystery. His anti-mystery emphasis was his main contribution to the development of deism.

In this connection, it is to be observed that Toland rejected[51] the distinction betwen above reason and contrary

---

42) Toland, *Christianity Not Mysterious*, pp. 16–17.
43) *ibid.*
44) *ibid.*
45) *op. cit.*, p. 19.
46) *ibid.*
47) *op. cit.*, p. 25.
48) *ibid.*
49) *op. cit.*, p. 43.
50) Locke, *Works*, vol. 3, p. 96. This statement is in a postscript to Locke's *Letter to the Bishop of Worcester.*
51) Toland, *Christianity Not Mysterious*, p. 77. cf. p. 6.

to reason which Locke had recognized.[52] Locke had insisted
that things contrary to reason could not be accepted but
that things above reason, which he termed mysteries, should
be accepted when found in a well-attested revelation. Tol-
and did not say that the Scriptures contain nothing mysterious or above reason but he did say that true Christianity
contains nothing of this character and that nothing above
reason can be accepted.[53] If Locke's definition of miracles
was less supernaturalistic than the usual one, Toland's was
even less so for he defined miracles as actions "exceeding
all human power and which the laws of nature cannot per-
form by their ordinary operations" but nevertheless "produced according to the laws of nature, though above its ordinary operations."[54]

Toland claimed to accept Christianity but to reject those
things in historical Christianity and in the Scriptures which
appeared to him to be mysteries or above reason. As indicated above,[55] he regarded most of these things as corruptions that had crept into Christianity and the Scriptures
from various sources. He hints that some of the offending
passages of Scripture should be allegorically and not literally interpreted.[56] But Toland did not develop this suggestion. Collins[57] and other later deists did so.

Toland's main contributions to the development of the
deistic movement were: building deism on the foundation
of a Lockian theory of knowledge, criticism of the canon of
Scripture, and making deism more distinctly and openly an
anti-mystery and anti-supernatural cult. Toland's work
ushered in that flourishing period of English deism in which
Locke's influence is most evident. Leslie Stephen has well
indicated the position held by Toland's book *Christianity
Not Mysterious* by saying it was "the signal gun which
brought on the general action."[58]

---

[52] LOCKE, *Essay*, IV:xviii:10.   cf. *Second Reply to the Bishop of Worcester, Works*, vol. 3, p. 341.   cf. also p. 96.

[53] TOLAND, *Christianity Not Mysterious*, p. 6.   Note title.

[54] *op. cit.*, pp. 144, 150.

[55] above, p. 121.

[56] TOLAND, *Christianity Not Mysterious*, p. 115.

[57] This was the main line of Collins' argument in his book, *The Ground and Reason of the Christian Religion*.

[58] STEPHEN, LESLIE, *History of English Thought in the Eighteenth Century*. New York, G. P. Putnam's Sons; London, Smith, Elder & Co., 1902.   Third Edition, 2 vols.   vol. 1, p. 105.

ANTHONY ASHLEY COOPER,
EARL OF SHAFTESBURY

Anthony Ashley Cooper, Earl of Shaftesbury (1671-1713), was the next writer after Toland whose works constituted an important contribution to the English deistic movement. This Shaftesbury was the grandson of Locke's patron. He was educated in accordance with Locke's educational scheme. He himself was acquainted with Locke and visited him when Locke was an old man. But, while speaking of Locke with great respect, he expressed disagreement with some of that famous philosopher's views.[59] In 1699 Toland had, without Shaftesbury's permission, published a weighty and precocious work by the latter entitled *Inquiry Concerning Virtue or Merit*.[60] In 1709 Shaftesbury published an *Essay on the Freedom of Wit and Humor* which soon appeared also in French and German translations.[61] Another of his works bore the title, *Several Letters Written by a Noble Lord to a Young Man at the University*. Much the largest and most famous of his works was his *Characteristics of Men, Manners, Opinions, Times*. This work, which contained some of the best of his earlier writings, appeared in 1711. Another work, especially valuable for the biographical material contained in it, was *The Life, Unpublished Letters and Philosophical Regimen of Anthony, Earl of Shaftesbury, Author of the Characteristics*.

Shaftesbury should be classed as one of the deists. Because he put a considerable portion of his discussion of religion into the form of a dialogue between two fictitious characters, his critics could not prove that the views expressed by either of these characters were Shaftesbury's own views. Moreover, he was much given to the use of witty ridicule and satire and irony and because of this, though the reader might feel reasonably assured in his own mind that he understood what Shaftesbury was teaching, he could not prove beyond question that Shaftesbury did hold just that view. Perhaps it was to tease and bait his critics and perhaps it was to avoid persecution, for religious toleration was not yet complete, that Shaftesbury made use

---

[59] *The Life, Unpublished Letters and Philosophical Regimen of Anthony, Earl of Shaftesbury.* London, Swan Sonnenschein & Co., Limited; New York, The Macmillan Co., 1900. pp. 403–404. Here Shaftesbury calls Locke his friend but also accuses him of striking a blow for deism.

[60] *Characteristics*, Editor's Preface, p. xiii.

[61] *op. cit.*, p. xiv.

of these methods. Shaftesbury also spoke ill[62] of the deists, accusing them of a lack of straightforwardness and of practical atheism. He accused "free-thinkers," a name assumed by some deists, of libertinism.[63] He professed to be an orthodox Christian theist[64] whose orthodoxy could not be doubted or questioned. But in the light of his extensive attacks upon the Bible and many of its contents and of his extensive use of ridicule and irony it is highly probable that his profession of orthodoxy was itself ironical. It was put in a form which at the same time ridiculed orthodox religion for its mysteries and gave a sly stab at such legalized religion as Hobbes had proposed.[65] Shaftesbury did differ also from some of the more prominent deists who had preceded him in the nature of the ethics that he proposed and in his views on a future life. Such considerations as these have led some, like Ueberweg, to claim that Shaftesbury should not be ranked as one of the deists.[66] On the other hand, most writers who have made a special study of deism do class him among the deists.[67] In the year 1736, when the deistic agitation was at high tide, a book entitled the *Cure of Deism* made Shaftesbury and Tindal to figure on its title page as "the two oracles of deism."[68] Robertson is authority for the statement that some half century later, at the time of the French revolution, the older writers who mainly represented deism for the English people were Shaftesbury and Bolingbroke.[69] Pope is said to have made the statement that Shaftesbury's *Characteristics* had done more harm to revealed religion than the other works of infidelity put together.[70] The weight of opinion both in his own time and since, seems to support the view that Shaftesbury was one of the deists. However, the question should be decided by examining his teachings and comparing them with the characteristic teachings of the deists, for names

---

[62] SHAFTESBURY, *Characteristics*, vol. 2, pp. 52–54.
Life, Unpublished Letters, etc., p. 39. *Characteristics*, vol. 2, p. 53.
[63] SHAFTESBURY, *Characteristics*, vol. 2, pp. 52–54. cf. *Life, Unpublished Letters*, etc., pp. 38–39.
[64] *op. cit.*, pp. 39, 353. *Characteristics*, vol. 2, pp. 54, 352.
[65] SHAFTESBURY, *Characteristics*, vol. 2, p. 352.
[66] UEBERWEG, *Geschichte d. Philosophie*, b. 3, s. 125.
[67] LELAND, *A View of the Principal Deistical Writers*, p. 54 ff.
FARRAR, *A Critical History of Free Thought*, p. 132.
ROBERTSON, *A Short History of Freethought*, pp. 310–311.
[68] SHAFTESBURY, *Characteristics*, vol. 1, Preface by Editor. John M. Robertson, p. xiv.
[69] *op. cit.*, p. xxviii.
[70] *op. cit.*, p. xxvii.

such as atheist, deist, infidel, skeptic and the like have often
been loosely used, especially in the heat of controversy.

When Shaftesbury's positive teachings are compared
with the positive tenets of deism, such as Cherbury's five
articles of natural religion, it is found he had much in common with them although differing on some points. He said
man "is not only born to virtue, friendship, honesty, and
faith; but to religion, piety, adoration, and a generous surrender of his mind to whatever happens from that Supreme
Cause or order of things, which he acknowledges entirely
just and perfect."[71] These he declared to be his "formal
and grave sentiments."[72] In another place he declared the
"sense of right and wrong to be natural to men."[73] Elsewhere he puts ethics or morality above religion,[74] insofar
as religion is conceived of as other than ethics. In these
teachings there lie embodied the teachings that men by reason can and do reach the beliefs that there is a Supreme
Being or God, that he ought to be worshipped and that
ethics is the principal part of religion, which constitute
three of Herbert's five articles. Shaftesbury had little or
nothing to say about repentance as a way back to God for a
sinner. Nor was he very clear or positive in his teaching
about a future life of rewards and punishments.[75] He
seemed to believe feebly[76] in a future life and to regard a
belief in it as some help toward making men live moral
lives,[77] although he did not regard conduct based on desire
for reward or fear of punishment truly moral.[78] Shaftesbury was also at one with the deists in his devotion to toleration.[79] Of course this did not make him a deist, for
many non-deists have championed toleration.

Turning from the positive to the negative aspects of
deism, it will be found that Shaftesbury had much in common with the deists here also. The whole spirit of his rea-

71) SHAFTESBURY, *Characteristics*, vol. 2, p. 295.
72) *loc. cit.*
73) SHAFTESBURY, *Characteristics*, vol. 1, p. 260.
74) *op. cit.*, pp. 237–238.
75) SHAFTESBURY, *Life, Letters, and Philosophical Regimen*, p. 347.
76) *loc. cit.* cf. *op. cit.*, p. 261 ff.
77) SHAFTESBURY, *Characteristics*, vol. 1, p. 270.
78) In his *Characteristics*, vol. 1, p 267, Shaftesbury wrote: "If on
this account, through hope merely of reward, or fear of punishment, the
creature be incited to the good he hates, or restrained from doing the ill
to which he is not otherwise in the least averse, there is in this case —
no virtue or goodness whatsoever." "There is no more of rectitude, piety,
or sanctity in a creature thus reformed, than there is meekness or
gentleness in a tiger strongly chained."
79) SHAFTESBURY, *Characteristics*, vol. 1, pp. 50 ff., 57–58; vol. 2, p.
345. *Life, Unpublished Letters*, etc., pp. 353, 403.

sonings on the things of religion and ethics was naturalistic.
But at times his attitude of hostility to supernaturalism
crept out[80] although he evidently sought to guard himself
carefully from attack at this point and boasted irreproach-
able orthodoxy.[81]   He did not take up a discussion of specific miracles as did some deists, but he expressed an attitude unfavorable to the use of miracles in support of Christianity when he wrote:[82] "We sicken and grow weary with
the orderly and regular course of things. Periods and stated
laws, and revolutions, just and proportionable, work not
upon us, nor win our admiration.   We must have riddles,
prodigies, matter for surprise and horror!   By harmony,
order, and concord we are made atheists; by irregularity
and discord we are convinced of deity!   'The world is mere
accident if it proceeds in course, but an effect of wisdom if
it runs mad'!"   Thus ironically he ridiculed the looking to
miracles as proofs of Deity.   He expressed his disbelief in
modern miracles[83] but added, probably ironically, "no matter, said I, how incredulous I am of modern miracles, if I
have a right faith in those of former times by paying the
deference due to sacred writ."[84]   However, the deference
he showed to sacred writ elsewhere in his writings was
small indeed.   He professed to believe as far as possible for
one never having seen a miracle or received any divine
communication.[85]   He subjected the Bible to ridicule,[86]
especially attacking the Bible accounts of the departure of
the Israelites from Egypt under Moses,[87] the story of the
conquest of Canaan by Joshua,[88] the story of Jonah,[89] the

---

[80] SHAFTESBURY, *Characteristics*, vol. 1, pp. 98, 231; vol. 2, p. 200.
cf. p. 299 ff.

[81] *op. cit.*, vol. 2, p. 352.

[82] *op. cit.*, vol. 2, p. 94.

[83] *op. cit.*, pp. 87, 89.

[84] *op. cit.*, p. 87.

[85] *op. cit.*, p. 200.

[86] *op. cit.*, vol. 1, pp. 230–232.   cf. p. 10 ff.

[87] *op. cit.*, vol. 1, p. 230.   cf. *op. cit.*, vol. 2, pp. 189–194.   The type
of Shaftesbury's attack is well illustrated by his criticisms on this
point.   He wrote: "The wit of the best poet is not sufficient to reconcile
us to the campaign of a Joshua or the retreat of a Moses by the assistance of an Egyptian loan."   He also suggested that the Jews were
exiled from Egypt for leprosy and pursued because of robbery on their
part.   Above citations, q. v.

[88] *op. cit.*, vol. 1, p. 230.

[89] Shaftesbury's style of mocking ridicule is also well-illustrated in
his treatment of the story of Jonah.   He wrote as follows: " 'Arise
(said his gracious Lord) and go to Nineveh.' 'No such matter,' says
our prophet to himself, but away over sea for Tarshish.   He fairly
plays the truant, like an arch school-boy playing truant, hoping to hide
out of the way.   But his Tutor had good eyes and a long reach.   He
overtook him at sea, where a storm was ready prepared for his
exercise, and a fish's belly for his lodging." *Characteristics*, vol. 2, p. 229.

account of the birth of Christ[90] and the record of the coming of the Holy Spirit on the day of Pentecost.[91] Evidently he was hostile to the Bible conceived as a supernatural revelation. Like the deists generally, Shaftesbury was also quite anti-clerical in spirit, manifesting hostility to both religious writers and speakers. He made much fun[92] of authors of religious books bearing such titles as "meditations" or "thoughts." Of religious speakers he wrote, "Their froth abounds"[93] and called "that there be no answering back," "the law of sermon."[94] He dwelt on the idea that Israel learned its "priestcraft" from Egypt.[95] He accused pastors of seeking their own worldly greatness by persecutions.[96] How Shaftesbury made use of the division of Christians to ridicule both the divisions and the clergy who are leaders of the different divisions is illustrated by his representing an Indian prince as saying: "'If those (Roman clergy) therefore, . . . were ambassadors of the sun, these (Protestant clergy), I take for granted, are from the moon'."[97] Like most deists, Shaftesbury was anti-Jewish. He called the Jews a "cloudy race."[98] He spoke ill of their national heroes[99] such as Moses, Joshua and David. He compared their writers, the writers of the Bible, to the ancient philosophers to the discredit of the former.[100] He represented their priests as deceivers.[101]

Shaftesbury was certainly much more of a deist than Locke. His attitude toward revelation and the supernatural was much more hostile than that of Locke. From an intimate acquaintance with Locke,[102] he admitted the latter to be a man of integrity and a sincere Christian believer.[103]

---

90) SHAFTESBURY, *Characteristics*, vol. 1, pp. 231–232.
91) *op. cit.*, vol. 2, p. 198.
92) SHAFTESBURY, *Characteristics*, vol. 1, pp. 109–110, 151.
93) *op. cit.*, p. 111.
94) *op. cit.*, vol. 2, p. 61.
95) *op. cit.*, pp. 189–194.
96) *op. cit.*, p. 227.
97) *op. cit.*, p. 366.
98) *op. cit.*, p. 227.
99) *op. cit.*, vol. 1, pp. 230–231; vol. 2, p. 190, footnote.
100) *op. cit.*, vol. 1, p. 7; vol. 2, pp. 75, 150, 366.
101) *op. cit.*, vol. 2, p. 194 ff.
Shaftesbury even went so far as to hint that the gospel scheme itself was an invention of priests for their own aggrandizement. *Characteristics*, vol. 2, pp. 200, 355. cf. GIZYCKI, *Die Philosophie Shaftesbury's*, s. 169.
102) SHAFTESBURY, *Life, Letters*, etc., pp. 273–274, 287–299, 403. Shaftesbury was intimate with Locke, having known him as tutor in the household of his own grandfather and father, and also having visited and corresponded with Locke in the latter's old age.
103) *op. cit.*, p. 403.

But he charged Locke with walking in the same way with the deists and of having struck the main blow for the free-thinking liberalism of which Tindal was a prominent representative.[104]   However, Shaftesbury's pose as a defender of the faith against Locke and the deists will hardly do. Locke had based a strong argument for revelation on the fact of miracles. As against this Shaftesbury had in a guarded and indirect way implied his own disbelief in miracles[105] and had greatly discounted the value of miracles even if their occurrence were admitted.[106]   Locke had argued for the need of revelation to give such a sure knowledge of future rewards and punishments as would serve for a powerful sanction for heroic moral and Christian living. Shaftesbury discounted the value of any such sanction of rewards and punishments either here or hereafter.[107] Locke had argued against extending toleration to atheists because he regarded atheism as undermining the foundations of society and morality. Shaftesbury argued that atheism would not seriously affect morality and would not do nearly as much harm as holding a wrong conception of God.[108] However, he admitted that the natural tendency of atheism is not favorable to high morality and that the natural tendency of a worthy conception of God is favorable to morality.[109] Yet in his arguing against Locke's position, Shaftesbury seems almost to be favoring atheism, and atheists might well quote him in support of their position. However, he himself expressed belief in God, a belief based on reason and not on revelation.[110] These points indicate how much less favorable to orthodox Christian views Shaftesbury was than was Locke.

Shaftesbury developed an extensive system of naturalistic ethics. Most other deists made a naturalistic ethics the main part if not the whole of their religion of nature, but did not develop an ethical system. Shaftesbury more than any other deist did develop such a system.[111] The purposes

---

104) SHAFTESBURY, *Life, Letters*, etc., p. 403. Shaftesbury here charges Hobbes with having set a-foot the free-thinking ideas and then charges Locke as going in the self-same way with men like Tindal. He says: "It was Mr. Locke that struck the home blow: for Mr. Hobbes's character and base slavish principles in government took off the poison of his philosophy. 'Twas Mr. Locke that struck at all fundamentals," etc.

105) above, p. 125.
106) *ibid.*
107) SHAFTESBURY, *Characteristics*, vol. 1, p. 267.
108) *op. cit.*, vol. 1, pp. 261-262.
109) *op. cit.*, pp. 268, 275.
110) SHAFTESBURY, *Life, Letters*, etc., p. 403.
111) This done in *Characteristics* and his *Philosophical Regimen*.

of this study do not permit an extensive examination of that system. Suffice it to say that it had certain Platonic features, emphasizing the beautiful.[112)

One contribution of Shaftesbury to deism consisted in his treatment of the use of wit and mockery in religious and philosophical disputes and his own influential example in the use of the weapon of ridicule. While deists who had written before Shaftesbury had made some use of the weapon of ridicule, none of them had used it as extensively as did he nor as did such deists who followed him as Woolston, Bolingbroke and the famous French deist, Voltaire. Shaftesbury not only used mockery as a weapon but he also developed something in the nature of a philosophy of ridicule. As early as the year 1709 he published an essay on the *Freedom of Wit and Humor.*[113) In his *Characteristics* he argued that good humor is the best security against "enthusiasm" and the "best foundation of piety and true religion."[114) Ridicule is made a test of truth and gravity is declared to be of the very "essence of imposture."[115) He taught that a true religion would not only stand the test of humor but would be strengthened by it whereas a religion that was spurious or mixed with imposture would have its spurious character exposed by the test.[116) Truth should bear all lights, one of the most important of which is ridicule itself.[117) Perhaps he was giving a clue to the way in which his own use of ridicule and satire should be interpreted when he wrote: "If men are forbid to speak their minds seriously on certain subjects, they will do it ironically. . . . 'Tis the persecuting spirit has raised the bantering one. . . . The greater the weight is, the bitterer will be the satire. The higher the slavery, the more exquisite will be the buffoonery."[118) He certainly exposed the Scriptures to the test of ridicule[119) and no doubt influenced others to do the same.

Another indication of Shaftesbury's real attitude in matters of religion is found in the way he wrote of some of the early opponents of Christianity, especially of Julian, who is usually called "the apostate." While most Christian his-

112) SHAFTESBURY, *Life, Letters and Philosophical Regimen*, p. 245 f.
113) SHAFTESBURY, *Characteristics*, vol. 1, Preface by Edit. Robertson, p. xiv.
114) *op. cit.*, pp. 7–24.
115) *op. cit.*, p. 10.
116) *op. cit.*, p. 24.
117) *op. cit.*, p. 44.
118) *op. cit.*, pp. 50, 51.
119) above, p. 125. cf. footnotes 87 and 89.

torians give a very unfavorable opinion of the character and ability of this emperor who apostasized from Christianity, Shaftesbury lauded him[120] as virtuous, gallant, generous and mild.

Shaftesbury, whose more enduring fame rests on his work in ethics, is therefore to be classed as one of the deists who championed a naturalistic religion that was essentially ethical in character and who made an indirect attack upon the Bible and Christianity by the use of the weapon of ridicule. His influence was on the side of naturalism and against supernaturalism.

C. WILLIAM WHISTON

Although William Whiston (1667-1752) is scarcely to be classed as a deist, he provided an important element in the development of deism. Though not a deist, he was certainly also not an orthodox Christian. In seventeen hundred twenty-two he published an *Essay Towards Restoring the True Text of the Old Testament.* Accepting the deistic contention that the Old Testament had been corrupted by the Jews, he argued that the fulfillment of its prophecies in the New Testament could not be used as a valid argument for Christianity. So, getting his materials from extra-canonical sources, he attempted a restoration of the text of the Old Testament. His work was of little worth in itself but was noteworthy for two reasons. It marked the taking up of the discussion of prophecy in the deistic controversy and it served as the occasion for Anthony Collins' important deistic work, *A Discourse of the Ground and Reason of the Christian Religion,* in which the author of that work made an important attack on prophecy under the guise of a criticism of Whiston's work. Locke and Hobbes had referred to prophecy and miracles as the appropriate proofs of revelation. They and others had discussed miracles somewhat extensively, but until the publication of Whiston's book prophecy had not been given much consideration. Thereafter it received prominent attention, for a time being even more central in the arguments than miracles themselves.

D. ANTHONY COLLINS

Anthony Collins (1676-1729) gradually came to a position of prominence among the deists of England. During the last eighteen months of Locke's life, Collins enjoyed intimate friendly relations with that famous philosopher. Locke thought well of him.[121] However, Collins' deistic works did not appear until after Locke's death. Collins avowedly built on Locke.[122] In 1707-8 Collins contributed some pamphlets in connection with the Dodwell-Clarke controversy on immortality. In this discussion Collins argued for the materiality of the soul and against its immortality. While doing so he made use of Locke's statement to the effect that it is impossible to prove that matter might not be given the quality of thinking.[123] He made belief in immortality to originate in Egyptian priestcraft. These expressions of his position gave early evidence that he would be one of the more radical deists. Collins' two most important contributions to the literature of deism were his anonymously published books, *A Discourse of Free-Thinking, Occasion'd by the Growth of a Sect Call'd Free-Thinkers,* which appeared in 1713, and *A Discourse on the Ground and Reason of the Christian Religion,* which appeared in 1724. The author's identity was soon known and not denied. These two works established Collins' rank as a leading deist.[124]

The *Discourse of Free-Thinking* was primarily an argument for toleration and free-thinking. Some of its better arguments were derived from Locke's writings on toleration.[125] The last and more original part of this book is little more than a catalog of great thinkers from Socrates down through the centuries to Francis Bacon, Tillotson, Herbert of Cherbury and Locke, all of whom Collins claimed as "Free-Thinkers."[126] If Collins had used the term "free-thinker" consistently to mean original and independent thinkers, few would have questioned the right of most of those named by Collins to a place in such a list. But his right to claim all those named as free-thinkers when he made that new term denote theological radicals who rejected revelation and held to the deistic notions of religion was promptly questioned and denied,[127] and the author's candor and honesty in using the new term was challenged.[128]

---

121) vid. NOACK, *Die Freidenker in der Religion,* Bd. 1, s. 149.
122) COLLINS, *A Discourse of Free-Thinking,* pp. 85, 177.
123) LOCKE, *Works,* vol. 4, p. 32.
124) LELAND, *A View of the Principal Deistical Writers,* vol. 1, p. 99.
125) This statement can best be appreciated by comparing the first half of Collins' book with LOCKE'S *Letters on Toleration.*
126) COLLINS, *A Dis. on Free-Thinking,* pp. 123–178.
127) BENTLEY, RICHARD (penname, Phileleutherus Lipsiensis), *Remarks upon a late Discourse of Free Thinking.* London, (pub. not given), 1737. pp. 3–20.
128) *ibid.*

This book, however, contained a number of other arguments against the Bible and Christianity, if the latter be conceived as a supernaturalistic religion. He reasoned that if a book came from God it would be expected to be more exact and better written than books by men and then he pointed to different interpretations of the Bible to prove that the Bible was not thus superior to other books.[129] He made much of the differences in teaching by different priests and sects concerning the canon of Scripture and the meaning of different Scriptures.[130] He urged the impracticality of the Bible as a guide because "one needs to be a master in many lines before being a master in it." [131] He strongly hinted the unreliability of the Bible because it had long had priests for its guardians, and no reliance is to be put upon priests for they have been notoriously guilty of fraud.[132] He made use of the ancient method of trying to discredit Christianity by seeking to parallel its wonders from pagan stories. Thus he struck a blow at the doctrine of the virgin birth of Christ by saying that the Siamese say of a certain Sommonocondon that he "was born of a virgin, and was the god expected by the universe." [133] He classed the idea of God having favorite nations as a mere "superstition." [134] He sought to disparage the influence of priests as teachers by saying, "A layman wants to know the truth, and a priest desires to have him of his opinion." [135]

Collins' other important work, *The Ground and Reason of the Christian Religion*, which was published eleven years after the *Discourse of Free-Thinking*, repeated many of the lines of attack of the earlier book and added others. In an effort to weaken the credibility of the Scriptures he dwelt on the pious frauds and the gullibility of early Christians.[136] He quoted Grotius to the effect that church history tells of nothing but "the roguery and folly of bishops and churchmen." [137] He made much of the divisions among Christians.[138] He maintained that the Old Testament text is badly

---

[129] COLLINS, *A Dis. of Free-Thinking*, pp. 10, 56, 58–59.
[130] *op. cit.*, pp. 52–64.
[131] *op. cit.*, pp. 10–12.
[132] *op. cit.*, pp. 91–99.
[133] *op. cit.*, pp. 52–53.
[134] *op. cit.*, p. 38.
[135] *op. cit.*, p. 109.
[136] COLLINS, *Ground and Reason of the Christian Religion*, pp. 104–105.
[137] *op. cit.*, p. xxx.
[138] *ibid.*

corrupted.[139]   In support of this contention he cited a number of authors[140] and also pointed to differences of readings in ancient texts.[141]   He strongly hinted that much corruption of Old Testament religion had come from Egypt through Joseph and Moses.[142]   Having thus sought to discredit the Old Testament, Collins advanced to the next step in his argument by seeking to maintain that "Christianity is founded on Judaism, or the New Testament on the Old." [143]   Of course if the Old Testament and Judaism were so corrupt and faulty as Collins had presented them, they would supply a rather poor foundation for the New Testament and Christianity to rest upon.   That Christianity was grounded upon the Old Testament by the apostles themselves, since they sought to prove it from the Old Testament prophecies, was Collins' next contention.[144]   And he maintained that if these proofs from the Old Testament failed, then Christianity would be shown unfounded and false.[145]   This led Collins to his main attack which was to the effect that the prophecies of the Old Testament were not literally[146] fulfilled in the New Testament and could only be considered as fulfilled at all by the use of an allegorical method of interpretation,[147] a method of interpretation which Collins claimed was much used by many early Christians including Origen.[148]   Of course Collins realized that rejection of the literal fulfilment of prophecies and the substitution of allegorical interpretation greatly weakened, if it did not altogether destroy, the value of the argument from prophecy for the purposes of Christian evidences. So, under an exceedingly thin veil of seeming friendliness to Christianity, Collins sought to destroy its foundation and proofs.

In his discussion of the argument from prophecy and in his argument that prophecies of the Old Testament could only be regarded as fulfilled in the New Testament by the use of an allegorical method of interpretation, Collins pointed to the fact that Julian (the apostate Emperor), took the apostles and

---

139) COLLINS, *Ground and Reason*, etc., pp. 135–136.
140) *op. cit.*, p. 136.
141) *op. cit.*, p. 145.
142) *op. cit.*, pp. 22–23.
143) *op. cit.*, pp. 4, 5.
144) *op. cit.*, pp. 5, 26.
145) *op. cit.*, p. 31. cf. p. 26.
146) *op. cit.*, pp. 31, 39, 227 ff.
147) *op. cit.*, pp. 31, 39, 227 ff.
148) *op. cit.*, pp. 173–174.

early Christians to task for misapplying prophecies to Jesus[149] and that Celsus and Porphyry both accused Christians of allegorizing.[150]   These references give a hint of the source of Collins' line of argument against Christianity.

Collins not only attacked the canon and text of the Old Testament but also attacked the canon and inspiration of the New.[151]   He argued against the value of miracles as a proof of Christianity.[152]   He urged against Christianity the fact of the Jewish rejection of Christ.[153]   He suggested that Jesus and the apostles were but following the practice of heathen sects when they made use of the argument from prophecy.[154]   He repeatedly attacked the New Testament use of the prophecy of Isaiah about a virgin bringing forth a son.[155]   But, though Collins, in his book on the *Ground and Reason of the Christian Religion,* made use of a wide variety of arguments against Christianity, his main attack was against the argument from prophecy and this attack he made by advocating the substitution of an allegorical for a literal interpretation of prophecy.

In the year 1709 A. D., before the publication of either of his major works, Collins entered into the controversy that was then raging in the Church of England over the Thirty-Nine Articles by publishing a little tract bearing the significant title, *Priestcraft in Perfection.* In this early work, Collins not only revealed his anti-clericalism but also made use of the argument found in Blount's book against revelation and in behalf of natural religion that what is essential to salvation must be known and easily understood by all men.[156]

From the summary of Collins' arguments given above, it correctly appears that this author's work was mostly negative, consisting chiefly of arguments against the Bible and its prophecies and against Christianity and its clergymen.   Collins did little of a positive character.   The deistic religion or the religion of nature as he presented it was indeed a very meager faith.   He did argue against atheism as folly.[157]   He

149) COLLINS, *The Ground and Reason,* etc., p. 175.
150) *op. cit.,* pp. 172–174.
151) *op. cit.,* pp. 14, 20.
152) *op. cit.,* p. 32.
153) *op. cit.,* p. 36.
154) *op. cit.,* pp. 20, 27, 28.
155) *op. cit.,* pp. 42, 130.
156) vid. BLOUNT, *Miscel. Works,* p. 198.
157) COLLINS, *A Discourse of Free-Thinking,* pp. 104–105.

also sought to prove natural religion productive of good morality.[158]   But he argued for the materiality[159] and against the immortality of the soul,[160] thus dropping one of Herbert's five famous principles of natural religion. Several of the other principles Collins did not mention at all.

Collins' writings stirred up a storm of controversy. In the year 1713 alone twenty replies were made to his *Discourse of Free-Thinking*. Among the more notable replies made to it in England was one by Bentley[161] who, according to Lechler,[162] overwhelmed Collins. Bentley criticized Collins' inaccurate scholarship,[163] "blasphemous buffoonery,"[164] and for using the term freethinking in an ambiguous way.[165] Bentley also answered point by point most of Collins' arguments. *The Ground and Reason of the Christian Religion* alone called forth no less than thirty-five replies.[166]   The more famous among these answers were the replies by Chandler, Sherlock and Jeffrey.[167]   Thus Collins did much to spread and increase the intensity of the deistic agitation in England.

E. BERNARD DE MANDEVILLE

Bernard de Mandeville (1670-1733), a foreign born physician who lived near London, added his contribution to the deistic agitation by writing a short poem entitled *The Grumbling Hive, or, Knaves Turned Honest* and a larger work, partly in poetry and partly in prose, which bore the title *The Fable of the Bees; or, Private Vices Public Benefits*. The first work, which appeared about the year 1706 A. D., was severely censured for being an attack on morality and virtue and was charged with encouraging vice. Mandeville published the second work in the year 1714 A. D., as a defense of the first work. He incorporated the first work in the second and added much material to express and argue for his views on religion and ethics. The tone and ideas of

158) COLLINS, *A Discourse of Free-Thinking*, pp. 120, 121.
159) vid. above, p. 130.
160) *ibid.*
161) BENTLEY, R., *Remarks upon late Discourse of Free Thinking by Phileutheros Lipsiensis*. London, (pub. not given), 1737. cf. LELAND, *A View of the Principal Deistical Writers*, p. 100.
162) LECHLER, *Geschichte d. Eng. Deismus*, s. 238.
163) BENTLEY, *Remarks*, etc., pp. 37–40, 52, 53, 171, 190.
164) *op. cit.*, p. 5.
165) *op. cit.*, pp. 3, 20, 154, 190.
166) NOACK, *Die Freidenker in der Religion*, b. 1, s. 186.
167) LELAND, *A View of the Principal Deistical Writers*, pp. 107–109.

the poem which stirred up the criticism and led to the
second work can best be indicated by a short quotation.

> "Among the many priests of Jove,
> Hired to draw blessings from above,
> Some few were learned and eloquent,
> But thousands hot and ignorant:
> Yet all pass'd muster that could hide
> Their sloth, lust, avarice and pride."[168]

"The Moral"

> "Then leave complaints: fools only strive
> To make a great an honest hive."[169]

The dominant theme of the poem was anti-clericalism. But
the strange theory that vice in society is necessary to the
society's greatness was also taught. It was this doctrine
that led to the charge that the work encouraged vice and so
brought on the action taken against it by the grand jury of
Middlesex. The main theme of the second and larger work
was this same doctrine as it is expressed in the second title
of the book, *Private Vices Public Benefits*. In his defense,
the author professed to have written the poem merely for
diversion and to show of "what vile ingredients" the "wholesome mixture of a well-ordered society" is composed.[170]

Mandeville was bitterly anti-clerical. He criticized the
discords among them[171] and their readiness for higher
salaries.[172] He saw in them love of ease but no self-denial.[173]
He censured the social life of monks and nuns.[174] He wrote
of the "roguery of designing priests." He hated the papal
church and did not think the Reformation had done much
good.[175]

In the fifth dialogue of his larger work, Mandeville made
the argument to support natural as against revealed religion.
But by using the dialogue form he avoided assuming direct
responsibility for the views expressed. The author professed, at the end of the sixth dialogue, to be establishing

---

168) MANDEVILLE, BERNARD DE, *The Fable of the Bees; or, Private Vices
Public Benefits*, etc. London, Allen and West; Edinburgh, J. Mundell,
1795. p. 3.
169) *op. cit.*, p. 11.
170) MANDEVILLE, *The Fable of the Bees; or, Private Vices Public
Benefits*, preface, pp. vi–vii.
171) *op. cit.*, p. 87.
172) *op. cit.*, p. 90.
173) *op. cit.*, p. 88.
174) *op. cit.*, p. 87.
175) *op. cit.*, p. 228.

the necessity for revelation and for belief in and practice of Christianity.[176]   Readers did not take this profession very seriously as the theory that vice was necessary for a great society was regarded as hardly consistent with Christian doctrines and ideals.

Mandeville made a sharp attack upon the ethical teachings of Shaftesbury and also exposed the deistic and anti-Christian character of Shaftesbury's writings.   He wrote: "That boasted middle way, and the calm virtues recommended in the *Characteristics,* are good for nothing but to breed drones."[177]   He also asserted that Shaftesbury favored deism and, "under pretense of lashing priestcraft and superstition, attacked the Bible itself."   He also said of Shaftesbury that, "by ridiculing many passages of Holy Writ, he seems to have endeavored to sap the foundation of all revealed religion, with design of establishing heathen virtue on the ruins of Christianity."[178]   Thus Mandeville agreed in the main with the orthodox element in their estimate of Shaftesbury and his relation to deism and Christianity.   However, the reader of both Mandeville and Shaftesbury is likely to conclude that Mandeville was as much a deist as Shaftesbury and that he also was no friend of Christianity or revelation.   As Shaftesbury seemed to be employing the fox-like trick of seeking to cause pursuers to follow the trail of another when he criticized the orthodoxy of the relatively orthodox Locke and when he spoke ill of the deists, so Mandeville seemed to be using the same tactics when he attacked Shaftesbury.

Mandeville's work was mostly negative in character. Such natural religion as he did allow was very meager as compared with that set forth by Herbert of Cherbury. He made virtue to appear unreal and optimism a delusion. His work tended to spread deism in its negative destructive aspects among the rougher ribald class of society with which he was wont to associate.[179]   While Shaftesbury and most of the other deists maintained that the light of reason was abundantly sufficient in itself without need of revelation and opponents of the deists insisted on the need for the light of

176) MANDEVILLE, *The Fable of the Bees,* p. 519.
177) *op. cit.,* p. 211.
178) *op. cit.,* p. 519.
179) STEPHEN, LESLIE, *Free Thinking and Plain Speaking.* New York and London, G. P. Putnam's Sons, The Knickerbocker Press, 1905. pp. 279–305.

revelation as they minimized the worth of natural revelation, Mandeville seemed to desire to "put out both lights."[180]

F. WILLIAM WOLLASTSON

William Wollastson (1659-1724), a retired clergyman, published his book, the *Religion of Nature Delineated,* in the year 1722 A. D. This work was very unlike the book by Mandeville which appeared about the same time. Mandeville's work was negative and coarse and made its appeal to a coarser element of society. Wollastson's work was, as the name suggests, positive and appealed to the more refined and thoughtful. It had in it little or nothing of the nature of an attack upon the Bible or Christianity or the clergy. It was rather an effort to build up a positive religion of nature. It was suited to appeal to more serious-minded people whose faith in Christianity and revelation had been shaken by the attacks of other deists but who felt the need of a positive religion. The fact that a seventh edition was issued in the year 1746 indicates something of the popularity and influence of the book.[181] Locke had thrown out the suggestion that he thought it would be possible for the reason to work out a moral system that would have a certainty like that of mathematics. But Locke had not thought it necessary to attempt such a work because the Bible had provided a sufficient system of ethics. Wollastson sought to do what Locke had suggested could be done. So, by a process of reasoning and by quotation from philosophers, he attempted to build up a natural ethical religion.

The content of the ethical religion thus built up by Wollastson was much the same as that given by Herbert of Cherbury a century earlier. It included belief in God as the uncaused first cause.[182] In it, Wollastson maintained both the immateriality[183] and the immortality[184] of the soul. He reasoned that since God is just and since the good do not always receive in this life a full reward for their goodness and the wicked do not receive a just punishment for their wickedness, there must be another life to permit the rectify-

---

180) STEPHEN, *Free Thinking and Plain Speaking,* especially p. 305.
Stephen here calls Mandeville a "pothouse edition of Hobbes," and also connects him with the fetich theory of the origin of religion and with Darwinism.
181) WOLLASTSON, WILLIAM, *The Religion of Nature Delineated.* Glasgow, Une & Co., 1746. Seventh Edition.
182) WOLLASTSON, WILLIAM, *The Religion of Nature Delineated.* London, Samuel Palmer, 1726. p. 65.
183) *op. cit.,* p. 186.
184) *op. cit.,* p. 193.

ing of the injustices and inequalities of earthly life.[185]   He
also thought that a good God must give his creatures more
pleasure than pain and that since, in his opinion, this does
not always occur in earthly life, there must be another
life.[186]   In presenting this line of reasoning, Woolastson indicated a rather gloomy and pessimistic view of man's life
on earth which is in marked contrast with the optimism of
Shaftesbury.

Woolastson is not to be confused with Thomas Woolston,
the next important deist whose work calls for consideration.

G. THOMAS WOOLSTON

Thomas Woolston (1669-1731) was a vigorous, coarse,
voluminous writer on the deistic side of the controversies
that raged in his day.   Leslie Stephen speaks of him as
"poor mad Woolston, most scandalous of the deists."[187]
Farrar says his abuse of Christianity was the most open
since the early day of the pagan opposition to Christianity.[188]   Leland charged him with "Scurrilous buffoonery
and gross raillery."[189]   Even J. B. Bury, whose attitude
toward deists is very friendly, speaks of Woolston's writings
as "coarse" and "ribald," but also thinks them important.[190]
The titles and dates of Woolston's works are as follows:
*The Old Apology for the Truth of the Christian Religion
against the Jews and the Gentiles Revived* (1705); *Free Gifts
to the Clergy* (1723-1724); a series of six *Discourses on Miracles* (1727-1730); and *The Moderator between an Infidel and
an Apostate* (1721).   This Cambridge graduate was well-
versed in the writings of the Church Fathers[191] but seems to
have read them chiefly to imbibe the arguments of Celsus
and Porphyry against Christianity.

Hostility to the clergy, and especially to the protestant
clergy, reached its very peak in Woolston.   In his *Moderator
between an Infidel and an Apostate,* he acted as umpire between Collins and the clergy who wrote against Collins. But
he showed himself a very partial umpire and his partiality
was not in favor of the clergy.[192]   He expressed the view

185) WOLLASTSON, *The Religion of Nature Delineated*, p. 202.
186) *op. cit.*, p. 202 ff.
187) STEPHEN, *History of Eng. Thought in the Eighteenth Century*,
vol. 1, p. 77.
188) FARRAR, *A Critical History of Free Thought*, p. 137.
189) LELAND, *A View of the Principal Deistic Writers*, vol. 1, p. 113.
190) BURY, *A History of Freedom of Thought*, p. 144.
191) WOOLSTON, THOMAS, *Works of Thomas Woolston*.   London,
J. Roberts, 1733. 5 vols. vol. 1, p. vi, and throughout works.
192) WOOLSTON, *Works*, vol. 5.

that Collins excelled Porphyry and Celsus in subtlety and learning[193] and of course assumed familiarity with the works of all of these men in so doing. When discussing miracles, he wrote of "hired clergy" and their "greed."[194] But the bitterness of his hatred against the clergy best appears in his series of four *Free Gifts to the Clergy*. Here he declares that they don't deserve their food and that he plans to drive "all the protestant hireling priests from their tubs."[195]

Woolston's main work was his discussion of miracles. He revived the discussion of miracles which had for a time given place to arguments concerning prophecy. His work, however, was not a philosophical discussion of miracles as such but rather a taking up of a large number of specific miracles of Scripture and attacking them. Among the miracles which he discussed and ridiculed were: the changing of water to wine,[196] the transfiguration,[197] the feeding of the five thousand,[198] the cursing of the fig tree,[199] the raising of Lazarus,[200] and the resurrection of Christ.[201] The main feature and peculiarity of Woolston's treatment of miracles is that he sought to apply the allegorizing method developed by Collins in the discussion of prophecy. He tried to show that the early church fathers understood miracles as allegories.[202] Of one and another of the miracles which he considers he says that, if understood literally, it is absurd, incredible, improbable, monstrous, ridiculous and the like.[203] He referred to Celsus' arguments against the resurrection of Jesus and declared that they had never been answered.[204] He used the method of attack by trying to parallel the Bible miracle with a miracle from heathen story. Thus he sought to parallel Jesus' miracle of turning water into wine from the story of Apollonius Tyanaeus which Blount had made popular.[205] In the course of his discussion of Christ's miracles, Woolston found occasion to

---

193) WOOLSTON, *Works*, vol. 5, *Dedicatory Preface*, pp. v-vi.
194) *op. cit.*, vol. 2, pp. 24, 38.
195) *op. cit.*, vol. 3, *Third Free Gift*, pp. 70–71.
196) *op. cit.*, vol. 1, *First Discourse*, p. 51.
197) *op. cit.*, vol. 1, p. 40.
198) *op. cit.*, vol. 1, p. 52.
199) *op. cit.*, vol. 1, p. 55. cf. *Third Discourse*, pp. 5–33.
200) *op. cit.*, vol. 1, *Fifth Discourse*, p. 52, 24.
201) *op. cit.*, vol. 1, p. 57. cf. *Sixth Discourse*, pp. 5, 24. cf. *First Discourse*, p. 57.
202) WOOLSTON, *Works*, vol. 1, *First Discourse*, pp. 2–7.
203) *op. cit.*, vol. 1, *First Discourse*, pp. 4, 55, 57.
204) *op. cit.*, vol. 1, *Sixth Discourse*, p. 24.
205) *op. cit.*, vol. 1, *First Discourse*, p. 51.

declare that Christ was not even a good man.[206]   This indicates something of the radical character of his anti-Christian attitude for most deists professed high respect for Christ as a man even though they rejected the doctrine of his deity.

Woolston's work was altogether negative in its character. Just how influential his work was can hardly be estimated for many may have read him to laugh with him and many to laugh at him.   At least it is certain that he was widely read for his writings appeared in many editions and called forth some sixty replies.[207]

H. MATTHEW TINDAL

Of all the deists of England, Matthew Tindal (1656-1733) probably best represented the deistic movement.   He was a lawyer who lived most of his long life in close connection with Oxford University. He went from the Anglican church into the Roman Catholic church, but later returned to the Anglican fold.   The one book on which his fame as a deist rests was not published until he was about seventy-four years of age.   It bore the title: *Christianity as Old as the Creation; or The Gospel a Republication of the Religion of Nature*.   Because it so completely set forth the views held in common by most deists and because of the extent of its influence, this book has been called the "Deistic Bible,"[208] and its author, "The great Apostle of Deism."[209]   It called forth one hundred fifty replies and so formed the high water mark of excitement in England over deism.[210]   One of the replies was Butler's famous *Analogy*, the most important and enduring apologetic work produced against deism.

Tindal brought together in his book the various elements of deism of which earlier writers had only provided fragments.   Herbert of Cherbury and Wollastson had developed the positive content of natural religion.   Locke, though not a deist, had magnified reason.   Toland had repudiated the mysterious and the distinction between contrary to reason and above reason and had also begun an attack on the canon of Scripture.   Hobbes had made a beginning of naturalistic explanations of the origin of religion.   He had also criticized the canon of Scripture and began that negative Bible criticism which was carried farther by the continental

---

206) Woolston, *Works*, vol. 1, *Sixth Discourse*, p. 6.
207) Farrar, *A Critical History of Free Thought*, p. 137.
208) Noack, *Die Freidenker in der Religion*, b. 1, s. 272.
Lechler, *Geschichte d. Englischen Deismus*, s. 327.
209) Noack, *Die Freidenker in der Religion*, b. 1, s. 272.
210) Robertson, *A Short History of Free Thought*, p. 312.

writer Spinoza. In one of Blount's books, the idea had been advanced that what is necessary to salvation must be known to all men as no special revelation has been or could be. Blount had in another work drawn parallels between Christian story and pagan tradition. Shaftesbury had especially stressed ethics as against ritualistic religion and had advocated and used ridicule as a tool in the controversy. Hobbes and Locke had suggested that were there a special revelation miracles and prophecy would be the proper credentials for the bearer of it. But this assumed the literal interpretation of the passages that gave the prophecies and their fulfillment and the miracles. Collins then insisted prophecy must be allegorically and not literally interpreted. Woolston urged the same in regard to miracles. This, if allowed, would destroy the evidential value of prophecy and miracle. Deists, with the exception of Hobbes, had advocated toleration. Most of them, but especially Mandeville and Woolston, had been bitterly anti-clerical. Nearly all had presented themselves in the role of reformers rather than as enemies of Christianity. Tindal, by bringing together these various elements of thought and method in a greater degree than had been done by any other, became the representative deist. In at least the first part of his book, Tindal's tone was more restrained and philosophical than the writings of most other deists. "Deism," as it is understood in philosophy, is better exemplified by Tindal than by most of his predecessors.

Tindal's main line of argument is developed from his conception of God. God is perfect, therefore any religion he gives to men must be perfect and incapable of improvement.[211] From this he concluded that no later revelation such as the Bible could improve on the religion given man at the creation. God is immutable, therefore he cannot be conceived as changing the religion first given.[212] God is impartial and therefore would not have a chosen people or give advantages to one age or race that he did not give to all.[213] A special revelation would constitute partiality. From the justice of God, Tindal reasoned that God "at all times has given mankind sufficient means of knowing what he requires of them."[214] Having concluded that the natural religion given by God at the creation was perfect and un-

---

211) TINDAL, *Christianity as Old as the Creation*, pp. 3, 49, 58, 59, 118.
212) *op. cit.*, pp. 2, 59, 115.
213) *op. cit.*, pp. 17, 363.
214) *op. cit.*, p. 1.

changeable, Tindal concludes that any religion revealed by
God can only be a republication of this original natural religion and must be identical in content with it. Hence the
title of his book.

But Tindal evidently anticipated the query, Why reveal
this religion in a book if it was already universally known?
His answer was that revealed religion could only be to free
men from the load of superstition that had been mixed with
natural religion.[215]   He does not seem to have faced the
natural objection to this that the freeing of some men by a
special revelation would be as much partiality as the giving
of a new religion. However, that Tindal did not regard the
Bible as a whole or any section of it such as the New Testament or the "Gospels" as in reality constituting a revelation
suited to free men from a load of superstition is apparent
from his later statements concerning these Scriptures. For
he later represents the Scriptures of both the Old and the
New Testaments as being very far from the kind of a work
that would clear away superstition and make the one true
religion shine forth in its unmixed purity and beauty.[216] He
makes it out that the Bible is full of unworthy things and
that it is far from as clear as natural religion.[217]   Such a
book as Tindal pictured the Bible to be could not be seriously presented as a revelation from God given to remove a
load of superstition that had accumulated upon natural religion. By picturing the Bible as full of errors, as much less
clear in its teachings than reason and as unable to add any
good thing to the religion which reason gives, Tindal actually left no worthy place for the Bible.

In the light of these facts, it is not strange that the contemporaries who answered Tindal's book accused him of
having given his work a misleading title. From their standpoint it certainly did appear to be a misleading title,
whether or no Tindal intended it to be misleading. The
book was not, as they evidently thought the title gave promise that it would be, a work to prove all of the New Testament teaching as old as the creation. It was rather an effort
to prove that the few principles which constitute natural religion are as old as creation and that these constitute genuine
Christianity and the true gospel. It allowed, indeed, that
these principles are found in the New Testament but
claimed that they were mixed with many errors.

215) TINDAL, *Christianity as Old as the Creation*, p. 7.
216) *op. cit.*, pp. 23, 54, 225.
217) *op. cit.*, pp. 22, 23, 225, 185.

It remains to note what content Tindal actually gave to the religion of nature which he called "Christianity" and what he had to say about the Bible and historical Christianity.

The articles of natural religion[218] given by Tindal are: belief in God; worship of God; doing what is for one's own good or happiness; and promoting the common happiness. Elsewhere, Tindal indicated that he also believed in a future life.[219]   The second, third and fourth of these articles of natural religion were derived by Tindal from a consideration of the natures and interrelations of God and men.[220]

Taken as a whole, Tindal's teaching about the Bible seems to be that it is worthless and worse than worthless.   The title of his book would seem to require that he would at least admit that the Bible contained the articles of natural religion.   In an early statement he ascribes to the Gospel the design of freeing religion from a load of superstition.[221] But he adds that the Gospel could not be more plain than reason,[222] that it has to be interpreted by reason and not vice versa[223] and that it cannot add to what reason gives.[224] This would seem to leave no worthwhile place for revelation.   Tindal quoted a wit as saying, "The truly illuminated books are the darkest of all."[225]   By quoting Charron he asked what is the use of all the tables, codes and the like and of all the labor of reading them.[226]   In contrasting the law as it is given through reason with the law as given through revelation, he disparaged the latter and used language which summed up many of the insinuations and unfriendly criticisms made upon the Bible by his predecessors.[227]   He spoke of the law as given by reason as "A law, which does not depend on the uncertain meaning of words and phrases in dead languages, much less on types, metaphors, allegories, parables, or on the skill or honesty of weak or designing transcribers (not to mention translators) for many ages together."[228]   He threw doubt upon the gen-

---

[218] TINDAL, *Christianity as Old as the Creation*, pp. 11–18.
[219] *op. cit.*, p. 21.
[220] *op. cit.*, pp. 11–18.
[221] *op. cit.*, p. 7.
[222] *op. cit.*, p. 22.
[223] *op. cit.*, p. 23.
[224] *op. cit.*, p. 27.
[225] *op. cit.*, p. 23.
[226] *op. cit.*, pp. 52–54.
[227] Ideas of Locke, Hobbes and Collins are woven into this brief statement by Tindal.
[228] *Christianity as Old as the Creation*, p. 54.

uineness of the Bible or any other claimed revelation by pointing to the number of works claiming to be revelations.[229] He argued that there is neither proof that there ever was revelation nor that there is a correct transmission of what is claimed to be such. He made use of Locke's remark to the effect that testimony weakens with the passage of time and with the increase of the number of men through whom it is handed down.[230] Against giving miracles recognition as credentials of bearers of revelation, he advanced an argument from Huetius having found parallels for many Bible miracles in pagan story,[231] and also quoted the old saying, "Miracles for fools, the reasons for wise men."[232] He ridiculed a number of Bible stories[233] such as that of the garden of Eden, the Fall, Jacob's wrestling, and Balaam's ass. He accused the Bible of teaching low morality and dwelt on the vices of such Bible heroes as David.[234] He censured the cruelty of the orders given Joshua and Saul.[235] He found fault with the Scriptures and with Christ himself for making salvation depend upon beliefs to which most of mankind are strangers.[236] He objected especially to the doctrine of original sin, not only to the church doctrine but to the Bible teachings[237] on which the church doctrine is based. He accused the prophets of speaking falsely.[238] He pointed to the various readings of different versions of the Bible.[239] He vigorously presented the disagreements between the Scriptures and science to discredit the former.[240] This list of criticisms urged by Tindal sufficiently indicates his attitude toward the Bible. His book took highest rank among the deists, marked the high-water mark of that movement in England and called forth a host of replies.

I. THOMAS MORGAN

Thomas Morgan (d. 1743) was the author of a large three volume work entitled *The Moral Philosopher*, which did not add much of new thought-content to the deistic movement

229) TINDAL, *Christianity as Old as the Creation*, p. 163.
230) *op. cit.*, p. 163. Cf. LOCKE, *Essay* IV:xvi:10.
231) TINDAL, *Christianity as Old as the Creation*, p. 170.
232) *loc. cit.*
233) *op. cit.*, pp. 229, 340, 349.
234) *op. cit.*, pp. 2–9, 220.
235) *op. cit.*, pp. 237, 238.
236) *op. cit.*, p. 225.
237) *op. cit.*, pp. 340, 349.
238) *op. cit.*, pp. 231, 232.
239) *op. cit.*, p. 244.
240) *op. cit.*, p. 185.

but did vigorously restate and give new illustrations to some of its main ideas. Morgan was first a dissenter preacher, then a practicer of healing among the quakers and finally a writer. The first volume of *The Moral Philosopher* appeared anonymously in the year 1737 A. D. It is much the most important of the three volumes, the other two being mostly repetitions made in reply to critics of the first volume. Morgan reflected the arguments of Toland and Tindal.[241] His particular antipathy was against Judaism and the Old Testament, although he by no means accepted the New Testament and Historic Christianity.[242] Gnostic ideas and attitudes found favor with him.[243] Indeed he regarded the gnostics as the true Christians of the early Christian era. He particularly resembles Marcion. His argument against the authority of the apostles was like that of Celsus.[244] The more common orthodox Christians he styled "Christian Jews,"[245] and he hated the Jews and everything Jewish. He called himself a "Christian deist."[246] He followed Tindal in seeming to admit revelation as a parallel of natural religion,[247] but makes it apparent in his work that he did not accept the Scriptures.[248]

The positive part of Morgan's teachings included all of the articles of natural religion as formulated by Herbert of Cherbury.[249] But he somewhat weakened his position on the subject of belief in a future life by saying that beliefs in future rewards and punishments came in about the time of Ezra.[250] He professed Christianity, defining it so as to make it not a religion revealed in a book but rather a religion that "depends on the most plain and necessary truths, such as are found in the eternal, immutable reason and fitness of things; 'and which must, therefore, be always and everywhere the same.' "[251] Christian worship he made to consist in a strict regard to all the duties and obligations of

[241] STEPHEN, *History of Eng. Thought in the Eighteenth Century*, vol. 1, pp. 77–78.

[242] LELAND, *A View of the Principal Deistical Writers*, vol. 1, pp. 145–147.

[243] LECHLER, *Geschichte d. Eng. Deismus*, s. 373.

[244] FARRAR, *A Critical History of Free Thought*, p. 141.

[245] This is indicated in the sub-title of Morgan's book.

[246] MORGAN, *The Moral Philosopher*, vol. 1, pp. 393–394.

[247] *op. cit.*, preface, p. x.

[248] *op. cit.*, p. 404.

[249] *op. cit.*, vol. 1, pp. 146, 147, 152, 212, 393–394.

[250] *op. cit.*, vol. 1, p. 46.

[251] *op. cit.*, vol. 1, pp. 393–394.

moral truth and righteousness,[252] i. e., in ethical living
rather than in any rites or rituals. These latter he regarded
as hindrances rather than helps to religion.[253] He further
explained what he meant by Christianity by writing that he
took it "to be that scheme or system of deism, natural religion or moral truth and righteousness, which was at first
preached and propagated in the world by Jesus Christ and
his apostles, and has since been convey'd down to us by
probable, human testimony, or historical evidence, strengthened and confirm'd by the necessary, natural truth, and in-
trinsic goodness of the doctrines themselves."[254] In the
positive teachings of Morgan we find a somewhat higher
place given to Jesus[255] than in the works of most deists, a
place perhaps not fully consistent with philosophical deism.
But at most points his positive teachings were quite in
agreement with other deists. In the negative, critical aspects
of his teachings Morgan was wholly in agreement with
deists generally.

The negative part of Morgan's work was much more
extensive than the positive, including an attack upon the
Bible, especially upon the Old Testament. He disparaged
the characters of Joseph,[256] Moses,[257] Samuel,[258] and David,[259] men whom the Bible and friends of the Bible generally hold in high esteem. On the other hand, Morgan
praised Solomon, Ahab and others[260] for that for which they
are usually censured, their toleration of idolatry. Moses he
charged with imposture and cruelty.[261] David he accused
of getting the throne by a long process of fraud.[262] Morgan
set the prophets over against the priests.[263] He particularly
hated the priests and their whole ritualistic system of religion with its sacrifices, all of which he regarded as a political imposture.[264] He regarded Israel as having been corrupted in Egypt, "the mother of superstition."[265] However,

252) Morgan, *The Moral Philosopher*, vol. 1, pp. 393–394.
253) *op. cit.*, vol. 1, p. 415.
254) *op. cit.*, vol. 1, p. 412.
255) *op. cit.*, vol. 1, pp. 228, 393–394, 412.
256) *op. cit.*, vol. 3, chap. 1.
257) *op. cit.*, vol. 1, pp. 271, 393–394; vol. 2, pp. 27–28, 53, 65–66, 71, 256.
258) *op. cit.*, vol. 1, pp. 294–297.
259) *op. cit.*, vol. 1, p. 300.
260) *op. cit.*, vol. 1, pp. 303–314.
261) *op. cit.*, vol. 2, pp. 53–71, 256.
262) *op. cit.*, vol. 1, p. 300.
263) *op. cit.*, vol. 1, p. 282 ff.
264) *op. cit.*, vol. 1, pp. 114, 125, 281, 334; vol. 2, p. 256.
265) Morgan, *The Moral Philosopher*, vol. 1, p. 241 ff.

Morgan was hardly self-consistent on this point for elsewhere he represented Israel as corrupting Egypt.[266] He rejected as a national delusion the idea that the Jews were a
chosen people.[267]   Whether discussing the sacrifices of the
Old Testament or the death of Christ, Morgan was always
hostile to the doctrine of a blood atonement.[268] He regarded
Christ's death as simply that of a martyr.[269]   He not only
repudiated miracles but also argued that even did they take
place they would furnish no proof that man was inspired
or had a revelation from God.[270] Some prophecies, like that
of Jeremiah concerning the captivity,[271] he said were mere
shrewd observations. Only by an allegorical interpretation
could the others be said to be fulfilled.[272] He contrasted the
Old Testament with the New to the disparagement of the former.[273]   But in the New Testament itself he set Paul against
the other apostles, giving Paul the place of higher esteem.[274] Yet even Paul, whom he praises as a free-thinker
of his day, he accuses of accommodating his teaching to
please people of the day.[275] Thus, by saying unfavorable
things about leading characters of Old and New Testament,
by setting the two Testaments against each other, by setting
prophet against priest and apostle against apostle, Morgan
labored to discredit the Bible. In the latter part of his work
he came out openly denying that God had given any revelation.[276]

Though his bitterest attacks were upon the priests of the
Bible, Morgan spake evil also of the prophets. He charged
them with playing politics, with corruption and with accommodating their teachings to the errors of the people.[277]

This deist also brought the usual charges against the
Christian clergy, accusing them of greed and fraud. He
also became somewhat bitterly sarcastic against them. He
said: "To oblige a man in preaching to talk sense would be
most unreasonable nonsense."[278]

In the preface to the first volume of his book, Morgan tells

[266] Morgan, *The Moral Philosopher*, vol. 3, chap. 1.
[267] *op. cit.*, vol. 1, p. 257; vol. 2, p. 53.
[268] *op. cit.*, vol. 1, pp. 125–228.
[269] *op. cit.*, vol. 1, p. 164.
[270] *op. cit.*, vol. 1, p. 98; vol. 2, pp. 26, 27, 32, 53, 78.
[271] *op. cit.*, vol. 1, pp. 47, 289, 290.
[272] *op. cit.*, vol. 1, p. 47.
[273] *op. cit.*, vol. 1, preface.
[274] *op. cit.*, vol. 1, pp. 71, 79–80.
[275] *op. cit.*, vol. 1, p. 163.
[276] Morgan, *The Moral Philosopher*, vol. 2, p. 25.
[277] *op. cit.*, vol. 1, pp. 285–289, 308.
[278] *op. cit.*, vol. 1, pp. 116, 119, 432–433.

of a frequent meeting of free-thinkers at an English country estate. At these meetings they drew up some conclusions including this one: "The moral truth, reason and fitness of actions is founded in the natural and necessary relations of persons and things, antecedent to any positive will, law or authority whatever."[279] Another of their conclusions was that the only final proof that any teaching was from God was its correspondence with this primary truth.[280]

Leland, Chapman and others answered the first volume of Morgan's book and it was these answers that called forth the second and third volumes from Morgan's pen.

---

[279] MORGAN, *The Moral Philosopher*, vol. 1, preface, pp. viii-ix.
[280] *loc. cit.*

CHAPTER V

THE DECLINE OF ENGLISH DEISM
(1742–)

A LL classes of society had now been reached rather thoroughly with the teachings of the deists. The movement had been represented by writers from various ranks of society, including nobles such as Cherbury and Shaftesbury, middle class gentlemen such as Blount and Collins, and men of the lower class such as Toland. Some of the writers had presented the movement in a way suited to appeal to the philosophically minded. Such were Cherbury and Toland and Hobbes. Others had made their appeal to those interested in history or science. Such was Blount. Others, like Shaftesbury and Collins, appealed to the clever and witty. Some, like Mandeville, appealed to the coarser elements of society, with a coarser wit. Not only had the numerous writings by deists and by men who had much in common with deists, such as Locke and the continental writer Spinoza, spread deistic doctrines but also the much more numerous answers made to these men. While the abler answers no doubt helped to check deism, probably many of the weaker replies did little more than spread the ideas they were opposing.

But in the later deistic writings of the period just considered it was becoming noticeable that few new opinions or arguments were being advanced, the works of the later writers, being just an enlargement upon or a slightly different presentation of ideas already in print. As a thought-movement deism was slowing down rapidly. A few important deistic writers were yet to appear in England, but the movement had begun to decline. The causes of this decline call for attention in the present chapter. These causes can best be summed up at the end of the chapter. However, one cause undoubtedly was the appearance of the writings of two men who, while having much in common with deism in its negative, critical attitude toward the Bible and revelation, passed from the deistic position of confident assertion that reason can know God and the articles of natural religion to a position of skepticism. These two writers were Henry Dodwell, Jr., and David Hume. Dodwell's book appeared in 1742 A. D., and its apppearance may be taken as the date of the beginning of the decline of English deism. It clearly presented the position of skepticism toward the powers of reason in matters of religion. Hume's skepticism was more far-reaching, covering the whole field of metaphysical philosophy, and therefore has been much more famous in the field of philosophy than the work of Dodwell. These skeptical writers certainly hastened the decline of deism although that decline may have been largely due to other causes, including a kind of thought-exhaustion.

At this point, for the first time in this study of deism, it seems desirable to depart from the chronological order and to study a few writers whose dates are later than Dodwell before studying that writer. This is due to the fact that in the main these other writers are more akin to the earlier writings than Dodwell and because Dodwell and Hume took a position that undermined and tended to destroy deism, though themselves in many ways akin to the deists in thought.

A. PETER ANNET

Peter Annet (1693–1769), a broken-down schoolmaster[1] with some pretensions in the field of theology was the author of three small books that were openly and violently anti-Christian. Like Collins, he wrote anonymously, but the authorship of the books was known and not denied. The first was a book on the life of David entitled *The History of the Man After God's Own Heart* that went farther than even Morgan had gone in attacking the character and reputation of David. Annet viewed every event of David's life in the worst possible light.[2] *The History and Character of St. Paul* was the title of his second book. On the whole Morgan had spoken well of Paul. But Annet attacked Paul in much the same spirit as he had David. He pictured Paul as lazy, ambitious, greedy, self-seeking, dishonest and untruthful.[3] His third book was entitled *The Resurrection of Jesus Considered*. In it the author attacked the trustworthiness of the records and also the character of the evidence advanced in

[1] STEPHEN, *Hist. of Eng. Thought in the Eighteenth Century*, vol. 1, p. 77 f.
[2] ANNET, PETER, *The History of the Man After God's Own Heart*. London, (publisher not given; Anonymous), 1766. "A New Edition," pp. 17–69.
[3] ANNET, PETER, *The History and Character of St. Paul*. London, printed for F. Page (Author and date not given). pp. 19, 25, 30, 35, 36–37, 41, 61–62.

the Bible records of the Resurrection.[4]   He supported this
line of criticism with an attack upon miracles as such in
which he insisted upon the uniformity of nature and upon the
unchangeability of God as both against belief in miracles.[5]

Annet was, like other deists, hostile to the clergy[6] and
strongly in favor of toleration.[7]   He was especially critical
of the early Church Fathers,[8] whom he accused of being
weak, credulous and dishonest.   He was bitter against them
for destroying the works of Celsus and Porphyry.[9]   Something of his tone and spirit is indicated in the following remark made by him in this connection.   "The damning of
books and men, for the sake of opinion, proves their opinions
to be damnable bad that do it." [10]

While Annet's treatment of the lives of David and Paul deserve for him the low opinion and slight attention given him
by most historians of deism, it seems to the present writer
that his criticism of the Resurrection[11] of Jesus and his brief
statement of the positive[12] aspect of deism show some shrewd
ability and call for more attention to his work than is usually
given.   Few of the arguments advanced against the much
attacked story of the resurrection of Jesus escaped Annet's
attention.   His arguments against miracles from the unchangeability of God and the uniformity of nature and his contention that, "natural powers are fit to answer all the ends of
virtue and religion; therefore supernatural powers are needless," [13] were quite in line with the fundamental principles
and assumptions of deism.

Unlike Collins who argued that the New Testament and its
religion was founded on the Old Testament, but more like
Morgan who had set the New Testament over against the Old,
Annet insisted that the New Testament had no necessary con-

---

4) ANNET, PETER, *The Resurrection of Jesus Considered; In Answer
to the Tryal of the Witnesses*. London, printed for Author, 1744. (Published under penname "Moral Philosopher".)
5) ANNET, *The Res. of Jesus Considered*, pp. 91–94.
6) ANNET, *The Res. of Jesus Considered*, pp. 18–19.
7) *op. cit.*, p. 19. cf. p. 8.
8) *op. cit.*, p. 8. cf. *Hist. and Character of St. Paul*, pp. 2–11.
9) ANNET, *The Resurrection of Jesus Considered*, p. 8.
10) *loc. cit.*
11) *op. cit.*, pp. 21–68.
12) *op. cit.*, pp. 18–19, 91–94.
Leslie Stephen calls Annet "a rather disreputable link between Woolston and Thomas Paine." *Hist. of Eng. Thought in the Eighteenth Century*, vol. 1, pp. 77–78.
13) ANNET, *The Resurrection of Jesus Considered*, pp. 91–94.

nection with the Old as Old Testament prophecies were not literally fulfilled in the New.[14]

Annet also made a short argument against the New Testament canon. He pointed to divergences of views on the canon in the early period of church history, especially to the divergences of the Manichæans, Marcionites and Ebionites from the more commonly accepted canon.[15]

Gilbert West's reply to Annet's attack on the resurrection was perhaps the most noted of the several replies called forth by Annet's works.[16] West had himself once been a free-thinker.[17] Lyttleton, who had also once been a free-thinker, made a reply to the attacks made by Annet[18] and others upon the Apostle Paul.[19]

B. THOMAS CHUBB

Thomas Chubb (1679–1747) was a candle-maker who had little education but some natural ability as a writer which he used to present deism in clear vigorous language to the masses. Naturally his writings are mostly a repetion of ideas and arguments already advanced by earlier deists. The most important of his many short works, *The True Gospel of Jesus Christ Asserted* etc., appeared in London in the year 1739 A. D., when deism was at its height and helped to propagate deistic notions among the lower classes. His numerous short works were gathered together and published in the year 1748 A. D. with the title *The Posthumous Works of Mr. Thomas Chubb* and so belong to the period when deism was already declining. This two volume work shows Chubb to be one of the more radical deists who made the religion of nature more scant in content than that of Cherbury and who attacked many parts of the Bible and of Bible Christianity.

Belief in God,[20] recognition that there is a moral law in

14) ANNET, *The History and Character of St. Paul*, p. 2.
15) *op. cit.*, pp. 3–11.
16) *Infidelity.* Comprising JENYN'S *Internal Evidence*, LESLIE'S *Method*, LYTTLETON'S *Conversion of Paul*, WATSON'S *Reply to Gibbon* and Paine, a Notice of Hume on *Miracles*, and an Extract from West on the *Resurrection.* New York, American Tract Society, (Date of publication not given). p. 450.
17) *op. cit.*, p. 104. cf. LECHLER, *Geschichte d. Englischen Deismus*, s. 314 f.
18) By a curious turn of fortune, Annet, who had so violently attacked the Scriptures and Christianity, was buried by the charity of a Christian church. NOACK, *Die Freidenker in der Religion*, Bd. 1, s. 268 f. cf. ANNET, *The History and Character of St. Paul*, pp. 2–11, 103.
19) *Infidelity.* p. 104.
20) CHUBB, THOMAS, *The Posthumous Works of Mr. Thomas Chubb.* London, R. Baldwin, 1748. 2 vols. vol. 1, pp. 155–157.

the very nature of things by which one ought to shape his life,[21] acknowledgement that only the life shaped in accordance with this natural moral law is acceptable to God and will pass his judgment,[22] and that repentance and reformation are the way back to God[23] for the wrongdoer to take, are the elements of natural religion as Chubb states them. He argued for materialism[24] and seemed a bit skeptical of a future life of rewards and punishments, although he sometimes seems to admit such belief.[25] This "natural religion" he regarded as clear and sufficient, leaving no need for revelation.[26]

Most of Chubb's work, however, was of a critical nature, being an attack upon the Bible, its characters and its doctrines. A recent writer who is himself not noted for favoring the Bible or supernaturalism writes with humorous contempt of Chubb as the tallow-chandler "who ingeniously confesses, whilst criticizing the Scriptures, that he knows no language but his own." [27] Chubb talked of "disagreeing parts" and teachings of the Bible.[28] He regarded some of its contents as too trivial for deity to have given it.[29] Like his predecessors he objected to the treatment of the Canaanites and added objection to the "malevolent" psalms.[30] He bitterly criticized the doctrine of the atonement and also sacramental religion.[31] The doctrine of the Trinity he ridiculed as giving a "Triangular God." [32] The resurrection of Jesus he holds to be incredible.[33] The Mosaic laws, he will not admit worthy of divine origin.[34] The apostles he accuses of hypocrisy[35] and also speaks contemptuously of Christ and his miracles.[36] He rejected both miracles[37] and prophecy[38] as proofs of revelation. He threw serious doubts upon the Bible records being

---

21) CHUBB, *Posthumous Works*, vol. 1, pp. 98–99.
22) *op. cit.*, vol. 1, p. 99.
23) *loc. cit.*
24) *op. cit.*, Section iv.
25) *op. cit.*, vol. 1, pp. 19, 309–366, 394, 400.
26) *op. cit.*, vol. 1, pp. 7–17.
27) STEPHEN, *Hist. of Eng. Thought in the Eighteenth Cent.*, vol. 1, pp. 77–78.
28) CHUBB, *Posthumous Works*, vol. 1, pp. 7, 9–18.
29) *op. cit.*, vol. 1, p. 8.
30) *op. cit.*, vol. 1, pp. 7, 190, 216–231; vol. 2, p. 29.
31) *op. cit.*, vol. 1, pp. 37–38, 249, 252–253.
32) *op. cit.*, vol. 1, p. 178.
33) *op. cit.*, vol. 1, pp. 327, 337.
34) *op. cit.*, vol. 1, p. 90.
35) *op. cit.*, vol. 2, pp. 57, 98, 119–120.
36) *op. cit.*, vol. 1, pp. 21–24; vol. 2, pp. 189–190. cf. p. 251.
37) *op. cit.*, vol. 2, p. 175 ff.
38) *op. cit.*, vol. 2, p. 153.

at all historical by talking about the corruptions of books and
fraud of early Christian clergy.[39]   He taught that clergy in
general are selfish, unscrupulous and not to be trusted.[40]   He
ridiculed the doctrine of the virgin birth of Jesus.[41]   He concluded that the Bible is an unsafe guide for mankind.[42]

Chubb was, like most deists, anti-Calvinistic[43] and anti-
Jewish.[44]   This brief survey of Chubb's position indicates
how much he had in common with deists who preceded him
and also indicates that his work was more along the line of
Bible criticism than of philosophy and was more negative or
destructive than constructive.

Chubb did not deny or hesitate to admit that he was a deist.
He regarded himself as a Christian deist. He claimed Jesus
as a deist. As was pointed out above,[45] some deists claimed
Jesus because Jesus is pictured in the Bible as stressing ethical
religion as opposed to the formal ritualistic and sometimes
not highly ethical religion of the pharisees. That Jesus did
emphasize ethical religion and that the deists did also is true.
But that hardly makes a man a deist. Many who are certainly
not deists have stressed ethical religion. That the attitude of
Chubb and other deists toward prayer, miracles, the Scriptures, the deity of Christ, the resurrection of Christ and
supernaturalism in general was radically different from that
of the Christ of the Gospel narratives, the only historical
Christ known, is at once evident when a comparison of teachings is made. How Chubb could claim to tell what was the
True Gospel of Jesus in consistency with his arguments
against the trustworthiness of the Bible records is not apparent. He might, logically enough, have declared what he,
Chubb, thought *should be* the Gospel according to Jesus or
have written with the title *The True Gospel of Thomas
Chubb Asserted*. But, in the light of his treatment of the
Bible, his treatment of many of the teachings of Jesus given
in the Bible, and his conception of the way of salvation, the
title Chubb used for his chief work, *The True Gospel of
Jesus Christ Asserted*, was misleading and his claim that
Jesus was a deist was without merit. Of course contemporary
critics of Chubb pointed out these facts. Nevertheless there

---

[39] CHUBB, *Posthumous Works*, vol. 2, pp. 57 ff., 221.
[40] *op. cit.*, vol. 1, pp. 42–55.
[41] *op. cit.*, vol. 2, p. 193.
[42] *op. cit.*, vol. 2, p. 326.
[43] *op. cit.*, vol. 1, p. 131; vol. 2, p. 315.
[44] *op. cit.*, vol. 1, pp. 90, 200.
[45] above, pp. 31–32.

was a clarity, a cleverness and a forcefulness about Chubb's style, — a style that had some similarity to that of Thomas Payne, — that gave his writings large circulation and influence among the masses of the people.

C. HENRY ST. JOHN, VISCOUNT BOLINGBROKE

Lord Bolingbroke (1672–1751), being one of the later deist writers, summed up in his works a great many of the ideas already circulated by earlier deists. Bolingbroke's high rank in society, his brilliant mind and his considerable literary ability, tended to make his works influential. Had his writings appeared early in the history of the deistic movement they would undoubtedly have created a great stir. But the novelty and excitement had passed, so far as deism and its arguments were concerned, when Bolingbroke's posthumously published works appeared. Interest in deism was rapidly fading when Bolingbroke's works appeared. The more radical deists were going on into the skepticism suggested by the writings of such men as Dodwell and Hume. The more conservative element were turning disgustedly from the movement as they saw the radical extremes to which it was leading. As few new arguments were being advanced and as other interests, especially in the political sphere, were absorbing the attention of the people, the writings of Bolingbroke did not create any great excitement or have any marked influence in England. The dark, gloomy character[46] of his views did not increase the popularity of Bolingbroke's works. Undoubtedly the influence of Bolingbroke was greater upon the continent,[47] where deism was on the increase, than in England. His summing up with some literary ability and with an extensive use of the weapon of mockery of already familiar arguments was his main contribution to deism.

The positive element of deism is not prominent in the works of Bolingbroke, yet he did state belief in God,[48] based on reason and not on revelation. He makes no reference to some of the articles of natural religion given by Herbert of

---

[46] BOLINGBROKE, HENRY ST. JOHN, VISCOUNT, *The Works of Lord Bolingbroke.* Philadelphia, Carey and Hart, 1841. 4 vols. vol. 1, p. 85, Editor's introduction.

[47] Leslie Stephen says, "Bolingbroke's blunderbuss missed fire, because discharged when the controversy was nearly extinct." *Hist. of Eng. Thought in the Eighteenth Century*, vol. 1, p. 77 f. But the shot that missed in England took effect in France.

[48] BOLINGBROKE, *Works*, vol. 2, p. 504; vol. 3, p. 33.

Cherbury. But he does indicate that he doubted the article on a future life and that he denied future punishment.[49]

Bolingbroke's works abound in destructive and unfriendly criticism of nearly everybody[50] and everything he mentions but especially of the Bible, the Church Fathers and the clergy. He held that Christianity must stand or fall as an historical religion[51] and therefore his attack took the form of a critical philosophy of history, especially of Bible history and the history of the transmission of the Bible to modern times. He accused the authors and transmitters of Bible history of selfish frauds and thus made the Bible history untrustworthy.[52] Against Protestants, he used the Roman Catholic arguments for the need of tradition in addition to revelation. Against the Catholics he used the Protestant arguments against unreliable tradition. Thus he made use of the division of Christianity into the Roman Catholic and Protestant camps to attack Christianity itself.[53]

Bolingbroke denounced the Scriptures on many grounds. He argued that the conception of the universe given by such men as Kepler, Copernicus, Galileo and Newton was far more worthy of the wisdom and power of God than that given by Moses.[54] The pentateuch, he accused of being full of falsehood.[55] He made similar charges against all the Scriptures and rejected all as not the word of God.[56] He particularly attacked the stories of the creation, of the flood, of Jacob and Esau and of the conquest of Canaan.[57] He attacked the doctrine of inspiration as borrowed from Egypt and utterly irrational.[58] Men who thought themselves inspired "were only mad,"[59] while men who were thought to be inspired were only "cheats." [60] Though he usually praised Locke more highly than any other writer and built upon Locke's theory of knowledge, he condemned Locke for speaking of a need

[49] BOLINGBROKE, *Works*, vol. 4, pp. 360–362 and elsewhere.
[50] Of many, Bolingbroke says that they were "mad." Others he called "delirious." Wollastson he called a "whining philosopher." *Works*, vol. 3, pp. 22, 307, 381, 390, 427; vol. 4, p. 96.
[51] *op. cit.*, vol. 2, p. 231.
[52] *op. cit.*, vol. 2, pp. 231, 490; vol. 3, pp. 15, 23, 234, 381.
[53] *op. cit.*, vol. 2, pp. 232–233.
[54] *op. cit.*, vol. 2, p. 495. cf. above, pp. 26 ff.
[55] *op. cit.*, vol. 3, pp. 15, 20.
[56] *op. cit.*, vol. 3, pp. 32, 33, 38.
[57] *op. cit.*, vol. 3, pp. 16–17, 35–37.
[58] *op. cit.*, vol. 3, pp. 139, 142.
[59] *op. cit.*, vol. 3, p. 381.
[60] *ibid.*

for revelation.[61]　While at times speaking of Paul as a reasoner and superior to other Bible writers and apostles, he yet
accused him of "theological cant" and of being "a loose para-
phraser, a cabalistical commentator." [62]　He attacked both
Paul's style as a writer and the substance of his writings as a
disproof of inspiration.[63]

Bolingbroke not only attacked Christianity on the ground
of the to him unacceptable character and history of the Bible,
but also on the ground that it had been corrupted by philosophers and particularly by those of the Platonic school.[64]　He
particularly disliked Plato.[65]　Christian theology was, he considered, a product of this influence of philosophy on religion.
And he said, "Theology has made Christianity ridiculous to
men of sense." [66]　Some of the Christian doctrines that especially aroused his ire were,[67] the trinity, the natures of Christ,
the atonement and election.

This author also argued for the materiality of the soul.　In
doing so, he made use of Locke's suggestion that we could not
say matter could not be given the power of thinking.[68]

In the course of his extensive writings, Bolingbroke found
occasion to make frequent references to other deists, to famous philosophers of ancient and modern times, to many of
the Church Fathers and especially to the early literary and
philosophical opponents of Christianity such as Porphyry and
Jamblichus.[69]　When seeking to discredit Bible miracles, Bolingbroke, like earlier deists, made use of the story of "Apollonius Thyana" and his miracles.[70]　He had something bad to
say about most of those he mentioned, especially the Church
Fathers, but nevertheless he evidently made use of arguments
suggested by such men as Porphyry.　Charron, the early
French deist, he quoted with approval.[71]

Though Bolingbroke was of high social rank and had
prominent friends among the great literary men of his day,
such as Pope, Swift and the Frenchman Voltaire, his political activities and his social life were such as to detract

61) BOLINGBROKE, *Works*, vol. 3, pp. 406, 319.　cf. pp. 33, 72, 84, 118.
62) *op. cit.*, vol. 3, pp. 393, 427, 384–385.
63) *op. cit.*, vol. 3, pp. 429–431.
64) *op. cit.*, vol. 3, pp. 201, 207 ff. vol. 4, p. 96 f.
65) *op. cit.*, vol. 3, p. 438; vol. 4, pp. 95–96.
66) *op. cit.*, vol. 4, p. 6.
67) *op. cit.*, vol. 4, pp. 6–7, 9, 306, 491.
68) *op. cit.*, vol. 3, pp. 172–173.
69) *op. cit.*, vol. 3, pp. 244, 287, 462; vol. 4, p. 256.
70) *op. cit.*, vol. 3, p. 382.
71) *op. cit.*, vol. 3, p. 396.

rather than add to his influence as a writer.[72]   Johnson, in his somewhat violent and exaggerated style, expressed about the opinion of Bolingbroke held by the more orthodox element of English society. "He was a scoundrel and a coward; a scoundrel for charging a blunderbuss against religion and morality; a coward because he had no resolution to fire it off himself, but left a half crown to a beggarly Scotchman to draw the trigger after his death."[73]   Johnson is here referring to the fact that Bolingbroke left his works to be published after his death, which was done in the year 1754.   The delay in publishing no doubt greatly lessened the influence of Bolingbroke in England for interest in deism had begun to decline very rapidly before these works appeared.

D. CONYERS MIDDLETON

Conyers Middleton (1683-1750) wrote an extensive and famous criticism of ecclesiastical miracles. His attack was almost entirely directed against miracles or claimed miracles of later date than the Bible. In the year 1747 A. D. Middleton published a small work bearing the title *An Introductory Discourse to a Larger Work, etc.*, which not only gave promise of a fuller treatment of the subject of Church miracles in a later work, but which itself condemned many of them as unreliable,[74] maintained that many of the early church clergy promoted belief in miracles for selfish ends,[75] and drew the conclusion that there is no sufficient reason to believe "that any miraculous powers did ever actually subsist in any age of the Church after the times of the apostles.[76] But having thus rejected post-apostolic miracles, Middleton seemed to give guarded acceptance to those of the Bible itself. He wrote: "As far as miracles can evince the divinity of a religion, the pretensions of Christianity are confirmed by the evidence of such, as of all others on record, are the least liable to exception, and carry the clearest marks of their sincerity."[77]   Then he added his reasons for these statements about Bible miracles: "Being wrought by Christ and his apostles, for an end so great, so important and so

---

[72] BOLINGBROKE, *Works*, vol. 1, pp. 16–17, 83; Vol. 3, p. 53.
[73] FISHER, GEORGE PARK, *History of the Christian Church*. New York, Charles Scribner's Sons, 1903. pp. 606–607.
[74] *An Introductory Discourse to a Larger Work, etc.* London, R. Manby and H. Cox, 1747. pp. 13–36.
[75] *op. cit.*, pp. 39, 43.
[76] *op. cit.*, p. 41.
[77] *op. cit.*, p. 43.

universally beneficial, as to be highly worthy of the interposition of the Deity; and wrought by the ministry of mean
and simple men, in the open view of the people, as the testimony of that divine mission, to which they pretended."[76]
Furthermore they are, "delivered to us by eye-witnesses,
whose honest characters exclude the suspicion of fraud, and
whose knowledge of the facts, which they relate, scarce admits the probability of a mistake."[79] The larger work that
Middleton had promised appeared in the year 1749 A. D.,
bearing the title *Free Inquiry into the Miraculous Powers,
Which Are Supposed to Have Subsisted in the Christian
Church*, etc. This is the work which Hume was chagrined
to find attracting more public attention than his own *Treatise on Human Nature*.[80] In the *Free Inquiry*, Middleton
more fully stated the same positions already maintained,
rejecting post-apostolic miracles on much the same grounds
as Locke had suggested their rejection in his *Third Letter
on Toleration*.[81] Middleton first took up an extensive examination of the Fathers of the early Christian centuries to
show their credulity and untrustworthiness as evidence for
Church miracles. Here he showed great erudition and
gained a reputation as one of the most scholarly of the writers engaged in the deistic controversy.[82] He then contrasted
Church miracles with those of Christ and the apostles to the
discredit of the former.[83]

Middleton argued that the credibility of primitive church
miracles must rest on the two grounds of testimony and
credibility. He said further, "If either part be infirm, their
credit must sink in proportion; and if the facts especially
be incredible, must of course fall to the ground: because no
force of testimony can alter the nature of things."[84] He attacked the testimony ground of such miracles by maintaining the unreliability of early church fathers, including such
men as Jerome and Augustine.[85] In urging incredibility as
an objection to be regarded as fatal, Middleton was practically on the same ground as Hume took in regard to all

[78] MIDDLETON, *An Introductory Discourse*, p. 43.
[79] *ibid.*
[80] STEPHEN, *Hist. of Eng. Thought in the Eighteenth Century*, vol.
1, pp. 77–78. cf. HUME, *An Enquiry*, etc., p. viii.
[81] MIDDLETON, CONYERS, *Free Inquiry into the Miraculous Powers,
Which are supposed to have subsisted in the Christian Church.* London,
R. Manby & H. S. Cox, 1749. pp. iii–iv.
[82] *op. cit.*, pp. 1–71. cf. BURY, *A Hist. of Freedom of Thought*, p. 150.
[83] MIDDLETON, *Free Inquiry*, p. 94.
[84] *op. cit.*, p. ix.
[85] *op. cit.*, pp. 39–40, 133 ff., 158, 161.

miracles. Deists generally claimed that this objection would hold against all miracles. Urging it and attacking the credibility of the church fathers constituted Middleton's main contributions to deism. Yet, staying in the church as a clergyman, he said, "The History of the Gospel, I hope may be true, though the History of the Church be fabulous."[86]

Attacks upon his *Free Inquiry* led him to publish in the year 1751 A. D. *A Vindication of the Free Inquiry, etc.,* in which he seemed to be drifting nearer to the deists and farther from the orthodox Christian position.

E. HENRY DODWELL, JUNIOR

Henry Dodwell, Jr. (d. 1784), son of the orthodox writer Henry Dodwell, published in the year 1742 A. D. a book bearing the title *Christianity Not Founded on Argument; and the True Principle of Gospel-Evidence Assigned,* which, though short, holds an important place in the history of English deism. Hitherto both the deists and their orthodox antagonists had assumed that true religion is rational and capable of defense *in foro rationis*. The deists had sought to show that those things in current and historical religions which they rejected were incapable of a reasoned defense. The defenders of the Bible and of Christianity had sought to show that these and their parts were capable of a reasoned defense and tacitly admitted that were it not so, one would be justified in giving up what could not be rationally defended. Dodwell departed radically from this position by asserting that religion is something absolutely out of the proper jurisdiction of reason.[87] This he stated clearly and vigorously. "I am fully persuaded, that the judging at all of religious matters is not the proper province of reason, or indeed an affair where she has any concern."[88] He attempts to show: "First, that reason, or the intellectual faculty, could not possibly, both from its own nature and that of religion, be the principle intended by God to lead us into a true faith. Secondly, that neither is it so in fact from the plain account given us of it in Holy Scripture. And, thirdly, by tracing plainly from the same indisputable authority

---

[86] MIDDLETON, *Free Inquiry*, p. 162.
[87] DODWELL, HENRY JR., *Christianity Not Founded on Argument; And The True Principle of Gospel-Evidence Assigned: In a Letter to a young Gentleman at Oxford.* London. Printed for M. Cooper, 1743. The Third Edition, p. 7. This work was published anonymously, but the author was known.
[88] *ibid.*

what it positively is, and by ascertaining the proper and prescribed means to come at the knowledge of divine truths."[89]   This was an attempt to prove what would in effect destroy the deistic religion of nature, for its champions claimed to derive it exclusively by the use of the reason, and also the elaborate defenses of orthodox Christianity, for these were reasoned defenses. Deism suffered more than orthodox Christianity from the blow. For the latter, though its defenders claimed its reasonableness, neither was nor claimed to be founded solely on reason. Answers came to Dodwell from both[90] the deist and the orthodox Christian sides as both felt themselves attacked. As a matter or fact the argument of the book would be likely to lead to skepticism rather than to an acceptance of either Christianity or the deistic religion of nature. Indeed the book did constitute the first important indication[91] of the tendency of deism to give way to skeptciism. Hume carried that movement much farther.

Dodwell argued that it is evident from the nature of reason and the nature of religion that God never intended reasoning to be the method by which men should be led to a true faith. Religion requires men to think alike while reason does not require conformity or agreement.[92]   Religion prejudices decisions by doctrines of rewards and punishments while reason requires that no such prejudicing influences be exerted.[93]   The baptism of infants before the age of reason is not consistent with reason being regarded as the road to true faith.[94]   A reasoned faith must depend upon an increase of evidence whereas religion teaches to pray for an increasing of faith.[95]   Religion is to be taught in childhood before reasoning powers have developed.[96] Reason calls for neutrality and the withholding of decision until all the evidence is in whereas religion abhors and con-

---

[89] DODWELL, *Christianity Not Founded on Argument*, pp. 7–8.

[90] Chubb wrote an answer from the standpoint of deism. cf. LECHLER, *Geschichte Des Englischen Deismus*, s. 423. Stebbing, Brine, Cookesey, and Benson wrote answers from the Christian standpoint. These, of which Benson's is the more extended and able, are incorporated in the same volume with the third edition of Dodwell's work from which quotations are made in this book. q. v.

[91] Lechler says of Dodwell's book, "Wir betrachten diese Schrift als Epoche machend, als einen wesentlich neuen Standpunkt beziechnen'd, und nehmen sie als den Anfang einer neuen Periode des Deismus, namlich seiner Auflösung in Skepticismus." LECHLER, *Geschichte*, etc., s. 412.

[92] DODWELL, *Christianity Not Founded on Argument*, p. 8.

[93] *ibid.*

[94] *op. cit.*, p. 9.

[95] *op. cit.*, pp. 10–11.

[96] *op. cit.*, pp. 11–12.

demns all neutrality.[97] Faith is needed all through life and
men cannot afford to be without it while giving reason time
to make her decisions.[98] It is needful that men be ready
for death at all times and without faith they are not ready.
They cannot afford the risk of unpreparedness while reason
makes her slow decisions.[99] Most men are for one reason
or another incapable of much reasoning and yet all are held
responsible for their possession or lack of faith. A just God
must not therefore require faith to be on a reasoned
basis.[100] Not all men are able to follow the reasoning of a
Butler's *Analogy*.[101] Necessary truth can hardly depend
upon such "far-fetched" and "labored" apologies.[102] Even
the best thinkers would be disqualified for sound reasoning
on matters of faith by prejudices.[103] The command to believe makes no time allowance for reasoning processes.[104]
Moreover even were one to attain to a reasoned faith, such
a faith would be too cold. "A zeal according to knowledge,
will scarce ever deserve the name."[105] Again, reasoned decisions must ever be subject to change, but the believer is
admonished not to be turned about with every wind of doctrine.[106] Reasoning about holy things tends to destroy reverence,[107] and religion demands reverence. He who never
asked himself one single question about his faith is the one
who enjoys it with greatest confidence and tranquility.[108]
A reasoned faith would not have sufficient force to control
human passions and so would not be practical.[109] Much
less would it be able to give men the martyr spirit,[110] which
religion requires of men.

Dodwell's second line of argument was that the Bible
itself does not teach that the appeal to reason is the way to
faith or right religion. It speaks of understanding with the
heart rather than with the intellect.[111] Christ did not appeal to reason but rather spoke as one having authority.[112]

97) DODWELL, *Christianity Not Founded on Argument*, p. 12.
98) *op. cit.*, pp. 13–15.
99) *op. cit.*, p. 17.
100) *op. cit.*, pp. 17–18.
101) *op. cit.*, pp. 20–21.
102) *op. cit.*, p. 21.
103) *op. cit.*, p. 23.
104) *ibid.*
105) *op. cit.*, p. 25.
106) *op. cit.*, p. 26.
107) *op. cit.*, p. 28.
108) *op. cit.*, p. 29.
109) *op. cit.*, pp. 30–32.
110) *op. cit.*, pp. 32–34.
111) *op. cit.*, p. 36.
112) *op. cit.*, p. 37.

Christ and his apostles alike called for quick decisions of acceptance or rejection of their doctrines and did not tarry to allow the slow processes of reasoning. The dust was to be shaken off the shoes against those refusing acceptance.[113] The apostles were not particularly qualified to promote faith by reasoning processes.[114] Miracles could not be appealed to as the reason for faith because lying wonders were admittedly wrought by imposters.[115] The care taken by Jesus not to have some of his miracles made public and his efforts to dissuade men from seeking miracles show miracles were not intended for to lead men to a reasoned faith.[116] But even if miracles were to be regarded as reasons for belief on the part of those that saw them, they must lose their value as such with their increasing antiquity.[117]

Dodwell's third line of argument is that the Scriptures themselves say faith comes only by the Holy Spirit.[118] Faith is a gift of God.[119] The Spirit is to lead into all truth.[120] The Scriptures make the want of faith criminal. But it could not be criminal if simply due to want of information or ability.[121] And few have ability, opportunity and information enough to decide surely on questions of text, canon, translation and interpretation.[122] Scripture represents like-mindedness as a gift of God rather than an achievement of sound reasoning.[123] Thomas was rebuked for seeking evidence while those who believe without seeing were praised by Jesus.[124] It is declared that the things of the spirit are only spiritually discerned.[125] The Scriptural admonition is, "My son, trust thou in the Lord with all thy heart, and lean not unto thine own understanding." With this quotation Dodwell closed both his argument and his book.[126]

Particularly prominent in Dodwell's book is his insistence that faith and reason are contrary in nature and in effect. "The foundation of philosophy is all doubt and suspicion,

---

113) DODWELL, *Christianity Not Founded on Argument*, pp. 38–39.
114) *op. cit.*, pp. 39–40.
115) *op. cit.*, p. 46.
116) *op. cit.*, pp. 48–49.
117) *op. cit.*, p. 51.
118) *op. cit.*, p. 56.
119) *op. cit.*, p. 57.
120) *ibid.*
121) *op. cit.*, p. 63.
122) *op. cit.*, pp. 62–63.
123) *op. cit.*, p. 65.
124) *op. cit.*, p. 78.
125) *op. cit.*, p. 103.
126) *op. cit.*, p. 118.

as the foundation of religion is all acquiescence and belief."[127]   There has always been antipathy between the
philosopher and the believer, the former scoffing at the latter and the latter proscribing the former.[128]   The wisdom
of men has always been reputed foolishness with God and
with God's servants.[129]   The world fails by wisdom to know
God and the brightest reasoners are likely to be found without any notion of saving faith.[130]   The believer, being sure
that he has the one thing necessary, despises the meaner
pursuits of the philosopher and scientist.[131]   The philosopher's mind is trained to argue and test and this disquali-
fies him for the appreciation of religion.   Julian, when he
sought to check Christianity by forbidding the education of
Christians, made a mistake.[132]   What he should have done
to gain his end was to educate them in philosophy as he
himself had been educated.   Even the apostle warned
against being spoiled by philosophy.[133] Men like Dr. Clarke,
however ingenious and however good their intentions raise
more doubts than they remove by their reasonings in defense of Christian faith.[134]   Champions of Christianity who
have sought to defend her by argument and reason have
only fatally betrayed the cause of religion by mistaking
their proper weapons and their ground.   They have forgone
"their advantage of an eminence, and the hill country" to
"prepare a defense for her, upon the level, of which she is
no way capable."[135]   English history testifies "that there
never has been seen less of zeal and steadiness in the cause
of religion, than at those particular junctures, when the circumstances of the times necessarily led men to the closest
enquiry into its merits."[136]

The reader has now before him a sufficient resume of the
arguments of Dodwell's little book to make plain how different was that author's position and mode of reasoning
from that of early deists as well as from that of their opponents.   The subtlety and skill of this lawyer's attack upon
Christianity must also be apparent.   Unlike the deists who
had put forth a natural religion or religion of reason, Dod-

127) DODWELL, *Christianity Not Founded on Argument*, p. 71.
128) *ibid.*
129) *ibid.*
130) *op. cit.*, pp. 72–73.
131) *op. cit.*, p. 73.
132) *op. cit.*, pp. 74–75.
133) *ibid.*
134) *op. cit.*, p. 81.
135) *op. cit.*, p. 85.
136) *op. cit.*, p. 82.

well had no such religion to propose himself and regarded all such proposed by others as worthless. Unlike the deists who had preceded him, he also made no accusations of fraud against the clergy, made no effort at destructive Bible criticism, made no attempt to disprove any prophecies and miracles, although he did attempt to show that miracles were not intended as means of producing faith, and made no plea for toleration. Indeed he wrote as though intolerance were the wise course for the champions of a religious faith to take.[137] The deist who had championed a rationalistic religion of nature and attacked Christianity could find little comfort or support for his position in the work of Dodwell. Yet he might secretly rejoice that Dodwell had represented Christianity as a faith wholly irrational and suited only to flourish in an age of ignorance and unreasoning credulity. The defender of Christianity, on the other hand, might rejoice in seeing Dodwell undermine the whole position of Christianity's deistic opponents, yet he could get little comfort from writings which made all his reasoned defenses of Christianity worse than useless and which represented his Christian faith as suited only to an age of ignorance and wholly incapable of reasoned defense. He felt that this shrewd and clever reasoner Dodwell who seemed to be championing Christianity from the standpoint of a thorough-going mystic was in reality a rationalist sneering[138] at Christianity as an utterly irrational faith suited only to the ignorant and unreasoning.

F. DAVID HUME

David Hume (1711-1776), the famous Scotch philosopher, holds an important place in the history of deism. Hume, though an able and acute reasoner, was not, and made little effort to be, a consistent writer.[139] For this reason it is not difficult to refute one part of Hume's writings from another part or to claim Hume's support for several different and inconsistent types of philosophical thought.[140] No doubt many of the people of his own time thought of him as just another of the many deist writers because they found in him the same anti-clergy, anti-Bible, anti-miracle, anti-Christianity attitude that they found in other deists and also

---

137) DODWELL, *Christianity Not Founded on Argument*, pp. 96–99.
138) cf. LECHLER, *Geschichte Des Englischen Deismus*, p. 422.
139) HUME, DAVID, *An Enquiry Concerning the Human Understanding, and An Enquiry Concerning the Principles of Morals.* Oxford, Clarendon Press, 1894. Editor's Introd., p. vii.
140) *loc. cit.*

because much of what he had to say about religion that was of a postive character was also quite in line with the position of deism. Indeed few, if any, of his deist predecessors had made so strong an attack or an attack so durable in its influence as was Hume's attack upon the Bible and the miraculous. And few, if any of them, had stated the fundamental positive positions of deism as well as he. But elsewhere in his works Hume advanced arguments that underminded the postive part of his deistic teachings and gained for him classification as a skeptic rather than a deist. And these arguments, which deal with causation, being the very ones that give Hume his important place in the history of philosophy, his abiding influence is on the side of skepticism rather than deism. From the Christian standpoint, Hume was not nearer but farther from the Christian position than were the regular deists. Though Hume did not descend to the scurrilous type of attack upon Christianity which such writers as Woolston and Annet had made use of but kept his work on a more dignified and philosophical plane, his hostility was none the less real nor his attack the less important.

The evidence in support of the position that Hume was a deist consists chiefly in what he wrote that presents him as a believer in the fundamental and positive articles of deism. He wrote: "The whole frame of nature bespeaks an intelligent Author; and no rational inquirer can, after serious reflection, suspend his belief a moment with regard to the primary principles of genuine theism and religion."[141] He also wrote: "There surely is a Being who presides over the universe; and who, with infinite wisdom and power, has reduced the jarring elements into just order and proportion."[142] Again he wrote: "Though the stupidity of men, barbarous and uninstructed, be so great, that they may not see a sovereign Author in the more obvious works of nature to which they are so much familiarized; yet it scarcely seems possible, that any one of good understanding should reject that idea, when once it is suggested to him. A purpose, an intention, a design is evident in everything; and when our comprehension is so far enlarged as to contemplate the first rise of the visible system, we must adopt, with the strongest conviction, the idea of some intelligent cause or

---

141) HUME, DAVID, *Essays, Literary, Moral and Political.* London, Ward, Lock & Co., Limited (date not given). p. 514.
142) *op. cit.,* p. 90.
143) *op. cit.,* pp. 551–552.

author."[143] Thus it appears that Hume agreed with the first article of the positive creed of deism, that there is a God known by reason without the assistance of revelation. Hume also agreed with the second article of deism for he wrote: "Can we be so blind as not to discover an intelligence and a design in the exquisite and most stupendous contrivance of the universe? Can we be so stupid as not to feel the warmest raptures of worship and adoration, upon the contemplation of that intelligent Being, so infinitely good and wise?"[144] Here is the second of Herbert's articles, that men ought to worship God. Hume did not so definitely or clearly state acceptance of the article concerning a future life, yet he did seem to imply belief in it when he wrote: "But it is our comfort, that, if we employ worthily the faculties here assigned us, they will be enlarged in another state of existence, so as to render us more suitable worshippers of our Maker: and that the tasks, which can never be finished in time, will be the business of an eternity."[145]

However the strongest reason a deist might have for claiming Hume as one of the deists were such reasonings advanced by him as the following. Teaching divine interference with nature minimizes instead of magnifying the attributes of God.[146] It argues more power in the Deity to delegate some power to creatures than to work all by his own immediate volition.[147] "It argues more wisdom to contrive at first the fabric of the world with such perfect foresight that, of itself, and by its proper operation, it may serve all the purposes of providence, than if the Creator were obliged every moment to adjust its parts, and animate by his breath all the wheels of that stupendous machine."[148] This is as clear a statement of the fundamental position of deism as is found in the writings of any of the deists.

Yet Hume differed in some of his positive teachings from the deists. He did not, like them, regard monotheism as the original religion of men that later became corrupted into polytheism. Instead he regarded polytheism as the first form of religion and monotheism as a much later development.[149] Man's reasoning powers were not sufficiently developed or directed to give monotheism first.[150] Religion

144) HUME, Essays, Literary, Moral and Political, p. 92.
145) op. cit., p. 93.
146) op. cit., p. 351.
147) ibid.
148) op. cit., p. 351.
149) op. cit., pp. 515–519.
150) ibid.

did not originate in reason but in fear of future events.[151]
The inferior precedes the superior. Huts come before pala-
ces.[152]   But somewhat inconsistent with this argument by
Hume for the priority of polytheism because of its inferior-
ity, is his argument that polytheism is superior to monotheism in that it is tolerant and promotes courage while theism
is intolerant and promotes abasement.[153]   Hume also was
not in agreement with the deists in their denial that there
are any atheists or people without religion. Rather he
agreed with Locke that there are some such,[154] though not
many.

Hume also had much in common with the deistic movement in its negative critical aspect toward Christianity and
the Bible, as well as toward later historical forms of Christianity. He ridiculed scholastic religion as utterly irrational.[155] He drew attention to the resemblance of the Jewish to the Egyptian religion,[156] evidently with the purpose
of suggesting, as earlier deists had done, that the Jewish religion was derived from the Egyptians. He rejected[157] and
argued against[158] miracles. He argued against the Bible,
especially against the Penteteuch,[159] on the ground that it
could not be accepted because so full of miracles. For the
same reason he also rejected Christianity itself, which, he
declared, a reasonable person could not believe without a
miracle.[160] Most of the deists had claimed to be reformers
of Christianity, rejecting only the unreasonable things that
had been fraudulently introduced by selfish priests and
keeping the rest. They had maintained that true Christianity is wholly rational. Dodwell had forsaken this position and maintained that Christianity itself is not a religion
that can stand trial in the court of reason, but that Christianity must be taken on faith alone. Hume now took up this
position of Dodwell. He wrote: "Our most holy religion is
founded on faith, not on reason; and it is a sure method of
exposing it to put it to such a trial as it is, by no means,

---

151) HUME, *Essays, Literary, Moral and Political*, pp. 515–519.
152) *op. cit.*, p. 516.
153) *op. cit.*, pp. 536–539.
154) *op. cit.*, p. 514.
155) *op. cit.*, p. 541.
156) *op. cit.*, p. 542, footnote.
157) *op. cit., Of Miracles*, pp. 556–557, 565.
158) *op. cit., Of Miracles*, pp. 554–565.
159) HUME, *An Enquiry Concerning the Human Understanding, And
an Enquiry Concerning the Principles of Morals*, p. 130.
160) *op. cit.*, p. 131.

fitted to endure."[161]   He called such as attempted to defend Christianity by reason "dangerous friends or disguised enemies to the Christian religion."[162]   Perhaps both Dodwell and Hume were just ridiculing, in a guarded way, Christianity as an irrational religion.

Most of the deists made attacks upon either miracles or prophecy. Hume made his great attack upon miracles, just briefly indicating that he regarded prophecy as but a form of miracle. Indeed Hume's attack upon miracles is more subtle and skillful and has had a more enduring influence than the attacks made by his deist predecessors. His attacks upon the characters of the witnesses to such miracles as have been recorded,[163] his raising suspicion against all miracles by pointing to the number of forged miracles,[164] his statement that miracles have abounded most among the ignorant,[165] and his asking why miracles do not occur now, were all intended to raise doubt and unbelief in miracles on the part of his readers. But such arguments were much like those of earlier enemies of the miraculous. Hume's main line of attack was different. He started with Tillotson's proposition that "a weaker evidence can never destroy a stronger."[166]   Then he asserted that a wise man proportions his belief to the evidence.[167]   Next he defines a miracle. "A miracle is a violation of the laws of nature."[168]   "There must - - - be a uniform experience against every miraculous event, otherwise the event would not merit that appellation."[169]   From this definition of a miracle, Hume advanced to the conclusion that, "as a firm and unalterable experience has established these laws, the proof against a miracle, from the very nature of the fact, is as entire as any argument from experience can possibly be imagined."[170]   Naturally those who answered this attack by Hume on miracles were quick to point out that Hume begged the question at issue in his definition, for the very question at issue is the "uniformity" and "unalterable" character of experience. Hume was

161) HUME, *An Enquiry Concerning the Human Understanding, and an Enquiry Concerning the Principles of Morals*, p. 130.
162) *ibid.*
163) HUME, *Essays, Literary, Moral and Political. Of Miracles*, pp. 557–559.
164) *op. cit.*, p. 559.
165) *ibid.*
166) *op. cit.*, p. 553.
167) HUME, *Essays, Literary, Moral and Political. Of Miracles*, p. 554.
168) *op. cit.*, p. 556.
169) *ibid.*
170) *ibid.*

ruling miracles out by definition. But this was not all of
Hume's reasoning against miracles. He went on to say: "No
testimony is sufficient to establish a miracle, unless the testimony be of such a kind that its falsehood would be more
miraculous than the fact which it endeavors to establish."[171]   This was to put the weight of a uniform experience, or nearly uniform, if the question at issue is not
begged, into one side of the evidence scale against the ability and truthfulness of the limited number who testify to
any miracle. Hume's conclusion was, of course, that no
claimed miracle had sufficient evidence in its support to
outweigh the general uniformity of nature.[172] It is a question whether or not this argument of Hume would not bear
against any strange or unusual events as well as against
miracles. Hume's argument against miracles has been famous and has probably been regarded as the best statement
of the position of those whose thinking has been so dominated with the idea of the uniformity of nature and of the
exclusive reign of naturalism that they cannot and will not
admit the supernatural or the miraculous.

As considered so far, Hume was just one of the abler
deists. But an element in Hume's teaching remains to be
considered which constitutes his main contribution to philosophical thought and which constitutes his chief claim to
fame. This element was his discussion of causality or "necessary connection." The association of different things
comes to us only from experience. But experience gives
only association and sequence but never cause.[173] Even
when we examine our wills and the events that follow our
willing all we find is sequence. We do not find any secret
connection which binds the willing and the events together
and that renders them inseparable.[174] Examine billiard-
balls hitting each other and all you will find will be that
motion of the one and its contact with the other is followed
by the motion of the other. You will find nothing to suggest
the idea of power or necessary connection.[175] Thus Hume
ruled out the conception of causality as power or force, as
push or pull, and in so doing paved the way for a deep-cut-
ting skepticism.

Although Hume did not himself avowedly discard what

[171] HUME, *Essays, Literary, Moral and Political*, p. 557.
[172] *ibid.*
[173] *op. cit.*, p. 327.
[174] *op. cit.*, p. 347.
[175] HUME, *An Enquiry Concerning the Human Understanding*, etc.,
p. 63. cf. pp. 60–79.

he had written from the deistic standpoint upon belief in
deity and in other articles of natural religion, others were
quick to see that his position on the subject of causation cut
the foundation from under the structure of natural religion
which he himself as well as deistic predecessors had
erected. Hume had rejected the idea of an innate or in-
stinctive knowledge of God and the principles of natural religion.[176] He had then built natural religion on reasoning
from the evidence of a creator's wisdom, power and purpose in the universe.[177] But, if the idea of causality is ruled
out, the ideas of a Creator, of power and of a purpose that
is able to effect anything, are ruled out with it. And since
Hume refused to accept revelation this left only skepticism
or agnosticism. He had rejected innate ideas or principles,
the foundation on which Herbert of Cherbury had founded
his deistic natural religion. He had also rejected the idea
of causation and the right to reason from the idea of either
a first or a final cause, thus destroying the foundation upon
which deists after Herbert had built their natural religion.
Thus deism in its whole postive and philosophical side was
mined and only its negative and critical side was left. With
this element in deism Hume had no quarrel. The logic of
Hume's philosophy was such as to dissolve deism into skepticism.[178]

G. CAUSES OF THE DECLINE OF ENGLISH DEISM

The deistic movement in England which began with Herbert of Cherbury in the year 1624 A. D. and developed very
slowly during the seventy years following and which then
suddenly flourished forth and became a thing of intense
popular interest for a period of nearly fifty years, calling
forth an almost incredible volume of controversial literature, died down very quickly. The year 1742 A. D., when
Dodwell published his *Christianity Not Founded on Argument*, marks the beginning of the rapid decline of deism.
By the year 1760 A. D. the movement had practically come
to an end in England, though a few belated works such as
those of the English-born deist Thomas Paine and the
deistic-in-tone History by Edward Gibbon appeared after

---

[176] HUME, *Essays, Literary, Moral and Political*, p. 515.
[177] *op. cit.*, pp. 90, 92, 514.
[178] STEPHEN, *Hist. of Eng. Thought in the Eighteenth Century*,
vol. 1, p. 77 f.
LECHLER, *Geschichte d. Englischen Deismus*, s. 425.

that date. Paine belonged more to America and France than to England. Gibbon, in the fifteenth and sixteenth chapters of his great work, *The Decline and Fall of the Roman Empire*, treats the history of early Christianity from the viewpoint of a deist and gives a naturalistic explanation of the growth and spread of Christianity.[179] Because of the lasting fame of this work it has probably done more to propagate deistic ideas than many other works by other deists that were given wholly to deistic argumentation.[180] There have been a considerable number of English books since the decline of deism that have been opposed to orthodox historical Christianity, but they have usually been written from the standpoint of a skeptical, agnostic or atheistic attitude rather than from the standpoint of deism. So rapid was the decline of interest in deism in England that before the end of the eighteenth century Burke could say, referring to the deists, "Who ever reads them now?"[181] At the present time even the names of most of the once famous deists are unknown to the public and their books that once stirred up so great an excitement can only be located in a few of the older and larger libraries and are only read by a few persons doing research work. The question naturally arises as to the reason or reasons for this rapid decline of deism.

The answer that would be given to a question seeking the reason for the decline of deism would be likely to vary greatly according to the viewpoint of the one questioned. Those who wrote against the deists would be likely to give a great part of the credit for its decline to the able and scholarly refutations of the deistic writings by their orthodox Christian opponents. They would probably point with some pride to the number of such answers that were made, to the fact that the weight of scholarship was against the deists,[182] and especially to such able defences of historical Christianity as were made by men like Berkeley, Law, West, Leland, Butler and Paley. This was undoubtedly the richest period for apologetical works in all the long history of Christianity. But, while some intellectual folks are cer-

---

179) Gibbon, Edward, *The Decline and Fall of the Roman Empire*. New York and London, The Co-Operative Publication Society (date not given). Six vols. vol. 1, pp. 522–681. cf. Hamilton, Floyd E., *The Basis of Christian Faith*. New York, George H. Doran Co., 1927. pp. 126–130.
180) Bury, *A Hist. of Freedom of Thought*, p. 166.
181) Stephen, *Hist. of Eng. Thought in the Eighteenth Century*, vol. 1, p. 90.
182) Stephen, *op. cit.*, vol. 1, pp. 86–87. cf. Robertson, *A Short History of Free Thought*, pp. 314–315.

tainly won over by argument and debate, it is likely that
those who engage in such argumentation overestimate the
effect of that kind of thing.   Other things than arguments
influence opinions. Oftentimes arguments and criticisms but
advertise the thing attacked.   Benjamin Franklin records
that it was reading answers to deists that led to his own acceptance of deism.[183]   Others would add to the work of the
men who replied to the deists the essential weakness and
falsity of the deistic position as a cause for its decline.   Orthodox Christians and atheists, skeptics and agnostics would
agree in giving this as one reason for the decline of deism.
The orthodox Christians would be thinking particularly of
the negative, critical side of deism as weak and false while
the others would be thinking of its positive element, its religion of nature, as its weak and false element.   Thus we
find Stephen saying: "The English rationalism of the
eighteenth century—was founded upon a decayed system of
philosophy" which resulted in a "deeply seated delicacy of
constitution."[184)   We also find him saying: "Deism of the
constructive kind wanted any true vitality."[185)   The orthodox critic of deism would give the apologists for Christianity the credit for exposing the weakness of deism whereas
the others would give the credit to such skeptical writers as
Dodwell and Hume.   Probably most philosophers would
credit Hume with causing the decline and practical disap-
pearance of deism.[186)   But it is easily possible to exaggerate
Hume's part in the decline of deism.   For, though it is true
that Humian skepticism both undermined deism and also
attracted the more radical opponents of historical Christianity, it is also true that deism was already rapidly declining before Hume's works were published and therefore
those works could not logically be credited with being the
main or first cause of the decline.   Hume himself testified
that his *Treatise* "fell dead-born from the press without
reaching such distinction as even to excite a murmur among
the zealots."[187)

Just as the division among Christians gave the deists quite
an advantage in attack, so the divisions and differences that

---

[183) FRANKLIN, BENJAMIN, *Autobiography*.   Ginn & Co., Boston, 1891.
p. 79.
[184) STEPHEN, *Hist. of Eng. Thought in the Eighteenth Century*,
vol. 1, p. 34.
[185) STEPHEN, *Freethinking and Plainspeaking*, p. 363.
[186) LECHLER, *Geschichte d. Eng. Deismus*, s. 425.
[187) HUME, *An Enquiry Concerning the Human Understanding*, etc.,
p. viii.

developed among the deists weakened their own position. Herbert of Cherbury had maintained that the articles of natural religion were innate whereas most later deists had opposed the idea of their being innate and maintained that they were the conclusions of a reasoning process. They differed also among themselves about the number of the so clear and plain principles of natural religion, especially dividing into rival camps over the question of a future life. Most of them argued that true Christianity is a highly rational religion while such later writers as Dodwell and Hume presented Christianity as irrational and a religion for faith only. Such divisions undoubtedly seriously weakened the position of deism with its claims to clear and universally known principles of natural religion.

One important thing that undoubtedly helped to bring about the rapid decline of English deism, a thing usually overlooked in stating the causes of that decline, was an exhaustion of the subject. The few arguments for the very limited number of articles of natural religion were soon given so that later deists were but repeating ideas already often advanced. The various modes of attack upon historical Christianity had also been so thoroughly presented that little new was presented by later writers. The attack had been made from the standpoint of history, of comparative religion, of science, of Bible criticism and of philosophy. The modes and spirit of attack had also varied from the mode of grave and dignified discussion to the modes of witty ridicule and flippant mockery. The movement therefore declined partly through a sheer intellectual exhaustion of the subject.

The moral and social laxity for which the period of Walpole was especially notorious[188] was laid by some at the door of a worldly clergy and by others it was blamed on the deists and their breaking down of old religious sanctions. The lives of a number of the deists being far from above reproach, gave appearance of justification to the charge made against their teachings. Thus, whether justly or unjustly, the blaming of the moral corruption of the times upon the deists probably made many turn against deism, and so became one cause for the decline of deism.

But far more important than this cause of the decline of deism, was the rapid development of the great religious re-

---

188) GREEN, JOHN RICHARD, *History of the English People*. New York, The Edward Publishing Co. (date of pub. not given). 4 vols. vol. 4, pp. 88–89.

vival led by Whitefield and the two Wesleys.[189] This was not a meeting of deism with debate and argument but a confronting of it with a religion of zeal and fervor and power. The type of life lived by the ascetic leaders of this new religious movement made the charges brought against the clergy fall utterly ineffective. Undoubtedly the great religious revival had much to do with the decline of deism. The revival began about 1736.[190]

Still another cause for the decline was the turning of popular attention to stirring political events in England, upon the continent and in America. The "Pretender" of the House of Stuart was making unavailing efforts to get the throne. Wars over royal successions were also developing in Europe. In America, French and British rivalry for colonial empire was becoming bitter and warlike. Such topics or the spread of the religious revival became the themes of conversation instead of the latest anti-Christian, anti-Bible or anti-clergy witicisms of the deists.

It is evident that there was not one only but that there were several causes working together to bring about the rapid decline of deism in England. The exhaustion of the movement itself, the weakness caused by differences among the deists themselves, the arguments of many able and learned opponents, who wrote in defense of Christianity, the undermining of the deist position by the skepticism of Dodwell and Hume, the blaming of deism for the widespread public immorality, the coming of the great methodist religious revival, and the turning of popular attention to absorbing political and military events, were all causes that worked together to bring about the rapid decline and almost the complete extinction of deism in England.

The remarkable English deistic movement had run its course and become a matter of history. But its influence was not ended. It spread from England to the continent of Europe, especially to France and Germany. It also leaped the Atlantic and had a considerable influence in the British colonies which were in the process of becoming the United States of America. And after deism had practically ceased in even these lands, the influence of deistic views and arguments entered into new types of Bible criticism and into new types of philosophical and theological opinion.

---

[189] GREEN, *History of the English People*, vol. 4, pp. 105–108.
[190] NINDE, E. S., *George Whitefield*. New York, The Abingdon Press, 1924. p. 48.

In Part I the reader was invited to consider the roots of English deism. In Part II he was asked to examine the rise, progress and decline of English deism itself. He is now invited in Part III to consider the fruits of eighteenth century English deism as it contributed to the rise of deistic movements in France, Germany and America and also as it has influenced thought-movements of later date down to the present time.

PART III

THE FRUITS OF ENGLISH DEISM

CHAPTER VI

THE INFLUENCE OF ENGLISH DEISM UPON THE DEISTIC MOVEMENTS IN FRANCE, GERMANY AND AMERICA

THE transit of ideas from one land to another is made by many routes. The following are among the more important of them. Books, in the original language or in translation, magazines, papers and private letters, are all important in the movement of ideas from one land to another. These writings need not champion the ideas that are transferred. Indeed they may have been written to refute and oppose such ideas. Franklin informs us that it was the writings of opponents of deism that influenced him to become a deist.[1] Books written as refutations of deism probably did as much to spread knowledge concerning English deists and their arguments in the lands of France, Germany and America as did the books of the deists themselves. International travellers also carry ideas from one land to another. Many English deists such as Herbert of Cherbury, Hobbes and Shaftesbury travelled in France. Many Frenchmen, including the most influential of French deists, Voltaire, travelled in England and there absorbed English deistic ideas. Moreover travellers from both these lands often met and exchanged ideas in Holland which was a land of refuge at the time under consideration for persecuted political and religious radicals of all lands. Writings and travel were the two chief ways in which English deistic ideas found their way into France. There was not so much travel in the seventeenth and eighteenth centuries between Germany and England. So it was more through French travellers in Germany, such as Voltaire, and through both English and French writings on the subject of deism, than through any direct travel connection between England and Germany, that English deistic ideas found their way into the land East of the Rhine. In the case of the American colonies it would be necessary to add immigration from the motherland to writings and travel as an important way in which deistic ideas were transferred from England to

---

[1] FRANKLIN, *Autobiography*, pp. 23, 28.

American soil. America was filling up with English colonists who brought their knowledge of deism with them from the old country.

It is not to be supposed that all the deistic ideas that appeared in France, Germany or America were either direct or indirect importations from England. The same causes that were operating to produce deism in England were also, in great measure, working to produce it in other lands. It has already been noticed that deism really had a start in France before it arose in England.[2] Later French deism undoubtedly owed much directly to the earlier French deism and to the influence of such French writers as Montaigne, Bodin and Charron.

Deism as a thought-movement first reached its maturity of development in England, then in France, next in Germany and last of all in America. The English influence was more directly exercised upon France than upon Germany to which it was largely mediated through France. It is fitting therefore to give first consideration to the influence of English deism upon France and French deism.

A. THE INFLUENCE OF ENGLISH DEISM UPON EIGHTEENTH CENTURY FRENCH DEISM

Lechler and Farrar are scarcely correct when they make French deism to be the direct offspring of English deism. For, as noted above, deism arose in France before it did in England and French deism was one of the many roots of English deism. Yet it is true that the early deism of France was comparatively weak and undeveloped, that deism first reached its maturity of development in England and that the later and more fully developed French deism did owe much to influences from across the channel.

The French were more radical in their free-thinking than the English. They were the fanatics of free-thought.[3] Montaigne was more skeptic than deist. Truly deistic ideas made their appearance in the works of Bodin and Charron. Locke, while in Holland, had extensive friendly intercourse with Le Clerc and Bayle, two influential French liberals. In Rousseau and Voltaire, the two most famous and influential French deists, the English influence was most marked. For a time deism became the characteristic mode of French thinking to a degree never equalled in England.[4] A much

[2] above. pp. 49–50.
[3] NOACK, *Die Freidenker in der Religion*, b. 2, s. viii.
[4] *op. cit.*, b. 2, s. 5.

larger proportion of the French than of the English free-
thinkers went over to skepticism, materialism and outright
atheism.[5]   Whereas in England the weight of scholarship
and literary ability was at all times on the side of historical
Christianity in its struggle with deism, in France, for a
considerable length of time, scholarship and literary genius
were mostly on the side of deism and the more radical forms
of opposition to historical Christianity.[6]   These radical
forms of religious philosophy and the radical forms of
political philosophy with which they were closely associated
had much to do with the bringing on of the great French
Revolution.   In that revolution, it was the radical religious
views that caused a so-called "Religion of Reason" to be
substituted for a time for Christianity.   Reaction and revul-
sion against the great extremes and cruelties of the revolution undoubtedly had much to do with the decline of deism
and other forms of religious radicalism about the beginning
of the nineteenth century.

A complete list of French deists would be a long one and
would include, among others, Bodin, Charron, Tissot de
Patot, Boulainvilliers, D'Argens, Mademoiselle Huber,
Toussaint, Jean Martin de Prades, Helvetius, Rousseau and
Voltaire.   A number of writers, such as Bayle and Diderot,
passed through a deistic stage in their thinking but later became skeptics.   La Mettrie and d'Holbach were atheists
rather than deists.   The skeptics and atheists doubted or
denied the positive teachings of the deists but were generally at one with the deists in the attacks upon the Bible and
historical Christianity.   During the deistic period a number
of large and influential works appeared in which many
different writers had a part.   Among these were Diderot's
Encyclopädie, Bayle's *Dictionnaire* and the anonymously
published *Systeme de la nature*.[7]   Deistic, skeptical and
atheistic views found expression in these works.

In character, content, spirit and methods, English and
French deism were essentially alike.   In the writings of
each there was a negative and positive element.   In the
writings of each the negative element occupied much more
space than did the positive element.   The positive element

---

[5] NOACK, *Die Freidenker in der Religion*, b. 2, s. 355 ff.   Also ROBERT-
SON, *A Short History of Freethought*, vol. 1, pp. 338–348.
[6] ROBERTSON, *A Short History of Freethought*, vol. 1, pp. 334–344.
STEPHEN, *History of Eng. Thought in the Eighteenth Century*, vol. 1,
pp. 86–89.
[7] NOACK, *Die Freidenker in der Religion*, vol. 2, is good on French
deism.

was more scant in the writings of the later than of the
earlier English deists. French deism, developing late and
having much connection with the writings of later English
deists, was also scant in positive content. The negative element in the writings of the French deists was also essentially the same as the negative element in English deism except
that the French was perhaps somewhat more radical and
bitter in spirit and expression, especially against clergy and
ritual.[8] The arguments that were used against miracles
were much the same in both countries.[9] So too were the
arguments used against belief in revelation.[10] Both English
and French deists attacked the doctrines of the Atonement,
the Trinity and Original Sin.[11] In both countries such Bible
characters as Abraham, Samuel and David were subjected
to ridicule.[12] The weapon of ridicule was extensively used
by a number of English deists such as Shaftesbury and
Bolingbroke but not with as much skill as shown by Voltaire. Of the use of this means of attack by Voltaire,
Macauley is quoted as saying: "Of all the intellectual
weapons that have ever been wielded by man, the most
terrible was the mockery of Voltaire."[13] Mademoiselle
Huber represented the Gospel as a republication of the
religion of nature just as Tindal had done in England. As
Blount and other English deists had revived the ancient
mode of attacking Christianity by seeking to parallel its
miracles and stories from heathen sources, especially the
life of Apollonius Tyaneus,[14] the French also used this
method.

As the purpose of the present section of this work is not
an exhaustive study of French deism but rather to show the
English influence upon it, only the work of the two most
outstanding French deists, Rousseau and Voltaire, need be
given in fuller detail. Though these two noted writers
represent quite different types of deism, Rousseau's being
an emotional or heart deism while Voltaire's was intellectual or head deism, both showed marked English influence.

---

[8] NOACK, *Die Freidenker in der Religion*, b. 2, s. 83. Anti-ritualism
was especially prominent in Rousseau.
[9] *op. cit.*, b. 2, ss. 76, 87, 114, 174.
[10] *op. cit.*, b. 2, ss. 81, 83, 114, 188.
[11] *op. cit.*, b. 2, ss. 77, 81, 83.
[12] VOLTAIRE, F. M. A., *The Works of Voltaire* (Collectors' Edit.).
Paris, London, & New York, E. R. Du Mont, 1901. vol. 8, p. 61.
[13] VOLTAIRE, *Works*, vol. 1, Publisher's preface, p. 5.
[14] NOACK, *Die Freidenker in der Religion*, b. 2, s. 227.

1. JEAN JACQUESS ROUSSEAU.

Rousseau (1712-1778) gained great fame in the fields of the philosophy of education and the philosophy of religion as well as in the field of political philosophy. His philosophy of education is found chiefly in his *Emile*. His political philosophy, which bears marked evidence of the influence of Hobbes and Locke, is mostly to be found in his *Social Contract*. His philosophy of religion is found in Book IV, Chapter VIII, of the *Social Contract*,—a chapter that deals with "Civil Religion,"—in his *Letters from the Mountains* and especially in that part of his *Emile* which contains the confession of faith of a Savoyard vicar.

Rousseau's deism was an integral part of his whole teaching that men should return to nature. The elaborate organization and rituals and dogmas of historic Christianity were for him but a part of that artificial civilization which he thought should be given up for a return to the simplicities of nature. Natural religion was attractive to this devotee of Nature and fitted in well with his general philosophy. However, the natural religion he favored was less intellectual, less of the head and more of the heart than that championed by most deists. While presenting his own religion of nature, Rousseau took occasion to write against revelation, miracles, dogmas, ceremonies and clergy in much the same spirit and with much the same arguments that are found in the writings of English deists.[15] Like Hobbes, he regarded civil religion as a part of politics.[16] Genuine Christianity he regarded as anti-social and not suited to this world.[17] He showed familiarity with the writings of Hobbes[18] and a liking for some of Hobbes' teachings on the subject of religion.[19]

Rosseau lived a very irregular life, roving in Switzerland, where he was born, France, where most of his work was done and where his influence was greatest, Italy, where he was for a time secretary to the French ambassador at Venice, and England, to which he was attracted by the

---

[15] These teachings are most clearly stated in the confession of faith of the Savoyard vicar for which vid. SCHINZ, ALBERT, *Vie et Oeuvres de J. J. Rousseau.* Boston, New York, and Chicago, D. C. Heath & Co., 1921. pp. 274–312.

[16] ROUSSEAU, JEAN JACQUESS, *The Social Contract*, or *The Principles of Political Rights.* New York and London, G. P. Putnam's Son, 1893. 2nd Edition revised. p. 218.

[17] *op. cit.*, p. 213.

[18] *op. cit.*, pp. 5, 209–211, 218–221.

[19] *ibid.*

philosopher Hume.[20]　Since most of his deistic views had already found expression before his visit to England, that visit cannot be credited with producing the views.

Rousseau has been generally credited by historians with exercising an influence second to none in the bringing on of the French revolution with its various political and religious excesses.

2. FRANÇOIS MARIE AROUET VOLTAIRE.

Voltaire (1694-1788) was the leading literary man of Europe for a period of over fifty years.　He early gained a great reputation as a writer of dramas.　To this he soon added a great reputation as a conversationalist, famed especially for witty repartee.　It was, however, his *Philosophical Dictionary,* which constitutes the contents of volumes five to thirteen, inclusive, of his *Works,*[21] that gave him his reputation as a philosopher and scholar of encyclopedic width of information.　Voltaire's literary output was enormous.　His assembled works constitute forty-two large volumes.　The skill of Voltaire in the use of the weapon of mockery, to which reference has already been made, far excelled that of any other deistic writer of either England or France.　Perhaps it has never been equalled by any writer of any age.　Although it was aimed at many things, most of its sharpest darts were against the Bible and historic Christianity in both its Roman Catholic and Protestant forms.　In his plays as well as in the articles selected for discussion in his *Philosophical Dictionary,* the Bible and Christianity are the chief objects of his mocking attack.

Voltaire became the leader of the French deists early in life.　That he very early in life showed a bent in the direction of deism is indicated by the fact that a Jesuit teacher whom the boy Voltaire had angered predicted future leadership among the deists for his pupil.[22]　After having been twice incarcerated in the Bastile, Voltaire fled to England. He lived there for nearly three years and, during that period, assimilated thoroughly about the whole of English deism.　Upon his return to France he wrote on England with such evident partiality for English government and philosophy and with such sly thrusts at the church and the

[20] GUIZOT, M. & DEWITT, *France.*　New York & London, The Co-Operative Public. Society, 1876.　8 vols.　vol. 5, p. 237.

[21] VOLTAIRE, FRANÇOIS MARIE AROUET, *The Works of Voltaire.*　Paris, London, New York, and Chicago, E. R. Du Mont, 1901.　Collector's Edition.　42 vols.

[22] GUIZET, *France,* vol. 5, p. 184.

religion of France that he soon found it expedient to seek
refuge in Switzerland. But ere long he was back in France
writing plays that spread his fame. It was not long till he
was recognized as the outstanding leader of the enemies of
Christianity and, particularly, of the Roman Catholic
Church.[23]

The rest of his life was spent in Prussia, Switzerland and
France, but mostly in Switzerland. Becoming offended because refused admission to certain French Academies, he
went to the court of Frederick the Great at Potsdam and
became the center of that brilliant group of free-thinkers,
mostly French, that the Prussian king had gathered about
him. After a short time he quarreled with Frederick and
fled back to France and then on to Switzerland. From
Ferney, near Geneva, he sent forth an enormous literary
output most of which contained attacks upon Christianity
or the church. Among these writings were articles on religious subjects for the encyclopedia of D'Alembert and
Diderot, the poem on the earthquake that destroyed Lisbon,
the *Candide* and the *Socrates*. While at Ferney he quarreled with Rousseau. Just before his death he enjoyed a
veritable triumph in Paris. His life had been that of a rest-
less, roving, quarrelsome man of genius. During his long
career he attained great fame and an almost unmatched
influence.[24]

Critics disagree in their estimate of Voltaire. All recognize his vast energy, his great productivity, his literary
genius, his matchless cleverness of wit and his rendering of
a real service to society in exposing and opposing and help-
ing to destroy certain evils and abuses that had crept into
the State and Church and social life of his day. All condemn
his vanity, his quarrelsomeness, his inconsistency, his
irregular social life and his notable lack of the martyr
spirit. Christians and especially Roman Catholic Christians
see in him an arch enemy of the faith and a most dangerous
man. Freethinkers, especially those of deistic viewpoint,
regard him as their great captain and champion. A close
examination of the works of Voltaire discloses that he was
neither a thorough scholar nor an original thinker. Diderot
and Bayle surpassed him in scholarship. His ideas and
views were those prevalent about him in deistic circles.
Nearly all of them are found in the works of English deists

[23] GUIZOT, *France*, vol. 5, p. 192.
[24] *op. cit.*, vol. 5, pp. 194–213.

who wrote before Voltaire. His wit and style were his own.
Most of the other abler French writers of his day went on
into skepticism or atheism. Rosseau remained a deist but
was an eccentric one with a deism that emphasized the
heart rather than the head, the emotions rather than the
reason. Characteristic deism was rationalistic as was Voltaire. Voltaire justly is esteemed the ablest, most representative and most influential of French deists.[25]

There need be no reasonable doubt that Voltaire was a
deist. So much did he enjoy attacking things and using his
clever wit and so little did he care for consistency that at a
few points his words suggest that he might have been an
atheist. But repeatedly he declared his belief in God and
in the worship of God according to reason.[26] He openly
quarreled with skeptics and atheists.[27] Here and there
throughout his works it appears that he believed in worship-
ping God but doing so without the use of forms and ceremonies.[28] Voltaire seldom wrote on any subject without
touching upon some problem of religion and seldom without
shooting an arrow of mockery at some position in religion
to which he was unfriendly. His *Natural Religion, L'Infame* and *Candide* were directly on religious themes. The
Candide was an attack on the doctrine, set forth by Leibnitz
and others, that this is the best possible world. It involved
an attack also on the doctrine of providence. In the *Zaïre*
Mohammedans are represented as superior to Christians
while in the *Mahomet* the founder of Mohammedanism is
represented as a cruel fraud. It was, however, in his *Philosophical Dictionary* that he gave fullest expression to his
views on religion and that he used to the utmost his art of
mockery. In such articles as those on *Genesis*[29] and
Gospels,[30] Voltaire found opportunity to deny the authen-
ticity of the Pentateuch and the Gospels and to attack and
ridicule the contents of these sections of the Scriptures. He
found peculiar delight in mocking such characters as Abra-

---

[25] GUIZOT, *France*, vol. 5, p. 213. cf. DURANT, *The Story of Philosophy*, pp. 219–221.

[26] VOLTAIRE, *Works*, vol. 9, Article on *God-Gods*, in *Phil. Dict.*, pp.
212–252.

[27] *op. cit.*, vol. 9, p. 231 ff.

[28] In his poem on *Natural Religion*, the burning of which led to his
publishing *L'Infame*, Voltaire comes nearest to giving his religion of
nature. Vid. *Works*, vol. 1, p. 27.

[29] VOLTAIRE, *Works*, vol. 9, p. 159 ff.

[30] *op. cit.*, vol. 9, p. 268 ff.

ham, Lot, David, and Mary Magdalene.[31] Most English
deists had expressed respect for Jesus as a man, but, like
Woolston, Voltaire did not exempt even Jesus from his
mockery.[32] Like other deists he rejected the doctrine of
the Trinity[33] and championed Toleration.[34] Indeed one
finds in Voltaire just the characteristic views of the more
radical English deists.

The marked similarity of theme and spirit and method
between French deism, especially as it appeared in Voltaire, and the English deists of an earlier date does in itself
strongly suggest the fact and greatness of English influence
upon the French thought. The fact that most of the French
writers showed familiarity with the works of the English
deists and with those English writers like Locke who had
much in common with deism, indicates a main channel by
which this influence entered France. Thus Rousseau showed
great familiarity with the works of Hobbes as Voltaire
showed acquaintance with the works of most English deists
and fondness for Bolingbroke and Locke. The views and
writings of Locke and of the weightier writers among the
English deists were readily accessible to Voltaire and his
compatriots for some of them circulated in France in Latin
editions, some in French editions and some in English
editions. Cherbury's *De Veritate* was first published in
Paris in 1624 and appeared in a French edition with the
title *De La Verité* by 1639. Hobbes' *De Cive* was translated
into French by 1649 and his other works soon followed.
Locke's great *Essay* was translated into French and published by Coste in 1700. His *Reasonableness of Christianity*
appeared in the same language ten years later. Works of
Blount, Toland, Collins, Woolston, Chubb and Bolingbroke
were soon translated into French and widely circulated in
France.[35] Toland is said to have had a large influence
among the French.[36] The same is even more true of
Shaftesbury much of whose works were put into French by
Diderot.[37] Voltaire regarded Shaftesbury as one of the
greatest of English philosophers.[38] The works of the more

---

31) VOLTAIRE, *Works*, vol. 11, p. 205 ff.
32) *loc. cit.* cf. p. 249 ff.
33) *op. cit.*, vol. 5, p. 253.
34) *op. cit.*, vol. 14, p. 100 ff.
35) LECHLER, *Geschichte d. Englishen Deismus*, s. 446.
36) UEBERWEG, *Geschichte d. Philosophie*, b. 3, s. 123.
37) *op. cit.*, s. 126. cf. s. 179.
38) LECHLER, *Geschichte*, etc., s. 263.

skeptical Hume were also soon translated into French[39] and no doubt helped to hasten the tendency of French deism to give place to skepticism. The views of these English deists were also extensively aired and widely circulated in France in such works as the *Encyclopedia* of Diderot and D'Alembert and the *Dictionary* of Bayle and the writings of Le Clerc.[40] Answers to deists by more conservative writers of England, France and Germany also found a wide circulation in France and spread acquaintance with deistic views. Thus Leibnitz, writing in French, answered Locke and Toland. No doubt this familiarity with the writings of English deists was the main way in which English thought influenced the development of French deism.

Yet the influence of the meeting of French and English travellers must be given large recognition. Not only did Rousseau and Voltaire and other French thinkers visit England and meet deists there from whom at least Voltaire absorbed deism like a sponge, but also many English deists and others who had some ideas in common with the deists visited and resided for considerable periods in France associating with the free-thinking element there. Herbert of Cherbury, Hobbes, Shaftesbury, Collins and Bolingbroke were among these deistic visitors to France.[41]

A factor that made the influence of the English deists upon the French greater than it would otherwise have been was the fact that, at the period of these contacts, there was a wave of admiration for almost anything English sweeping over France. Montesquieu had done much to promote pro-English sentiment. The French people, dissatisfied with their own political situation and with their lack of freedom of thought and expression, admired the relatively great civil and religious liberty to which the English had attained.[42] This made them receptive to English ideas, including deistic ideas. Voltaire, upon his return from England, could not refrain from praising things English to the extent of offending rulers of both Church and State in France.[43]

---

[39] *op. cit.,* s. 446.

[40] UEBERWEG, *Geschichte d. Philosophie,* b. 3, s. 108.

[41] Herbert of Cherbury wrote in *De Veritate* in France, and Hobbes also wrote his *De Cive* there. Shaftesbury had intercourse with French liberals in both France and Holland. Bolingbroke chummed with Voltaire both in England and France.

[42] GUIZOT, *France,* vol. 5, p. 179.

[43] *op. cit.,* vol. 5, p. 191.

B. THE INFLUENCE OF ENGLISH DEISM UPON EIGHT-
EENTH CENTURY GERMAN DEISM

Deism arose comparatively late in Germany.[44] When Herbert of Cherbury published his *De Veritate* in 1624, Germany was in the throes of the Thirty Year War which continued for 24 years after that date. Conditions in Germany were not then suited to the rise of such a movement as deism although the evils arising from the religious divisions were preparing the intellectual soil for seed of deism in its critical anti-dogma aspects. Characteristic views and attitudes of deism are not found championed in Germany until early in the eighteenth century. Among the earliest German writers who championed deistic ideas were Johann Conrad Dippel (b. 1673), Christian Wolff (b. 1679) whose modified Leibnitzian philosophy exercised great influence in Germany until displaced by Kantianism, and Johann Christian Edelman (b. 1698). Dippel denied revelation and opposed the use of external forms of worship. Wolff was not a full-fledged deist but, like Locke in England, he manifested an inclination in the direction of deism which gave much encouragement to deists. He was strongly biased against supernaturalism. He insisted on judging anything that claimed to be supernatural revelation by natural revelation. While not absolutely denying miracles, he allowed but few and ascribed them a place of little importance. Natural theology was emphasized.[45] Edelman was a deist. Quite in the manner and spirit of the English deists he insisted that there are no atheists and that miracles are unbelievable. In the manner and spirit of the English deists, he also attacked miracles, especially those of the virgin birth and the resurrection of Christ, and the doctrines of the deity of Christ and of original sin. The doctrine of original sin he regarded as a papal lie. He claimed the Bible had been corrupted by priests and filled with such fables as the story of creation and the story of the fall of man. Somewhat more in the spirit of Rousseau than of the English deists, he made feelings the test of truth. The appearance of Edelman's book, *Moses mit aufgedecktem Angesicht,* in the year 1740 marked the beginning of the flourishing period of German deism. Thus German deism was just beginning to

---

[44] By "Germany" is here meant the lands of central Europe occupied by German speaking people. Germany as a nation had not yet come into being at the time dealt with in this work.

[45] NOACK, *Die Freidenker in der Religion,* b. 3, ss. 30–44.

flourish when deism in England was starting upon its very
rapid decline.

But sometime before writings of German deists began to
appear, the writings of outside deists had been circulating
extensively in Germany. Spinoza is usually classed as a
pantheist rather than a deist. Yet it is almost correct to say,
as Leslie Stephen does, that Spinoza's *Tractatus Theologico-
Politicus* contains "The whole essence of the deist position."[46]   This work was published in Hamburg, Germany,
in the year 1670. It aroused a storm of disputation. This
Jewish Dutch philosopher had been a diligent student of
the English philosopher Hobbes and had adopted a number
of Hobbes' ideas in a somewhat modified form. Thus
Spinoza became the medium for the transfer of English
deistic ideas into Germany.[47]

A number of the works of Herbert of Cherbury and of
Hobbes as well as of some of the later deists were published
in Latin which was the common language of educated
Europe. These of course circulated among the educated
classes in Germany. Several of the early English deistic
works also soon appeared in French editions and French
was in general use in German court circles and among such
men as Leibnitz. Hobbes' works in both Latin and English
were available in Germany at the time of the rise of German
deism.[48]   Toland lived for a time in Hanover and Berlin and
his *Letters to Serena* was one of his works directed directly
to the queen of Prussia.[49]   Anthony Collins' works were
widely known and influential in Germany. His important
work, *A Discourse of Free-Thinking*, which was first published in English in London in 1713, soon appeared in a
French translation under the title *"Discours sur la Liberte
de Penser.* As early as 1714-'15 this work was the subject of
academic debates and controversial writings at both
Tübingen and Helmstädt.[50]   It was regarded as a work that
any select theological library should contain. With it went
also Bentley's and Whiston's criticisms of it. In this connection it is interesting to note that Tübingen soon became

[46] STEPHEN, *Hist. of Eng. Thought in the Eighteenth Century*, vol. 1,
p. 33.
    [47] SPINOZA, BENEDICT DE, *The Chief Works of Benedict de Spinoza*,
t. from the Latin with an Introd. by R. H. M. Lewes.   vol. 1.   *Introduction, Tractatus Theologico-Politicus, Tractatus Politicus.*   London, G.
Bell and Son, 1908.   p. xxii.
    [48] WEBER, ALFRED, *History of Philosophy*.   New York, Chas. Scrib-
ner's Sons, 1905.   p. 301.
    [49] UEBERWEG, *Geschichte d. Philosophie*, b. 3, s. 110.
    [50] LECHLER, *Geschichte d. Eng. Deismus*, s. 230.

famous for its liberal theology and Bible criticism giving its
name to the well-known school of thought known as the
"Tübingen School." Also when Lechler set about the task
of publishing (1841) his German history of English deism,
he found a special abundance of the then rather rare works
of the English deists in the University library at Tübingen.[51]
Christian Pfaff made an argument against Collins as his
inaugural address at Tübingen in 1717.[52] Tindal's famous
book that has been called "The Bible of English deism,"
*Christianity as Old as the Creation: or The Gospel a Repub-
lication of the Religion of Nature* was translated into German and published at Frankfurt and Leipsic in 1741.[53] The
first German translation of Shaftesbury's *Characteristics*
appeared in 1768 and frequent editions appeared thereafter.[54] Shaftesbury has enjoyed a greater reputation in
Germany than in his own country. A two volume French
translation of Bolingbroke's works came to Berlin in 1752
and a German translation of them was made six years
later.[55] The works of David Hume who had much in common with the deists although himself a skeptic began to
appear in German translations in 1755.[56] His influence
upon Kant constitutes a factor of major importance in the
history of philosophy. The above list suffices to make evident that German readers of the period when deism arose
in Germany had abundant opportunity to know the works
and views of English deists.

There were other opportunities for German readers to
learn the views of English deists. Many of the replies made
to the deists found their way into the hands of German
readers either in the original English or, as more frequently
happened, in German translations. Among these were the
works of Leland, Bentley, Whiston, Sherlock, Lyttleton,
Conybeare, Foster and Clarke.[57] These works would naturally get into the hands of many German readers whom
prejudice might keep from reading the works of the English
deists themselves. Nevertheless they spread acquaintance
with English deistic ideas.

[15] LECHLER, *Geschichte*, s. iii f.
[52] *op. cit.*, s. 447.
[53] LECHLER, *Geschichte des Englischen Deismus*, ss. 327, 360.
[54] UEBERWEG, *Geschichte d. Philosophie*, b. 3, s. 126.
[55] LECHLER, *Geschichte*, etc., s. 399.
[56] UEBERWEG, *Geschichte*, etc., b. 3, s. 183.
[57] vid. LECHLER, *Geschichte*, etc., ss. 4, 230, 312, 315 ff., 327, 358 ff.
vid. also NOACK, *Die Freidenker in der Religion*, b. 3, s. 2 and also UEBER-
WEG, *Geschichte*, etc., b. 3, s. 123.

Another method by which knowledge of English deism was spread in Germany was by German writings about, for and against the English deists. Histories, reviews and criticisms of their works were numerous.[58] As early as 1680, Christian Kortholt published his *De Tribus Impostoribus* which was chiefly a criticism of Herbert of Cherbury and of Hobbes. Leibnitz took notice in 1701 of Toland's *Christianity Not Mysterious*.[59] The historian Mosheim gave his countrymen much information on the life, works and views of Toland in a book bearing the title *Vindiciae antiquae Christianorum disciplinae,* a second edition of which appeared in Hamburg as early as 1722.[60] Jöcker wrote at Leipsic in 1734 against Woolston and Tindal.[61] Six years later Lemker wrote against Woolston.[62] As early as 1717 Buddeus wrote of Collins, Toland, Hobbes and Locke.[63] Between 1748 and 1751, Baumgarten published an eight-volume work with the title *Nachrichten von einer Hallischen Bibliothek* which contained much information from and concerning English deistic books.[64] Many excerpts from the works of English deists were also incorporated in Trinius' *Freidenkerlexicon,* published in 1759.[65] More important than any of the works named was Thorschmidt's four-volume compendium of information concerning the whole English deistic movement that bore the title *Engellandischen Freydenker-Bibliothek.* This full treatment of the English deists and their adversaries was published in Halle in 1765-7. Though not exhaustive, this dry list of German works that were available to make the German people acquainted with English deism before deism made much headway in Germany itself is sufficiently long to show that there was abundant opportunity for knowing the English movement.

Since English deism was older than the fully developed French deism, the English deistic influence reached Germany before the French arrived there. German deism started on an English basis, modified by the strong influence of the Dutch philosopher Spinoza who had himself been much under the influence of the Englishman Hobbes. The

58) NOACK, *Die Freidenker in der Religion,* b. 3, s. 1.
59) LECHLER, *Geschichte,* s. 447.
60) UEBERWEG, *Geschichte,* b. 3, s. 110.
61) LECHLER, *loc. cit.*
62) *loc. cit.*
63) BUDDEUS, JOAN F., *Theses Theologicæ De Atheismo Et Superstitione.* Jenæ, apud Joan F. Brelckium, 1717.
64) LECHLER, s. 6.
65) *loc. cit.*

first German interest in deism was manifested at the universities, especially at Tübingen and Halle. From first to last the English influence seems to have been stronger than the French in the German University centers while the French influence was probably greater and more direct in the Court circles where French language and wit were in style. Especially did Frederick the Great advance the French influence by gathering in his court a group of French free-thinkers that included Voltaire. Noack suggests that the serious-minded German people, especially of the University centers, took more kindly to the serious argumentation of English deists than to the witty jibes of the French.[66] Probably there is a grain of truth in the observation. But it should not be over-stressed. Probably Noack was a bit more pro-British than pro-French. Many of the English deists also had made extensive use of weapons of ridicule and mockery, Shaftesbury and Bolingbroke being notorious for doing just this.

The French travellers and visitors at the German Courts were indeed but another channel by which English deistic ideas and influences penetrated Germany. For it is to be remembered that Voltaire and his compatriots did not add much in content or idea to the deism derived by the French from England. At the time under consideration there was more travel between France and Germany than between England and Germany though it was not long until the connection between the English and Hanoverian courts increased the intercourse between the latter nations.

The further study of the influence of English upon German deism can best be made by a brief examination of the views and work of a few of the more outstanding German deists. Note has already been taken[67] of the presence of deistic ideas in the works of Dippel, Wolff and Edelman. A number of writers followed these whose viewpoints and arguments as well as quotations showed close connection with English deistic works.

1. MOSES MENDELSOHN.

Mendelsohn (1727-1786) was a Jewish writer who belonged to the Wolffian school. He was neither a deep nor an original thinker. However, he had literary ability and considerable influence. His deistic views are most fully ex-

[66] NOACK, *Die Freidenker in der Religion*, b. 3, s. 1.
[67] above, p. 189.

pressed in three works[68] bearing the titles, *"Phädon oder über die Unsterblichkeit der Seele," "Jerusalem oder über religiöse Macht und Judenthum,"* and *"Morgenstunden oder über das Dasein Gottes."* In these he argued for the existence of God and the immortality of the soul and natural religion and against atheism, revealed religion and Christianity. His manner of argument was very like that of the English deists from whom he differed chiefly in the fact that he was inclined to be pro-Jewish while they were generally anti-Jewish and more favorable to the New than to the Old Testament. Today (1933), with Nazi influence dominant in Germany, one would expect to find German writers more hostile to the Jews and things Jewish than English writers would be. But this was not so at the time of the deistic movement. English deists were much more hostile to the Old Testament and to things Jewish than were German deists. German deism was influenced in the direction of a more friendly attitude toward the Jew than characterized English deism by the fact that Spinoza and Mendelsohn who were themselves Jews exercised a strong influence upon German deism and by the additional fact that Lessing, greatest of German deists, was a great admirer of both Spinoza and Mendelsohn and that Goethe, greatest of all German writers, was profoundly under the influence of Spinoza.

Contemporary with Mendelsohn, Johann Bernhard Basedow (b. 1723), Gotthilf Samuel Steinbart (1738-1809), Jakob Mauvillon and Carl Freidrich Bahrdt (1741-1792) presented the deistic viewpoint in their writings. Basedow, without resorting to mockery or ridicule, contrasted natural with revealed religion to the discredit of the latter.[69] Steinbart of Halle University also was neither radical nor coarse in presenting his mildly rationalistic and deistic views. Nevertheless in his book, *System der reinen Philosophie oder Glückseligkeitslehre des Christentums für die Bedürfnisse seiner aufgeklärten Landsleute und Andere, die nach Weisheit fragen, eingerichtet* (1778), he argued for a getting away from the corrupted creedal statements of the church and back to a simpler Christianity more like natural religion. An anonymous work appeared in Berlin in 1787

---

68) For a complete list of Mendelsohn's writings, vid. UEBERWEG, *Geschichte der Philosophie,* b. 3, s. 158. For a fair estimate of Mendelsohn's importance among the deists, vid. NOACK, *Die Freidenker in der Religion,* b. 3, s. 137 ff.

69) NOACK, *Die Freidenker in der Religion,* b. 3, ss. 165–179.

bearing the title *Das Einzig wahre System der christliche Religion*. It was ascribed to Mauvillon. This was a much more radical deistic book and was quite in the spirit of such English deists as Tindal, Collins and Shaftesbury. It was bitterly anticlerical. It did not deny the possibility but the necessity for revelation. It insisted that were there a revelation it must be clear and general as the Bible is said not to be. It insisted that the Bible, having been handed down by a long tradition and in the hands of priests, no one can know what the original was. Bible miracles and prophecies are repudiated as not a sufficient ground for accepting the Bible as a true revelation. All religions are said to appeal to miracles. The worth of a miracle as evidence is said to depend on the genuineness of the document in which it is recorded and on the nature of the grounds on which the writer believed in it. This, it is argued, makes Bible miracles of little or no value as evidence. He would accept as of value only the testimony of eye-witnesses to the miracles and then points out that Mark, Luke and Paul were not eye-witnesses of Gospel miracles. In much the same way as Collins had done, he ruled out the evidential value of Bible prophecies. They must be clear and not subject to different interpretations to have value. Christian or Bible morals were criticised as slavish and duplex and lacking a proper emphasis on courage and friendship. This last charge was borrowed from Shaftesbury. It was also charged with intolerance. In fact this author said it would be a misfortune for the world were Christianity to become general. It is a priest-corrupted religion. Like the more radical deists of England and France this author was skeptical of a future life. Most of the other German deists mentioned above had argued for belief in immortality. Bahrdt, who at various times studied or taught at Leipsic, Halle and Giessen, gave his life to promoting deistic views. He declared against revelation and argued Christianity unworthy of divine origin. Such doctrines as Original Sin, Justification and the Atonement were special objects of his hostility. He gave Jesus high rank as a man but denied his deity. The idea of prayer being effective was repudiated by Bahrdt.

But though these men helped to spread deism in Germany, none of them compared in importance with Reimarus and Lessing whose works now demand attention.

2. HERMAN SAMUEL REIMARUS.

Reimarus (1694-1768) did much toward introducing and spreading English deistic ideas in Germany. Reimarus studied in Jena and Wittenberg and then taught Hebrew and Mathematics in the city of Hamburg. He was the author of two of the monumental works of German deism. The first of these which made him famous was published in 1774 and bore the title *"Abhandlungen über die vornehmsten Wahrheiten der naturlichen Religion."* The second was published between 1774 and 1777 by Lessing under the title *"Wolfenbüttelsche Fragmente eines Ungenannten."* These *Wolfenbüttel Fragments* became very famous in the history of Bible criticism. Reimarus championed Tindal's idea that creation is the only miracle to be admitted and that to say there were later miracles or a special revelation after creation would be to assert imperfection in the creation and lack of power or wisdom in the Creator. This was the fundamental philosophical conception characteristic of deism which some deists almost lost sight of in their many-sided critical attack upon historical Christianity and its clerical leaders.

Reimarus championed Reason and criticised and rejected special revelation quite in the manner and spirit of the English deists. Quite in the spirit of the English deists, he drew a distinction between the original teaching of Christ and the apostles, between the teaching of the apostles and of the Church Fathers and between each of these and the Bible and Church of the present. Repeating the arguments of Blount and Tindal he maintained that there could be no supernatural revelation to all mankind and yet that if all men are to be judged by a special revelation fairness required that all have it. A special revelation could not be trusted to be handed down by sinful and selfish men. Suspicion of all priests runs through his works. He thought early baptized and instructed men are lost to reasonable religion. Furthermore, like most of the English deists, he attacked various parts and characters of the Bible as unworthy of a revelation from God. Lot, Jacob, Abraham, Moses and Joseph are severely censured by him. He concludes that if an untrained and unprejudiced man were to read either the Koran or the Bible he would refuse to accept either as a revelation from God.

Reimarus argued for belief in God, for a religion of reason or nature known to all men and moral rather than ceremonial in character and for the immortality of the soul.

3. Gotthold Ephraim Lessing.

Lessing (1729-1781), a man of high rank in German liter-ature, was easily the ablest and most influential of all Ger-man deists. In him German deism reached its highest point. While librarian at Wolfenbüttel he rendered his first great service to the cause of deism by publishing Reimarus' fragmentary works. Then Lessing himself championed deism in a controversial debate with a pastor named Göze. While at Wolfenbüttel, Lessing also wrote his own two most important deistic works, *Die Erziehung des Menschenge-schlechts* and *Nathan der Weise*. Both works present rea-son as in rebellion against revelation, the characteristic atti-tude of deism.

The story of *Nathan der Weise* (*Nathan the Sage*) is built upon the story of the *Three Rings* told by Boccaccio in his *Decameron*,[70]—a story which may be older than Boccaccio. Boccaccio had used the story to suggest that Judaism, Mo-hammedanism and Christianity are all equally from God, or perhaps rather to suggest that none of the three is from God although all profess to be. Lessing used it for a similar purpose. The book, *Nathan der Weise*, arose out of bitter controversy.[71] Lessing aimed to show that Christianity produces no better men than other religions and therefore has no right to claim that it is peculiarly or exclusively from God. His making a Jew to be the noblest character in the story may have been in compliment to his friend Mendel-sohn or to Spinoza whom he greatly admired. The story stresses the deistic idea that true religion consists essential-ly in morality. It also teaches religious toleration. Many readers who do not accept the deism of the book neverthe-less admire it for its well-told story, its fine language and its excellent setting forth of the teachings of faith, love, charity, and toleration.

Lessing taught that Christianity existed before the Bible and independent of it. He named what he regarded as true or natural religion, or the religion of reason, "Christianity." In doing this he was but giving to the German people what Tindal had given to the English folk in his *Christianity as Old as the Creation,* a work which had been translated into German in 1741.

The general impression left by Lessing upon his reader is that he did not at all believe in revelation. His attacks up-

---

70) above, p. 48.
71) Lessing, Gottfried Ephraim, *Nathan der Weise*. Boston, D. C. Heath and Co., 1905, p. iii.

on miracles, prophecies, Bible characters and upon some
Bible teachings certainly indicate a low opinion of the Bible
and its claim to revelation. For him all so-called revealed
religions are alike true and alike false. They are alike true
insofar as they agree with natural religion or what is general
and true and they are alike false insofar as they disagree
with what is general and true. The best of the positive religions in his estimation is the one that does least to limit
natural religion and that adds least of convention to it. Yet
at times Lessing seems to make some concession to revelation for he says that revelation gives nothing reason would
not discover but gives it earlier.

Both Reimarus and Lessing were even more philosophical
in their presentation of deism than the English deists. They
resorted much less to witticisms and mocking ridicule than
did the French and much less than even some of the English
deists. Some of the free-thinkers Lessing said were but
"Schalen Kopfen." He charged that some of them would be
more tyrannical than the orthodox had they the power to be
so. Herder called Lessing "The rich-thinker among the
free-thinkers" and Noack called him the patriarch of the
German free-spirit.[72] His influence in Germany was very
great.

Just as it was necessary in the consideration of English
deism to give some study to such writers as Locke and
Hume who were not properly deists because of their influence upon English deism, so in the study of German deism
it is necessary to give some attention to Immanuel Kant,
though he also is scarcely to be ranked as a deist.

4. IMMANUEL KANT.

Immanuel Kant (1724-1804), seer of Königsberg and most
famous of modern philosophers, was in his earlier life an
adherent of the Wolffian rationalistic school of thought and
as such inclined toward deistic ideas. In his *Die Religion
innerhalb der Grenzen der bloszen Vernunft,* he taught that
practical reason is ground enough for morality. He was
always interested in questions of religion and ethics. He
was fond of reading English writers on ethics which makes
it probable that he read Shaftesbury. Certain it is that he
read the works of Locke and Hume. A magazine article
which he wrote was rejected by the Prussian censors and he
was forbidden by a royal order from writing as he had

---

[72] NOACK, *Die Freidenker in der Religion,* b. 3, s. 215.

done.[73]   This shows that he was not regarded by the
authorities as orthodox though it does not prove him a full-
fledged deist. Kant, having little taste for the mud-slinging
method of controversy used by both clergy and deists, did
not enter into the deistic controversy on either side. Nor
did he take up problems of Bible criticism. His taste caused
him to take up the more fundamental philosophical problems that lay at the foundation of the deistic controversy
but of which most deists seemed scarcely aware. He did
wrestle with such problems as the evidence for the existence of God and the ground for ethical conduct. But if it
was not natural for Kant to have sympathy with the bitter
controversial attitude of many deists, it was natural for him
to think very highly of the reasoning function and so to incline in the direction of theological rationalism.

Kant himself testifies that it was Hume that awakened him
from his "Dogmatic slumber." Before that awakening Kant
had assumed with the rationalists that the human mind is
capable of and does know substances and realities. Hume's
reasoning on causality led Kant to forsake his old position
and to develop that system of thought known as "Kantianism." In it there is a denial that the mind does or can know
substances or realities as they are in themselves. The mind
itself provides the time and space forms and the categories
of thought. Things are only known and knowable as the
mind has put these forms and categories upon them. The
thing-in-itself ("Ding-an-sich") is and must ever remain
unknowable. Since God and the human soul are things-in-
themselves or noumena they must forever remain unknowable to the human mind. Thus Kant's epistemological theory led him to a type of intellectual agnosticism. Despair-
ing of reaching a knowledge of God through perception, he
turned hopefully to Logic but there found himself confront-
ed with his fourth antinomy[74] which blocked that way to
the knowledge of God.

Deism had been very confident of the complete power of
the human mind to know God. Herbert of Cherbury had
considered such knowledge as innate. Deists after Locke
had considered knowledge of God not as innate but as
readily attainable by the Reason. By such arguments as
the ontological, cosmological and teleological deists had

73) Kant, Immanuel, *Critique of Practical Reason*. London, N. Y.,
etc., Longmans, Green & Co., Ltd. Sixth Edit., 1927, p. xi.
74) Kant, Immanuel, *Critique of Pure Reason*. New York, The Macmillan Co., 1925, pp. 370–371.

been sure men could know God. But from the standpoint of Kant's theory of knowledge, these arguments lost their validity.[75]) Thus deism found its foundations being shaken and perhaps destroyed by Kant. With this point in mind some have called Kant "The executioner of deism." Of course Kant's work undermined the position of the orthodox opponents of deism as well as the position of the deists. However the orthodox had not built so exclusively on the assumption of the sufficiency of the human Reason as had the deists. However, as was said in speaking of Hume's relation to English deism, it is doubtful if any man "executed" deism. The most that can be claimed is that he gave it a wound that should logically have caused its demise. Probably at the time it was hardly conscious of its wound. As in England, other factors than the philosophical reasonings of Hume, so in Germany, other factors, which do not concern this study, than the epistemological reasonings of Kant had to do with the decline of deism. Kant helped on that decline and was led to do so by the influence of the British philosopher Hume upon his own thinking. Since Kant, in his *Critique of the Practical Reason,* restores to men a practical knowledge of God, it could only be of the old, proud, rationalistic, self-confident deism that he could be called in any sense the "executioner."

C. THE INFLUENCE OF ENGLISH DEISM UPON EIGHT-EENTH CENTURY AMERICAN DEISM

The early colonists in what later became the United States were not deists. Deism had scarcely begun in England when the first English colonists settled in Virginia in 1607 or in New England in 1620. It will be remembered that Herbert's *De Veritate* did not appear until 1624. The early settlers in Virginia were men out for adventure or worldly gain and were not notably religious. This comparatively worldly class no doubt furnished better soil for the later seed of deism than did the more sternly and strictly religious type of settler farther to the north. The Pilgrim Puritans who first settled New England were far from deists. They were earnest Bible-loving Calvinistic Christians whose laws had an Hebraic Old Testament flavor and whose clergy were held in highest esteem. The whole spirit of the early New England colony was the antithesis of deism. Roger Williams' colony in Rhode Island had nothing in common with

---

[75]) KANT, *Critique of Pure Reason,* pp. 477–516.

deism except perhaps the championing of toleration. The Roman Catholic colonists in Maryland would naturally be unfavorable to deism for deism was anti-Romanist in both England and France. The earnest, quiet, reverent, mystic quakers of Pennsylvania who constituted the most important other early English colony in the New World were radically different in attitude and spirit from the deists. However the quaker doctrine of "Illumination," which put the "Inner Light" above the authority of the Bible, may have to some degree prepared the way for the deistic putting of Reason above Revelation. Thomas Paine came of quaker parentage. But at the beginning, deism had no place in Pennsylvania. The pietistic German immigrants, the Calvinistic French huguenots and the rugged Calvinistic Bible-loving Scotch and Scotch-Irish immigrants who soon came to America in considerable numbers were not deists nor were they likely soil for the seeds of deism.

However the type of colonists that came to America a century later were quite different. The religious motive for migrating had largely disappeared. Most colonists now came to better themselves in a worldly way. Some came for adventure. Some of them were earnest religious people. Others were worldly and deistic. The period when deism was flourishing in England (1695-1741) was a period of heavy emigration to America and undoubtedly many who were more or less tinctured with deism came among them. No records were then kept of the faith of immigrants but the probability is that with deism rampant in England many deists came to America. It is known that somewhat later such a materialistic philosopher, who had much in common with the deists, as Priestly, and the best known of all American deists, Thomas Paine, did come over from England bringing their views with them. Undoubtedly immigration from the mother country was one of the main ways in which English deism influenced the growth and development of deism in America.

During most of the colonial period the American colonists were largely dependent upon England for reading matter and, as the English press was soon publishing so much material on the subject of deism, it was natural that much of this kind of literature should reach and be read in America. As wealth increased and the harsh pressure of the raw pioneer life decreased, men of wealth and culture in America began building up considerable libraries. English works naturally predominated in these although there were also

Latin and French works in some of the private libraries of
men of learning and culture. John Adams informs us that
the literature of Great Britain was more thoroughly natural-
ized in New England than was her government.[76] He also
gives us the direct statement that "The writings of the free
thinkers had made their way across the Atlantic."[77] He
states that he himself had read Bolingbroke's works and
Morgan's *Moral Philosopher* and Leland's famous *View of
the Principal Deistical Writers* and he shows acquaintance
with the works of Hume and Priestly.[78] Benjamin Franklin
informs us that while a boy he had read the works of Collins and Shaftesbury as well as the answers made to deists
in *Boyle Lectures.*[79]   Thomas Jefferson is known to have
been fond of the writings of Conyers Middleton and Priestly
as well as of the French deists Rousseau and Voltaire.[80] He
also recommended such works to the reading lists of his
young friends Monroe and Madison.[81]   Political animosity
probably made Jefferson more partial to the French than to
the English thinkers but even when influenced by the French
deists he was but getting second-hand English deism.   If
such men as Franklin, Jefferson and Adams were reading
English deistic books, no doubt many other Americans of
that day of whose lives we have less information were doing
the same.

Another mode by which English and the similar French
deism was transferred to America was by travellers other
than immigrants. This was, however, as compared with the
literature from England and France, a comparatively unim-
portant channel of ideas.   Little or nothing is known of
transient English or French travellers in the American
colonies seeking to spread deistic ideas in the New World.
The number of Americans who travelled abroad was comparatively small.   Those who are known to have done so
were chiefly men prominent in public life such as Franklin,
Adams and Jefferson.   These did travel in England and

---

[76] ADAMS, JOHN, *The Life and Works of John Adams,* compiled by
his Grandson, Charles P. Adams.   Boston, 1856.   10 Vols., vol. 1, p. 40.
[77] *op. cit.,* vol. 1, pp. 41–43.
[78] *op. cit.,* vol. 1, pp. 41, 43, 44.   Vid. also WILSTACH, PAUL (Editor),
The Correspondence of John Adams and Thomas Jefferson, 1812–1826.
Bobbs-Merrill, 1925, p. 69.
[79] FRANKLIN, BENJAMIN, *Autobiography.*   Boston, Ginn & Co., 1891.
pp. 23, 28.
[80] Vid. *The Correspondence of John Adams and Thomas Jefferson,* p.
79.   cf. also LORD, JOHN, *Beacon Lights of History* (Second Series),
vol. 7, pp. 222, 224, 272.
[81] STODDARD, W. O., *The Lives of the Presidents.*   Third Edition. p. 11.

France and had intercourse with the free-thinkers of those lands.[82]

Records of religious conditions and of thinking along the lines of the philosophy of religion during the colonial period of American history are neither full nor exact. It is quite evident that most of the colonies and colonists during the 17th century were religious in character. This was true of the Puritans of New England, of the Huguenots who settled near New York, of the English Quaker and pietistic German elements that settled the Pennsylvania area, and of the Roman Catholic colonists of Maryland. It was perhaps somewhat less true of the Dutch colonists of New York, the English colonists of Virginia, the Swedes of the Delaware region and the English of Georgia. Yet though these latter were comparatively secular in character, they were far from being either irreligious or deistic. The immigrants of the 18th century were much less distinctly religious in type than those of the 17th century, although there were still many religious people among them and many who came to America primarily for religious reasons. The growth of toleration in England was probably the main reason for the change of the type of American immigrant. No doubt the growth of irreligion and religious liberalism of various types also had some part in producing the change. No doubt the change in type of immigrants and the importation of deism and other forms of free-thought had much to do with the widespread departure in New England from the stern rugged Calvinism that at first prevailed there and in the development there of a latitudinarian theology and of Unitarianism. The same causes also undoubtedly had much to do with the development of that deism and irreligion and prevalent immorality throughout the colonies which were complained of by such earnest religious leaders as Jonathan Edwards, George Whitefield and John Wesley. Just how much of the liberal thinking along religious lines that was prevalent in America just before, during and after the Revolutionary War was of the deistic type cannot be known because such terms as "deist," "unbeliever," "infidel" and "atheist" were used rather indiscriminately. It is known, however, that Thomas Paine, who had been popular in America during the Revolution because of political activities, was given a chilly reception[83] upon his return from France after he had published his deistic book, *The Age of Reason*. This fact does

82) LORD, *Beacon Lights of Hist.*, vol. 7, p. 237.
83) ROBERTSON, *A Short History of Freethought*, vol. 2, p. 385.

not seem to indicate that deism was so widely held or so
popular in America at the time as some historians would
have us believe.

America produced few outstanding deists. The names
usually mentioned in connection with American deism are
Ethan Allen, Benjamin Franklin, Thomas Jefferson and
Thomas Paine. The names of John Adams and George
Washington are added by some. It will at once be noticed
that all of these men, with the possible exception of Paine,
were chiefly famous for other things than their religious
views or writings. Ethan Allen, though he was undoubtedly a free-thinker, is scarcely known today except for his
heroic exploits as a soldier of the Revolutionary war. Benjamin Franklin is well-known as diplomat, statesman, scientist and as author of works in the field of homely, common-sense, practical philosophy. Yet his views in the field
of religious philosophy are not lacking in fame and require
attention in any discussion of American deism. Jefferson
is of course best known as a statesman and a writer in the
field of political philosophy. His authorship of the *Declaration of Independence* gave him a secure place among the
immortals. Though deeply interested in religious questions,
he did not seek fame as a writer in that field but rather
sought to avoid publicity in what he had to say on religion
and to keep out of religious controversy.[84] Yet Jefferson
was a deist and by his personal contacts and private correspondence used his great influence to spread deistic views.
Therefore he also requires attention in any study of American deism. Adams' fame rests upon his work as a diplomat
and a statesman and not at all upon his writings in the field
of religion. His views in religion are chiefly contained in
his private correspondence, much of it with Jefferson. His
letters show him to have been a liberal, anti-Calvinistic,
unitarian Christian but not a deist.[85] His position was
about half-way between Puritan-Calvinistic Christianity and
deism. His religious viewpoint was much like that of John
Locke. He shared to a large extent in the deistic anti-
clerical attitude, being especially hostile to Calvinistic

---

[84] HAMILTON, J. G. R., *The Best Letters of Thomas Jefferson*, p. 204.
Here, in a letter to Rev. Charles Clay dated Jan. 29, 1815, Jefferson
wrote: "Of publishing a book on religion, My dear Sir, I never had an
idea."

[85] *The Life and Works of John Adams*, vol. 10, pp. 235–236. cf. *op.
cit.*, vol. 1, p. 44. vid. also WILLSTACH, *Correspondence of John Adams
and Thomas Jefferson*, p. 21.

clergy.[86]   Yet he believed in the Bible as a revelation from God and also in the church.[87]   Washington's undying fame rests entirely upon his achievements as a soldier and statesman and not at all upon anything done in the field of religious philosophy.   Some liberals and free-thinkers have claimed that Washington was a deist.[88]   But they furnish little evidence to support their claim.   Indeed there seems to be no evidence of any worth to support this claim while there is much against it.[89]   Undoubtedly some of the earlier biographers of Washington, such as Pastor Weems, went too far in the direction of trying to prove Washington an ultra pious man of almost superhuman saintliness.   However, some of the "debunking" biographers have gone even farther in the opposite direction and have rebunked the life of Washington by dipping their pens in slimy muck which is not supplied by worthy historical records.   Although "The Battle of the Biographers" goes merrily on, the Washington that emerges from the smoke appears to have been just a normal member of the Church of England in his religious views.   He certainly left no writing that supports any position championed by the deists.

To bring out more fully the nature of American deism and its connection with the deism of England, it is now desirable to examine the lives and the teachings on religion of Franklin, Jefferson and Paine.

1. BENJAMIN FRANKLIN.

Benjamin Franklin (1706-1790), noted and influential diplomat, statesman, scientist and writer, has left a full and frank statement of his own religious experiences and views in his *Autobiography*.   His father was a strict and perhaps somewhat narrow Presbyterian, whose library consisted rather largely of polemic works in theology.   The son, being a great reader, read a number of these works but had little taste for them.   Late in life he expressed regret that he had been obliged to spend so much time on that kind of reading matter in his youth.[90]   Among the books that he read early and did appreciate were Bunyan's *Pilgrim's Progress* and Plutarch's *Lives*.   Referring to the time when he was about

---

86) *Life and Works of John Adams*, vol. 1, p. 39.   cf. *Correspondence of John Adams and Thomas Jefferson*, pp. 82–83.

87) *Life and Works of John Adams*, vol. 9, p. 636, and vol. 10, p. 235.

88) ROBERTSON, *A Short History of Freethought*, vol. 2, p. 381.

89) vid. JOHNSON, W. J., *George Washington the Christian*.   The Abdingdon Press, 1919.

90) *Autobiography*, p. 16.

sixteen years of age, Franklin says that he had become a
real doubter in many points of religious doctrine through
"reading Shaftesbury and Collins."[91] He also informs his
readers that he unsettled the faith of some of his com-
panions.[92] Elsewhere he gives the following important bit
of information concerning how he came to have deistic
ideas. "My parents had early given me religious impres-
sions, and brought me through my childhood piously in the
Dissenting way. But I was scarce fifteen, when, after doubting by turns, of several points, as I found them disputed in
the different books I read, I began to doubt of Revelation
itself. Some books against deism fell into my hands; they
were said to be the substance of sermons preached at Boyle's
Lectures. It happened that they wrought an effect on me
quite contrary to what was intended by them; for the arguments of the deists, which were quoted to be refuted, appeared to me much stronger than the refutations; in short,
I soon became a thorough deist."[93] The English source of
Franklin's deism is here very clearly indicated. The fact
that he did become a "thorough deist" in his youth is also
clearly stated. However many writers on Franklin make
the mistake of stopping the quotation at this point and of
also failing to adequately note his later teachings on religion. These show him not to have been in mature life so
thorough a deist as he was for a time in early youth. He
goes on in the same paragraph to state that the unworthy
conduct toward him of those whom he had influenced to
become deists and the unworthy conduct of other deists
whom he knew, including himself, caused him to seriously
doubt the usefulness of the deistic doctrine.[94] This practical criticism is quite Franklinesque.

Writing of a somewhat later period in his life when he
had issued a philosophical pamphlet in England (1725), he
says: "Revelation had indeed no weight with me as such;
but I entertained an opinion that, though certain actions
might not be bad because they were forbidden by it, or good
because it commanded them, yet probably those actions
might be forbidden because they were bad for us, or commanded because they were beneficial to us, in their own
natures," etc.[95] This passage shows that at that stage in his

[91] *Autobiography*, p. 23.
[92] *op. cit.*, p. 51.
[93] *op. cit.*, pp. 79–81.
[94] *loc. cit.*
[95] *loc. cit.*

early life Franklin was coming to appreciate the practical value of the Bible even though he did not ascribe to it any divine authority. This was a much less hostile attitude toward the Bible than characterized most English deists.

Writing when 66 years of age concerning his earlier life and religious views, Franklin says: "I had been religiously educated as a Presbyterian but I early absented myself from the public assemblies of the sect, Sunday being my study day. I, however, never was without some religious principles. I never doubted, for instance, the existence of the Deity; that he made the world, and governed it by his Providence; that the most acceptable service to God was the doing good to man; that our souls are immortal; and that all crime will be punished, and virtue rewarded, either here or hereafter."[96] The resemblance of this little creed to Herbert of Cherbury's famous five articles of natural or deistic religion will be at once noticed by the reader. It adds the article of divine providence and omits any reference to repentance. Otherwise it is almost identical with Herbert's list. That Franklin, like the English deists, thought his articles common to all positive religions and that the other things in the positive religions beside these were of little value if not harmful is evident from what he wrote after stating his little creed. "These I esteemed the essentials of every religion; and, being to be found in the religions we had in our country, I respected them all, though with different degrees of respect, as I found them more or less mixed with other articles, which, without any tendency to inspire, promote, or confirm morality, served principally to divide us, and make us unfriendly to one another."[97] This is quite the characteristic attitude of the deists. Franklin continues with the information that, as he thought all the religions or sects had some good effects he avoided speaking against any, and, as the country expanded he gave to the establishing of churches of various sects.[98]

Franklin while in Philadelphia attended church but irregularly because he found the preacher dry and polemic rather than morally helpful.[99] This is still the deistic emphasis on morality and the deistic disparagement of ceremony and doctrine. But he believed in the propriety of public worship and paid regularly to the support of the

---

[96] *Autobiography*, p. 103 f.
[97] *Autobiography*, pp. 103–105.
[98] *loc. cit.*
[99] *loc. cit.*

Presbyterian Church in Philadelphia.[100) Later in life he
very definitely urged his daughter Sarah, in a letter dated
1764, to go to church. "Go constantly to church, whoever
preaches."[101) Franklin found some preachers that pleased
him. In 1734 a young Presbyterian preacher named Hemphill came from Ireland and preached with the emphasis on
morality that suited Franklin who went to hear him until
Hemphill was deposed for plagarism.[102) Later Whitefield,
whom Franklin appreciated as an honest man,[103) so moved
Franklin by his preaching that he emptied his pocketbook
into the collection plate after having resolved previously to
give nothing.[104) Franklin's attitude toward clergy and
churches lacked the hostile and bitter quality common to
most English deists. He did not scatter charges of selfishness, dishonesty and corruption against the clergy but did
think they were, in many cases, too much concerned with
ceremonies and with doctrinal preaching and that they did
not preach enough practical moral sermons.

Whereas most English deists wrote much against miracles
and prophecy and against the doctrines of the inspiration of
the Bible and the deity of Christ, Franklin had very little to
say on these subjects. His mature views on these matters
are perhaps best expressed in a letter written to Ezra Stiles
in 1790. "Here is my creed. I believe in one God, Creator
of the universe. That He governs it by his providence. That
He ought to be worshipped. That the most acceptable service we render Him is doing good to his other children. That
the soul of man is immortal, and will be treated with justice
in another life respecting its conduct in this. These I take
to be the fundamental principles of all sound religion, and
I regard them as you do in whatever sect I meet with them.
As to Jesus of Nazareth, my opinion of whom you particularly desire. I think the system of morals and his religion,
as he left them to us, the best the world ever saw or is likely to see; but I apprehend it has received various corrupting
changes, and I have with most of the present dissenters in
England, some doubts as to his Divinity; though it is a
question I do not dogmatize upon, having never studied it,
and think it needless to busy myself with it now, when I
expect soon an opportunity of knowing the truth with less

100) *Autobiography*, pp. 103–105.
101) *op. cit.*, p. 105. Editor's footnote.
102) *op. cit.*, p. 125 f.
103) *op. cit.*, p. 138.
104) *op. cit.*, pp. 137–138.

trouble. I see no harm, however, in its being believed, if that belief has the good consequence, as probably it has, of making his doctrines more respected and better observed."[105] One familiar with English deism can readily detect a decidedly deistic flavor in this creedal statement by Franklin. The emphasis on the existence of God the Creator, on the fact that He should be worshipped and that the best and truest worship is morality and service to fellowmen, on the things common to various religions, on the immortality of the soul and on the idea that the religion of Jesus had been corrupted, were all very common features in English deism, though some of the English denied immortality. But it differs from the common position of English deists in only doubting instead of denying and definitely opposing the doctrine of the divinity of Christ. Nothing is here said directly on the question of inspiration or miracles or prophecy, though there might be a hinted doubt of these in the reference to the corruption of the religion of Jesus. His reference to sharing views of "Most of the present dissenters in England" is of significance in connection with a study of the influence of English deism upon American deism as it shows Franklin assuming familiarity with the liberal religious thought of England. Franklin evidently shared the view of those more conservative English deists who gave Jesus the highest position among great moral teachers rather than classing him among the imposters as more radical deists did.

As a boy, Franklin left Boston and went to Philadelphia where, by his gifts and by the putting into practice of his own homely maxims for success, he attained success as a printer. He worked for a short time in Britain where he is known to have met Hume[106] and probably did meet other liberals or free-thinkers. A word given out in England by Franklin to induce emigration to the American colonies is of interest both because of the light it throws on Franklin's religious attitude and on religious conditions in America. "To this may be truly added, that serious religion, under its various Denominations, is not only tolerated, but respected and practised. Atheism is unknown there; infidelity rare and secret. So that persons may live to a great age in that country without having their piety shocked by meeting with

---

[105] SMYTH (Editor), *The Writings of Benjamin Franklin*. Macmillan, 1907. 10 vols. vol. 10, p. 84.
[106] *Autobiography*, p. 237.

either an atheist or an infidel."[107] In early manhood, Franklin was the father of an illegitimate son but he soon married and settled down to a more creditable life in which both his morals and religion are said to have shown improvement.[108] When Franklin had already attained business success and quite a reputation as a scientist and practical philosopher, he was sent to France by the Colonies to work in their behalf during their troubles with England. Franklin was very acceptable to the French not only because of his genial personal traits and his reputation but because of his liberal theological views. He moved very comfortably among French free-thinkers. But so far as known Franklin's views suffered little change from these French contacts. After the revolutionary war was over and the colonies had gained their independence, Franklin was the honored and influential Nestor of the great constitutional convention that was called to plan a new government for the free states. Here, in making a plea for the opening of the meetings with prayer after the convention had long failed to make progress, Franklin gave expression to his views on providence and prayer in a manner that requires attention.

Franklin's words, addressed to the President of the convention, were as follows. "How has it happened, Sir, that we have not hitherto once thought of humbly applying to the Father of Lights to illuminate our understandings? In the beginning of the contest with Britain, when we were sensible of danger, we had daily prayers in this room for the divine protection. Our prayers, Sir, were heard; and they were graciously answered. All of us, who were engaged in the struggle, must have observed frequent instances of a superintending Providence in our favor. To that kind Providence we owe this happy opportunity of consulting in peace on the means of establishing our future national felicity. And have we now forgotten that powerful Friend? Or do we imagine we no longer need his assistance? I have lived, Sir, a long time; and the longer I live, the more convincing proofs I see of this truth that God governs in the affairs of men. And, if a sparrow cannot fall to the ground without his notice, is it probable that an empire can rise without his aid?"[109] He concluded by moving "That henceforth prayers, imploring the assistance of Heaven and its blessing on our deliberations be held in this Assembly every

107) *Writings*, vol. 8, pp. 613–614.
108) LORD, *Beacon Lights of History*, vol. 7, p. 61.
109) *Autobiography*, p. 290.

morning before we proceed to business: and that one or more of the clergy of this city be requested to officiate in that service."[110)

It may then be said, in conclusion: that Franklin became a deist early in life through reading the writings and arguments of English deists; that later experience and reflection caused him to retreat somewhat from the thoroughgoing deism of his early life; and that in his mature life, while still having many sentiments in common with the English deists and not at all an orthodox Presbyterian Christian, he became more conservative in viewpoint and held views on providence and prayer much more like those of orthodox Christians than like those of deists. Indeed Franklin's views on providence and prayer were quite inconsistent with the deistic conception of an absentee God who does not and who could not, in consistency with the perfection of his work of creation and his impartial nature, interfere in the affairs of men. Moreover a thoroughgoing deist would not only "doubt" the divinity of Christ as did Franklin but would positively deny that divinity in consistency with his fundamental deistic principle. Without doubt the fact that Franklin was known to be liberal in his religious views and was commonly regarded as a deist, together with his high standing and reputation as a scientist, philosopher and statesman and his genial personality, made him a great influence in favor of deism in his own age and in favor of liberal religious views in later eras.

2. THOMAS JEFFERSON.

Jefferson (1743-1826), writer of the *Declaration of Independence,* third President of the United States and revered founder of what later became the *Democratic Party,* was a deist. His fame however rests entirely upon his political writings and activities and not upon his religious philosophy. He definitely sought to keep out of the field of religious controversy[111)] and therefore his deistic views are found expressed in private memoirs and correspondence rather than in any published books. The only deistic principle for which he publicly contended was religious toleration, a principle which was by no means a monopoly of the deists.

Although the evidence in his writings is abundant to prove Jefferson a deist who shared the views and attitudes in matters of religion that were common to the English

110) *Writings,* vol. 9, p. 601.
111) above, p. 204, footnote 84.

deists, yet he was called by many titles of reproach such as
"Infidel" and "Atheist." Unfortunately such words were
then and are yet often used very inaccurately. No sect or
church made much claim upon Jefferson though he seems
to have been a nominal "Vestryman" in an Episcopal or
Church of England church.[112] But he spoke sharply against
that as well as other sects, his special antipathy being the
Presbyterian denomination.[113] If by "Infidel" is meant one
who does not believe in God, then Jefferson was not an
"Infidel." But if the term is used to denote one who does
not believe in the creed of any particular sect or in such
doctrines as the Inspiration of the Bible, the Divinity of
Christ or the Trinity, then he was an Infidel.[114] An "Atheist" he certainly was not for throughout his writings on
religion he consistently asserted or assumed his belief in
and worship of God.[115]

Jefferson belonged to a family of wealth and culture and
so had the opportunity of satisfying his thirst for knowledge
both by books and by association with people of culture.
Early in life he became acquainted with Francis Fauquier,
a cultured gentleman of the liberal French school who was
for a time Lieutenant Governor of the province of Virginia
and who introduced the writings of Diderot, Rousseau and
Voltaire into the colony.[116] The result was that Jefferson
became steeped in the philosophy of Rousseau.[117] Though
it is true that a dislike for England and things English[118]
characterized Jefferson during much of his life and caused
him to be more hospitable to French than to English ideas
and influences, yet he was fond of some of the liberal English writers. He expressed highest admiration for Bacon,
Newton and Locke,[119] whom he regarded as among the
greatest men the world had produced. One of his most
vigorously urged arguments for toleration is so nearly identical in thought and language with that urged by Locke as
to indicate that he was borrowing, consciously or uncon-
sciously, from Locke.[120] Jefferson read with hearty ap-

112) Hamilton, *The Best Letters of Thomas Jefferson*, pp. 204–205.
113) Lord, *Beacon Lights of History*, vol. 7, p. 236. cf. *Best Letters*,
p. 231 f.
114) *Best Letters*, pp. 230–232. cf. pp. 34–36.
115) *op. cit.*, pp. 21–23, 284–285.
116) *Beacon Lights of History*, vol. 7, p. 222.
117) Lord, *Beacon Lights of History*, vol. 7, p. 224.
118) *op. cit.*, vol. 7, p. 236.
119) *Best Letters of Thomas Jefferson*, p. 162.
120) vid. Locke, *Works*, vol. 6, p. 40, and *The Works of Thomas Jefferson*, vol. 2, pp. 237–239.

proval the works of Middleton and Priestly and recommended their writings on religious matters to Madison and
others.[121]   It is clear that Jefferson absorbed deistic ideas
directly from English deistic sources as well as through the
medium of the writings of French deists.

The positive aspects of Jefferson's position on matters of
religion were just those common to the deists.   He believed
in God (conceived in the Unitarian and not the Trinitarian
way) as the perfect and skilled Creator[122] who is to be worshipped chiefly if not exclusively by moral living.[123]   He
agreed with those deists who believed in the immortality of
the soul.[124]   Jefferson was a materialist even when he
thought Jesus opposed to that doctrine.[125]   Priestly led him
to think Jesus was also a materialist.[126]   Like most other
deists he was a thoroughgoing rationalist in the theological
sense of that word.[127]   Although he found many things in
the writings of great men of all ages with which he agreed
and though he found things he thought particularly fine in
the teachings of Jesus as recorded in the Gospel portion of
the New Testament, yet he regarded no writing and no person, not even Jesus as authority.[128]   Herbert of Cherbury
and most of the other English deists who followed him vigorously urged the doctrine that repentance makes a sinner
acceptable with God.   This they urged as against the doctrines of sacrifice and vicarious atonement.   Jefferson,
though he does not seem to have expressed himself on that
point, probably agreed with their attitude toward sacrifice
and atonement doctrines.   Yet he did not exactly agree with
their doctrine of repentance being sufficient to make the
wrongdoer acceptable with God.   He said: "He" (i. e. Jesus)
"teaches the efficacy of repentance toward the forgiveness
of sin; I require a counterpoise of good works to redeem
it,"[129] etc.   On this point Jefferson was less humble and less
inclined to trust to the goodness of God than his compatriot
Franklin who wrote: "He that for giving a draught of water
to a thirsty person, should expect to be paid with a good
plantation, would be modest in his demands, compared with

121) STODDARD, W. O., *The Lives of the Presidents*, 3rd Edition, p. 11.
cf. *Correspondence of John Adams and Thomas Jefferson*, p. 79.
122) *Best Letters of Thomas Jefferson*, p. 33.   cf. p. 138.
123) *op. cit.*, pp. 139–142.   cf. *op. cit.*, p. 10.
124) *op. cit.*, p. 146.
125) *Best Letters of Thomas Jefferson*, pp. 230–231.
126) *The Works of Thomas Jefferson*, vol. 10, p. 285.
127) *op. cit.*, vol. 9, p. 408 f.
128) *Best Letters*, etc., p. 230 f.
129) *loc. cit.*

those who think they deserve heaven for the little good they do on earth."[130]   In his discussion of conscience, Jefferson, who in most matters was a great champion of the Reason, seems to go back from the Lockian empiricism toward the Herbert of Cherbury doctrine of innate ideas.   He wrote: "The moral sense, or conscience, is as much a part of man as his leg or arm.   It is given to all human beings in a stronger or weaker degree.   It may be strengthened by exercise, as may any particular limb of the body.   This sense is submitted, indeed, in some degree, to the guidance of reason; but it is a small stock which is required for this; even a less one than what we call common sense.   State a moral case to a ploughman and to a professor.   The former will decide it as well, and often better than the latter, because he has not been led astray by artificial rules."[131] Rousseau's influence on Jefferson is evident in the last clause of the above quotation.

Jefferson's essential agreement in viewpoint with the English deists is even more evident when the negative phases of deism and of his attitude on religious matters is taken into consideration.   Like them he was bitterly anticlerical, accusing the clergy or priesthood of selfishness, greed, stupidity, bigotry, dishonesty and the corrupting of the Gospel and of pure religion.[132]   Unlike Franklin, he has no good word to say for any of them.   Their theologians he calls "crazy theologists"[133] and accuses them of causing the divisions of mankind into sects by their corrupting of natural religion and the pure precepts of Jesus with their "casuistries" and especially with the mysticism and "foggy" nonsense of Plato.[134]   This charge that Christianity and Christian theology had been grossly corrupted by Platonism reminds the reader forcibly of the view of the English deist Bolingbroke.[135]   Jefferson was so anticlerical that he favored a ministerless form of religion such as he found among the Quakers.[136]   Far from believing in the supernatural character or inspiration of the Bible, Jefferson spoke ill of some of its most prominent characters and writers.   Moses he charged with corrupting religion with idle ceremonies

130) *The Writings of Benjamin Franklin*, vol. 3, pp. 144–145.
131) *The Best Letters of Thomas Jefferson*, p. 33.
132) *The Works of Thomas Jefferson*, vol. 8, pp. 408–419.
Best Letters, pp. 139–142. cf. pp. 230–231. cf. also pp. 206–209.
133) In a letter to Ezra Styles dated June 25, 1819.
134) *Best Letters*, pp. 236–237.
135) above, p. 157.
136) *The Works of Thomas Jefferson*, vol. 9, p. 419.

and mummeries that were of no service to virtue. He disliked the Jews and the Old Testament religion of which he
regarded Jesus as a great reformer.[137] The God of the Old
Testament he regarded as "A Being of terrific character,
cruel, vindictive, capricious and unjust." A similar attitude
and similar charges were common among English deists,
and they too were wont to set the New Testament against
the Old. Jefferson also, far from believing in the inspiration of the Gospel writers, spoke of them as ignorant men
who corrupted, mutilated and misstated Jesus' teachings.
Jesus he regarded as unfortunate in his biographers.[138] As
he set the New Testament against the Old and Christ in
contrast to the Gospel writers, so also he set Paul up as a
corrupter of Christianity. He says: "Of this band of dupes
and imposters, Paul was the great Coryphaeus, the first corrupter of the doctrine of Jesus."[139] This too was an attitude
and method of several of the English deists. Some of the
English deists had represented Jesus as himself a very fine
man and greatest of moral teachers, but one whose teachings had been corrupted by ignorant and dishonest biographers and followers. Others, more radical, had represented
Jesus himself as one of the great imposters of history. In
the main Jefferson agreed with the less radical group and
spoke of Jesus in high terms as the best of men, one having
every human excellency and claiming no other, the great
reformer of Judaism, and the finest of all moral teachers.[140]
He thought he could separate the real teachings of Jesus
from the unworthy teachings ascribed to him by the "grovel-
ling authors" who were his biographers as one separates
gold from dross.[141] Yet Jefferson was inclined to think
Jesus himself guilty of some false and base teachings and
accommodations.[142] Jefferson, for his own pleasure, compiled a little book of Jesus' moral teachings from the four
Gospels and found it to contain gems of moral teaching far
better than those of the philosophers.[143] It is evident from
the general tone of his references to miracles that Jefferson
was a disbeliever in them. He would apply Hume's argument to them.[144]

137) *Best Letters*, pp. 136–137. cf. pp. 204–205.
138) *loc. cit.*
139) *Best Letters*, pp. 230–231.
140) *Best Letters*, pp. 139–142.
141) *op. cit.*, pp. 230–231. cf. *op. cit.*, p. 138.
142) *Best Letters*, pp. 230–231 and elsewhere.
143) *Best Letters*, pp. 139–142, 206–209, 230–231.
144) *op. cit.*, pp. 34–35.

While Jefferson did not enter into public controversy on religious matters other than toleration, he did, by his extensive private correspondence and direct personal intercourse do much to propagate deistic views.[145] He not only agreed with Priestly's views on the Bible and religion but also highly recommended that and other free-thinking books to Madison and other young friends.[146] His political fame naturally made Jefferson's religious influence large.

3. THOMAS PAINE.

Thomas Paine, or Payne, (1737-1809) was the chief controversial writer for deism in America. Paine was something of an international character as he was born an Englishman, migrated to America in 1774 and took an active part in the colonial agitation for independence, went to France and hurled himself into the activities of the French Revolution and finally returned to America where he died. He seemed to enjoy strife and controversy, whether political or religious. If, on the one hand, prejudice against him because of his radicalism on religious matters has caused religious conservatives not to give adequate recognition to his importance as a political writer and agitator for freedom during the era of the American Revolution, prejudice in his favor on the part of freethinking writers has probably led them to ascribe to him a greater influence and importance than he actually possessed.[147] He did not come to America until 1774, near the beginning of the Revolutionary war. His pamphlet *Common Sense* and some writings in the *Pennsylvania Magazine* did help to stir up the spirit that started and maintained the Revolution. His most famous political writing, *The Rights of Man*, was not published until 1791, after the war of the American Revolution was over. It was published in France and probably exercised considerable influence there. Paine also published his most famous deistic work while living in France. This work, *The Age of Reason*, appeared in 1795, being published in France. Since Paine was born in England and lived as an international character and since his book was published in France, it seems a bit odd to rank it as a work of an American deist. But Paine returned to and died in America

---

[145] vid. *The Best Letters of Thomas Jefferson* and *The Correspondence of John Adams and Thomas Jefferson.*

[146] STODDARD, W. O., *The Lives of the Presidents*, Third Edition, pp. 3–12. cf. *Best Letters*, pp. 34–36.

[147] ROBERTSON, *A Short History of Freethought*, vol. 2, p. 381.

and his work had wide circulation and influence in this country. He is usually reckoned to be an American deist.

There is no doubt about Paine having been a deist. He openly boasted that he was such. His views were the views common to deism in England and France and were expressed by him with blunt frankness as well as with great clearness and vigor.[148] He had great ability in the use of the English language. The clearness and forcefulness of his style probably had much to do with extending and perpetuating the influence of his book, making it the most influential and best known of American deistic works. Today the views on religion of Franklin and Jefferson would probably be unknown were it not for the great political fame of these men. Ethan Allen is remembered only as a soldier and his deistic *Oracles of Reason* are almost entirely forgotten. But Thomas Paine is known and is remembered chiefly as a deist and by his deistic book *The Age of Reason*. Like most of the English deists, Paine gave much more space in his book to negation and attacks on what he did not believe than to a direct setting forth and defence of his own positive beliefs. Yet he gave enough statement of positive beliefs to prove him a deist rather than a skeptic or atheist. He wrote: "I believe in one God and no more; and I hope for happiness beyond this life,—My own mind is my own church."[149] He rejected all books that claimed to be special revelations, saying bluntly that he "disbelieves them all."[150] But he made his special attack upon the Bible, first upon the Old Testament and then upon the New. Of the Bible he wrote: "It would be more consistent that we call it the word of a demon, than the Word of God." "It is a history of wickedness, that has served to corrupt and brutalize mankind; and, for my own part, I sincerely detest it, as I detest everything that is cruel."[151] In this book he could find "scarcely anything but a history of the grossest vices and a collection of the most paltry and contemptible tales."[152] At the end of his examination of the Old Testament he wrote: "I have now gone through the Bible, as a man would go through a wood with an ax on his shoulder, and fell trees. Here they lie; and the priests, if they can,

---

[148] vid. PAINE, THOMAS, *The Age of Reason — Being an Investigation of True and Fabulous Theology.* New York, G. P. Putnam's Sons, 1907. (First published in Paris in 1794.)
[149] *op. cit.*, pp. 21–22.
[150] *The Age of Reason*, p. 23.
[151] *op. cit.*, p. 34.
[152] *op. cit.*, p. 38.

may replant them. They may, perhaps stick them in the ground, but they will never make them grow. I pass on to the New Testament."[153] Paine's opinion of his own prowess was evidently no humble one. His attack upon the New Testament and its writers was even more bitter. The story of the Virgin-Birth of Christ he derided as on a par with Greek stories of gods co-habiting with men.[154] He called the writers of both Old and New Testaments perjurers. Paul he called a fool. He expressed himself as holding in abhorrence miracles, prophecy, the idea of a divine Christ and all priests.[155] On the subject of the deity of Christ he wrote further as follows: "He was a Jew by birth and by profession; and he was the son of God in like manner that every other person is; for the Creator is the Father of All."[156] He rejected all churches, Turkish, Jewish and Christian as alike human inventions "Set up to terrify and enslave mankind, and monopolize power and profit."[157]

Though, like Jefferson and most of the English deists, Paine was willing to concede that Jesus was the greatest of moral teachers, he did not allow him to be divine or virgin-born nor that he left the world by ascending as described in the New Testament. The ascension story he called a "wretched contrivance."[158]

There was nothing new in Paine's work except the directness, frankness and forcefulness of his language. The positions taken and the arguments used were but repetitions of those found in the English deists who had preceded him. His work with its coarseness and forcefulness was well suited to appeal to those of the masses who were already touched with infidelity toward Christianity and the Bible. But, on the other hand, it was likely only to disgust and offend those of more refined taste who still cherished reverence for the Bible.

Just how extensively deism was held in 18th and early 19th century America cannot be determined with much accuracy and that chiefly because of the loose use of such words as "infidel," "atheist," "skeptic" and "deist." That the rugged Calvinism of the early pilgrims and puritans soon gave place to an emasculated Calvinism, that unitarianism developed considerable strength in New England,

---

153) *The Age of Reason*, p. 151.
154) *op. cit.*, p. 25.
155) *op. cit.*, pp. 180–182.
156) *The Age of Reason*, p. 39.
157) *op. cit.*, p. 22.
158) *op. cit.*, p. 26.

that for a time there were few professing Christians in the eastern universities and colleges, that religious leaders complained much of the prevalence of irreligion, infidelity and low morality, is known. That Ethan Allen and Paine were vigorously and publicly propagating deism and Thomas Jefferson doing so in a more private way and that Benjamin Franklin was lending his winsome influence to favor views in the main deistic, is also known. Of the older eastern institutions of learning, Harvard seems to have been most influenced by the deistic movement.[159)] Woolastson's *Religion of Nature Delineated,* a work which Franklin had helped to print while in England as a youth, is known to have been influential at Yale.[160)] It is known that a considerable collection of deistic books including Shaftesbury's *Characteristics* were at Yale.[161)] Presidents Dwight and Stiles of Yale opposed the deistic movement in that institution[162)] while President Witherspoon was speaking against the writings of the English deists Collins and Woolastson[163)] at Princeton. Uzel Ogden answered Paine.[164)] President Stiles, who corresponded with Franklin and Jefferson on the subject of deism and who later complained of the spread of deism in the army and country, had himself already read the English deists Tindal, Collins and Bolingbroke as early as 1756.[165)] Yet the cold reception given to the once popular Paine when he returned from France after publishing his deistic book *The Age of Reason* does not suggest that deism was as popular in America as some of the above facts might lead one to suppose.

In America the deistic movement stood out less distinctly from other liberal types of thought on religion than was the case in England. One of its earliest American champions, Ethan Allen, seems to have been half deist half transcendentalist though it would probably be most correct to class him with the deists. Distinct deism did not last long in America even as it had declined quickly in England. In America it gave place chiefly to transcendentalism which like deism dispensed with an objective and external revelation. But whereas transcendentalism was reverent and

---

[159)] RILEY, I. WOODBRIDGE, *American Philosophy.* New York, Dodd, Mead & Company, 1907. p. 13.
[160)] *op. cit.,* p. 209.
[161)] RILEY, I. WOODBRIDGE, *American Thought From Puritanism to Pragmatism and Beyond.* New York, H. Holt & Co., 1923. p. 63.
[162)] RILEY, *Am. Phil.,* pp. 56–57, 213–216.
[163)] *op. cit.,* p. 227.
[164)] *op. cit.,* pp. 310–311.
[165)] *op. cit.,* p. 213.

mystical in tone, deism was generally coldly rationalistic and irreverent in spirit.

America produced no such philosophical "Executioner" of deism as Britain had in Hume and Germany in Kant. Of course the works of these, especially of Hume, were known in America. Deism never seems to have had so strong a hold upon the American people as it once had on the French and German and even the English people. Great religious revival movements may have had much to do with this fact. Stirring international interests such as those centering on the Napoleonic wars and the War of 1812, diverted the attention of the people from questions of religious philosophy. Internal political excitement, the vast economic task of developing a new continent, and the growing excitement over the slavery question, to a large degree took the thoughts of the people from such questions as the deists proposed. When, later, time and inclination favored the giving of attention to matters of religious philosophy, deism had already become rather out-of-date. But it is not to be thought that deism exercised no influence upon the thought of the nineteenth and twentieth centuries. That influence will be considered in the next chapter.

The conclusion may be drawn that American deism was mainly an importation from England, from whence it came by immigration of English deists, by the importation of English deistic books and books that were written in answer to English deists and by being carried by travellers who passed from one land to the other. The most important immigrant to bring it was Thomas Paine. A second-hand and somewhat modified English deism also came in the form of French deistic writings and travellers during the era of the Revolutionary War when relations between France and the American colonies were especially close and friendly. In the main American deism may be regarded as little more than a weak and belated and short-lived segment of British deism.

CHAPTER VII

THE INFLUENCE OF DEISM UPON THE THOUGHT OF THE NINETEENTH AND TWENTIETH CENTURIES

DEISM is almost invariably referred to in the past tense. It is regarded as a system of thought that began in the seventeenth century, flourished in the eighteenth century and ceased to exist early in the nineteenth century. It is to be admitted that this conception of the history of deism is, in the main, correct. But it is not altogether correct. For, as shown in Part I of this work, deism with its ideas and attitudes and methods did not spring suddenly out of the blue in its full-grown dimension in the seventeenth century as something absolutely new but had roots reaching far back into human history and spreading widely into many branches of man's intellectual activity. Nor did the fact that deism as a rather compact, organized system of thought with a fairly definite positive and negative content almost ceased to exist in the early nineteenth century cause it to cease to exercise a far-reaching and noteworthy influence upon other schools of thought even down to the present time. As in Part I an attempt was made to show the "Roots" so in Part III of this work an attempt is being made to show the "Fruits" of English deism. In the last chapter the "first-fruits" of English deism were shown to be the development of deistic movements very similar to English deism in France, Germany and America, these movements developing chiefly as a result of English influences. It was not intended by singling out these three lands for consideration to suggest that deism did not develop in other countries of the Western world as well as in them or that English influences were not at work elsewhere also. But these three nations were selected as perhaps furnishing the most significant and direct and easily traced early influence of English deism outside of England itself. In this chapter it is proposed to continue a study of the fruits of deism by showing its influence upon later schools of thought in the western world that do not bear the name "deist," schools of thought that are quite prominent even at the present time. In doing this it is not attempted to keep the English deism distinct from the deism of other nations and to show its influence exclusively. Since the deism of other lands was essentially one with the deism of England and since these other national deisms owe their origin and development so much to English deism, it seems best to simply seek to trace the influence of deism upon modern schools of thought, pointing out occasionally the evidence of direct English influence. It is believed that this study will show deistic ideas and influences constitute one of the very potent forces at work in the intellectual life of the world ever since the eighteenth century deists proclaimed their views. As the influences that produced deism went far back into the past, so the influences that have proceeded from deism have extended down to the present and give promise of going on into the future.

The fruits of eighteenth century deism can best be studied by examining its influence upon later schools of philosophic thought, upon various forms of later infidel or anti-Christian agitation, upon modern Bible criticism, and upon what is known as "modernism" in religion. In this examination an attempt will be made to point out the elements in these more modern thought schools that are the same as or very like elements in eighteenth century deism and, further, to trace where possible the route by which the deistic influence entered the modern school of thought. Of course it is not claimed that any of these modern schools of thought that show deistic influence is simply a restatement of deism or that it is entirely a product of the deistic influence. Like deism itself, each of these schools of thought springs from many roots that lead back into the remote past. But what is here claimed is that deism is one of the important roots of several of the recent and present-day schools of thought and that several of the up-to-date schools owe more to and have more in common with eighteenth century deism than is usually recognized. If one were to name some of the influences other than deism that have profoundly affected more recent thought, he would have to name the vast expansion of the physical sciences and of their prestige, the development of the sciences of psychology and sociology, and, most important of all, the far-reaching and pervasive influence of developed modern evolutionary theory. The influence of these alone, to name no other factors tending to modify thought, is sufficient guarantee that no modern school of thought would be a simple repetition of such an old system as deism.

A. THE INFLUENCE OF DEISM UPON NINETEENTH AND EARLY TWENTIETH CENTURY PHILOSOPHY

In the Medieval Era, Theology was regarded as the "Queen of the Sciences." Philosophy was regarded as the hand-maid of theology. The "glory of God" was the supreme aim of both. All this changed with the rise of modern philosophy and the development of the modern scientific era. Philosophy, under the leadership of Francis Bacon, declared her independence. Her thought became more of the glory of man than of the glory of God. Scientific investigations were carried on, not for the glory of God but to satisfy the curiosity of man, to express man's sense of mastery and to minister to man's pleasure during his life on the earth. The old God-centered, theology-controlled type of philosophic thought came to be regarded as a tether that hampered the intellectual freedom and the material progress of mankind. Liberty, not loyalty, became the watchword. The former reverence for things old in the field of thought gave place to high respect for things new. Deism was charged full with this new spirit and the deists did much to spread and perpetuate it. They had no reverence for the ancient book, the Bible, for the ancient institution, the church, or for the ancient doctrines, the creeds of the past. Consequently they greatly shocked conservative religious people of their day by their bold irreverent attacks upon the Bible and upon such Bible characters as Abraham, Moses, David, Paul and Christ himself. It was in this new atmosphere, of which deism was one of the most striking expressions, that modern philosophy passed through the first stages of its development in England, France and Germany. Most of the early modern philosophers were much influenced by it and these, in turn, have influenced the later modern philosophers and their systems of thought.

1. THE INFLUENCE OF DEISM ON MODERN ENGLISH PHILOSOPHY.

In England, where deism had its first full development, the spirit of rebellion against medieval theology and philosophy, the spirit of scientific investigation and empiricism in philosophy, and the desire to make man's intellectual activity secure glory and happiness for mankind, manifested themselves early. Their rudiments can be detected even in Roger Bacon. They are clearly manifest in the work of Francis Bacon, who wrote when deism was just taking form as a distinct movement in the thought world. Hobbes

the deist, though a bit cautious in his manner of expressing
himself because of the intolerance of the age, showed his
lack of reverence for the Bible and for the old creeds by his
writings on the canon of Scripture and in the field of Bible
criticism. He put his intellectual acumen at the service of
man in the field of political philosophy. Locke, though not
himself a deist and opposing some of the fundamental con-
tentions of the deists, yet shared with them in their hostility
to medieval philosophy and theology, shared with them
their boldness in dealing with sacred things, and sought to
put his knowledge into the practical service of men in the
fields of politics, medicine and education. He shared and
passed on much of the freethinking spirit of the deists.
Berkeley, who was an opponent of the deists and a more
speculative thinker than any of the others yet named,
naturally showed less of the deistic spirit and attitude.
Hume, though his keen speculative thinking on the material
handed him by Hobbes, Locke and Berkeley, led him to a
skepticism that cut the foundation from under deism,
shared very fully in the deistic attitude toward Bible, clergy
and church. Following the time of these famous English
philosophers who were contemporaries of the deists no
names of comparable rank in philosophy appeared in England. But the thought of England's philosophic thinkers
remained largely empirical, worldly and a bit agnostic. It
turned chiefly in the direction of ethics, or moral philosophy, and economics. And the dominant English ethics was
not authority ethics with God as the authority but was
rather of the utilitarian type as represented by Jeremy Bent-
ham and John Stuart Mill. Adam Smith made an important
contribution to English thought along the lines of economic
and social theory in his famous book, *The Wealth of
Nations*. Soon the great industrial development and the
rise of the Darwinian theory of evolution began to direct
and profoundly influence the intellectual life of the English
people. Streams of influence were also entering the land
from such French thinkers as Comte and such German
thinkers as Kant and Hegel. Herbert Spencer, intoxicated
with the strong wine of the evolutionary theory, tried to
gather up in his massive works the whole wisdom of the
ages. Probably he owed his unorthodox attitude toward the
Christian religion in some measure to the influence of deism
but in his case so many currents of influence had converged
into the one river of his elaborate system that it is not easy
to trace this particular stream of influence.

During the latter half of the nineteenth century, England did not produce many outstanding leaders of thought in the field of philosophy. She produced a number of famous scientists such as Thomas A. Huxley and John Tyndall who, as often happens among scientists, were at times tempted to step beyond the strict bounds of their scientific field into the neighboring fields of philosophy and especially into the field of the philosophy of religion. To a considerable degree, these men shared in the deistic attitude toward miracles and supernaturalism, though they did not, like the deists of earlier date, take up particular Bible miracles for special attack. But it was because of a wide observance of uniformity in nature and because it seemed necessary to them for the very existence of science that the uniformity of nature be accepted as axiomatic that they rejected the miraculous and not because of any deductions from the nature of God conceived of as a master-craftsman as was the case with the deists.

Of the prominent literary men of England during the nineteenth century several had something of a philosophical bent and showed some interest in the philosophy of religion. The earlier ones, Shelley, Keats and Byron, though not deists in the positive sense of the term, were rather sympathetic toward the negative aspects of deism and its unfriendly spirit toward revelation and orthodox Christianity. The later poets, Wordsworth, Browning and Tennyson, were more friendly toward revealed religion. Wordsworth, because of his intense and religious interest in nature, was inclined to favor natural religion. But his mystic spirit had little in common with such cold rationalism as that represented by the English deists and Voltaire. He had more in common with the spirit of Rousseau. He did not antagonize revelation. In Browning, orthodox Calvinistic Christianity and revelation found a staunch friend and rugged defender. Tennyson too was on the side of Christianity but not so sure of himself as Browning. His hesitancy was probably due to the impact on his mind of the rapidly developing evolutionary theory rather than to the influence of the earlier deists. The prose writer Henry Drummond was deeply interested in both science and the Christian religion and sought to reconcile the seeming quarrel between them. His *Natural Law in the Spiritual World* is a work in Christian apologetics worthy of a place beside Butler's *Analogy* and Paley's *Natural Theology*.

A number of important philosophers such as Balfour,

Alexander, Eddington, Haldene, Bertrand Russell and
Whitehead have gained prominence in England during the
first part of the twentieth century. Such thinkers in the
field of epistemology as Hobhouse and Bradley had preceded them. These twentieth century thinkers nearly all
enter the field of philosophy having a background of
specialization in mathematics or some of the physical
sciences. This fact has probably influenced their type of
thought on religion more than any deistic influence. Whatever the reason, the views on religion of none of them is
quite in agreement with historical, Biblical Christianity.
Balfour, champion of theism, and Alexander and Eddington
are more nearly so than the others. Bertrand Russell is
farthest from Biblical Christianity. His philospohical
position seems to change somewhat with each successive
work he publishes, but can probably be fairly classed as
materialistic, skeptical and unfriendly toward revelation
and toward historical Christianity. In preparing his book
on the philosophy of Leibnitz, he would naturally become
well acquainted with the works of the deists and skeptics
and atheists of the eighteenth century and he seems to have
absorbed something of their spirit. Haldene, outstanding
English biologist and physiologist, champions a spiritualistic
monism that is pantheistic.[1] He is frankly anti-supernaturalistic.[2] He makes religion and philosophy to be
one.[3] His spirit is more that of Spinoza than that of the
English deists. Whitehead's philosophy of religion is a
part and an important part of his whole great philosophical
system, a system that is perhaps the most elaborate and
significant produced in recent years. In this system, God
becomes "The principle of concretion"[4] rather than the
Creator of the universe as agreed upon by both deists and
their orthodox theistic Christian opponents. For Whitehead
the highest type of religion is, as for the deists, rationalized
religion. But for the deists the highest form of rationalized
religion is a religion of morality and service to fellow-men,
or socialized religion, whereas for Whitehead religion that
stresses society is degenerate and the highest religion is
found in solitude.[5] Both deists and Whitehead oppose the

[1] HALDANE, J. S., *The Sciences and Philosophy*. Garden City, N. Y.,
Doubleday, Doran and Company, Inc., 1929.
[2] *op. cit.*, pp. 293–302.
[3] *op. cit.*, p. 303.
[4] WHITEHEAD, ALFRED NORTH, *Science and the Modern World*. New
York, Macmillan Co., 1925. p. 243.
[5] *op. cit.*, p. 267.

dogmas of the church but the grounds of opposition in the two cases are entirely different. Deists hated the doctrines or dogmas themselves and opposed their claimed super-natural origin, assigning them rather to priestly corruption. There is no talk of priestly corruption in Whitehead. His criticism is rather that dogmas of religion like "laws" of science should not be static but subject to change and re-statement with enlarging knowledge.[6] It is apparent that Whitehead's attitude and method of reasoning is quite dif-ferent from that of the deists. Scientific considerations rather than deistic principles and prejudices seem to be the main factors in shaping his viewpoint.

2. THE INFLUENCE OF DEISM UPON MODERN FRENCH PHI-LOSOPHY.

Deism developed rapidly in France under the leadership of Rousseau and Voltaire. But the tendency in France was to pass on to a more radical religious philosophy such as the skepticism of Diderot and the materialism of La Mettrie and D'Holbach. Condillac, a great admirer of John Locke, de-veloped Locke's sensationalism but, as a priest of the Roman Catholic church, he naturally did not favor deism or deists openly. More evident and more important was the influence of deism upon the Positive philosophy of Auguste Comte.

Comte was born in Montpellier in 1798 and therefore grew to manhood at a time when deism and skepticism were very important factors in the intellectual life of France. The idol of Comte's young manhood was Benjamin Franklin.[7] Thus English deists influenced Comte through the medium of their American disciple Franklin. Comte shared the English empirical spirit. For him Philosophy was but a generalization of the results of the different sciences. He had a mania for reform and regarded the improving of the social, moral and political position of mankind as the proper task of philosophy. He held to the idea that there have been three stages in the history of human thought, a theological one, a metaphysical one and a positive or scien-tific one and he would repudiate the first two as childish and immature. This, of course, involves the rejection of both the Bible and historical Christianity. In this task of repudiation, Comte adopted common deistic arguments. In his later years, Comte proposed to substitute "Positivism"

6) WHITEHEAD, A. N., *Religion in the Making*. New York, Macmillan Co., 1926. p. 130 f.
7) DURANT, *The Story of Philosophy*, p. 381.

or the "Religion of Humanity," a Comte-made and man-centered religion, for the God-centered religion of the Bible. This new "Religion of Humanity" emphasizes the physical sciences and also the new science of sociology of which Comte has himself been called the "father."[8] Comte was a voluminous writer, his works being comparable in magnitude to those of Hegel and Spencer. His most important work was the five volume *Positive Philosophy* which appeared between 1830 and 1842. Next to it in importance is his four volume *Positive Polity* that was published between 1851 and 1854. This latter work contains his new religion. Although Comte's new religion gained few adherents, the influence of his theory of the history of thought and of his emphasis upon science and of his work in sociology spread widely and still persists. Thus through Comte, deistic ideas and attitudes spread their influence in France and elsewhere even down to the present day.

The dominant influence in the Philosophy of Bergson seems to be the theory of evolution rather than deism. Mathematics and modern science dominate the philosophic thinking of the more recent French philosopher Poincare. But deism, especially through the writings of Voltaire, still exercises a great influence in France. When the novelist and poet Anatole France makes a half-blind priest evangelize and baptize penguins by mistake, he is showing much of the same attitude toward Roman Catholic Christianity and much of the same mocking method of dealing with it that characterized the deist Voltaire. The spirit of deism and positivism in their attitude toward supernaturalism and revelation and toward the doctrines and rituals of the Roman Catholic church of France is by no means dead in that land.

3. THE INFLUENCE OF DEISM UPON MODERN GERMAN PHILOSOPHY.

Germany, by giving to the intellectual world such thinkers as Leibnitz, Wolff, Kant, Fichte, Schelling, Hegel, Schopenhauer, Nietsche and Haeckel, has held a dominant place in modern occidental philosophy. The earlier of these men lived during the age of deism and were strongly exposed to its influence. Leibnitz, contemporary of Locke and Toland, defended his philosophical rationalism against their empiricism. His doctrine that this is the best possible world

8) BOGARDUS, EMORY S., *A History of Social Thought*. Los Angeles, J. R. Miller, 1929. 2nd Edit. p. 222 ff.

aroused the ire and attracted the mockery of Voltaire. Leibnitz can properly be classed as an opponent of early deism. Wolff built up a system of rationalistic philosophy on the foundations laid by Descartes and Leibnitz. But in religious matters he was very much under the influence of the deism which was then spreading in Germany.[9] He helped to spread that influence. Kant, most famous and influential of modern philosophers, was the son of pietist parents. This fact probably prevented Kant from ever adopting the bitter or mocking attitude toward historical Christianity found in so many of the deists. Early in life Kant came under the dominating influence of the Wolffian school of thought which was nearly deist in its religious attitude. Some of Kant's writings during this period came under the unfavorable censorship of the Prussian authorities on matters of religion. Later Kant became an interested reader of Locke and Hume with the result that the latter awakened him from his "dogmatic slumber" and caused him to develop that famous system of philosophy known as "Kantianism." It is a system that combines and interrelates elements from the rationalism of the continent with elements from the empiricism of England. Like Hume's philosophy it cut the deeper philosophical and theological foundation from under the position of the deists and therefore Kant, like Hume, has been called "The executioner of deism." But no doubt, Kant, like Hume, though in less degree, was influenced in his attitude toward supernaturalism and historical Christianity by the deism around him. Fichte, Schelling and Hegel were subtle, speculative, idealistic philosophers quite different in spirit and method from the deists and from such empirical philosophers as Locke and Hume. Although all were theologically educated, they were too unorthodox to be in good standing in religious circles. Just how far this was due to the influence of the deism about them cannot be determined. They reveal more of the direct influence of Kant and Spinoza and of the old Greek thinkers who speculated on "being" and "becoming" than they do of the deists. Their religious philosophy was pantheistic rather than deistic in type. Buddhism had more influence than deism upon Schopenhauer, the philosopher of pessimism. His highly allegorical method of interpreting New Testament stories and doctrines reminds of the English

---

9) above, p. 189.

deist Collins. But his attitude toward the New Testament and his purpose in using the allegorical method of interpreting it do not seem to have been those of Collins. Nietsche manifested an attitude as hostile toward Christ and the religion of the New Testament as that of the deists. This can be readily seen in his famous book *Also Sprach Zarathustra*. His attack, however, was upon the principles and ideals of Christ and not upon the history and miracles recorded in the Gospels as was the case with the deists. The materialist Haeckel championed, developed and drew some of the philosophical inferences from the Darwinian theory of evolution. Evolution theories go back as far as Democritus. In the seventeenth century the English deist Blount made the observation that some folks of his day thought man nothing but a cultured ape. But the deists made practically no use of the evolution theory in their attacks upon historical Christianity and the Bible. With Darwin began the modern prestige and influence of the theory. Haeckel was one of the first to use it as a weapon in the warfare going on in the field of the philosophy of religion. He shared the antagonism of the deists toward supernaturalism. Though in the later German philosophers it is not possible to trace any direct influence of the deists as could be done with some of the earlier philosophers and though the fundamental deistic assumptions in regard to the nature of God and his relation to the universe are wanting in both the earlier and later modern German philosophers of note, yet the deistic bias against revelation and supernaturalism and historical Christianity are found to persist.

The influence of deism is more evident in the thought of Germany's philosophically minded literary men such as Goethe and Schiller and Lessing than it is in the works of the philosophers proper. As shown above, Lessing was himself one of the most outstanding of German deists. Goethe, most revered of Germany's literary thinkers, was a disciple of Lessing and of Spinoza, who in turn was much influenced by the English deist Hobbes. Schiller, friend of Goethe and disciple of Kant and patriot poet of Germany, though far from having the cold rationalistic spirit of the deists, was influenced by them to take an unfriendly attitude toward revelation and supernaturalism. The literary excellence of the works of these men give them, and through them give deistic attitudes, a wide influence.

4. THE INFLUENCE OF DEISM UPON AMERICAN PHILOSOPHY.

The earliest American philosophy was closely related to theology of the Calvinistic type. Jonathan Edwards was probably its ablest representative. Then, through change in the character of the new immigrants and through the influence of the writings of English and French deists, there came a marked change in the dominant philosophy. Philosophy ceased to be so exclusively of the nature of philosophy of religion or so entirely dominated by theology. Some of it turned to social and economic themes. Franklin's homely proverbs and wisdom literature such as is found in his *Poor Richard's Almanac* is the best illustration of this new type of American philosophy. But much more of it became political philosophy as represented by the more important works of such men as John Adams, Thomas Jefferson, Madison, Hamilton, and many others. This political philosophy developed as part of the revolt against England on the part of the colonies and as part of the effort to establish a new nation on the American continent. The chief influence that deism exerted upon this political philosophy was that element in deism that stressed toleration and argued for separation of Church and State. The deist Jefferson was particularly interested in this theme. But a considerable amount of the philosophical thinking of the age still dealt with religion. The strong, orthodox Calvinism of the earlier era gave place in large measure to a latitudinarian theology that was in some Arminian and even Pelagian and Socinian. This was the era of the development in New England of unitarianism with its denial of the divinity of Christ. John Adams was a prominent representative of this anti-Calvinistic unitarianism.[10] Deism itself as represented by Jefferson and Paine and to a large degree by Ethan Allen and Benjamin Franklin was but a more extreme form of this theological reaction. Unquestionably this change of theology and of religious philosophy that took place in America during the eighteenth century was largely due to the impact upon American thought of English and European deism.

The next important development in philosophical thought in America was the rise of transcendentalism. Emerson was a prominent representative of this school of thought. It arose as deism faded out. It was more vague and mystic in character and not so bitter and controversial in spirit as

[10] WILSTACH, *Correspondence of John Adams and Thomas Jefferson,* pp. 82–83.

deism. But, like deism, it "denied need of miracle, revelation and dependence upon an objective standard of faith."[11]

An important name in the history of more recent American philosophy is that of William James. He is important as one of the early leaders in the development of psychology and in the application of this new science to old philosophical problems. He is important also as one of the founders of the new philosophical school of pragmatism or instrumentalism. He was interested in religion and religious philosophy as indicated in such works as his *The Will to Believe* and *Varieties of Religious Experience*. Though not regarded as orthodox in religious viewpoint, he never was regarded as being hostile to the church and Christianity as were the deists. There is no evidence of any direct influence of deism upon his thinking. He was radically empirical in his thought, being thoroughly hostile to metaphysics. He was also utilitarian in his attitude. In these respects his spirit was akin to that of most of the deists.

John Dewey (1859-) has developed the pragmatism of James into what is now usually called "Instrumentalism." He is fully as hostile to metaphysics as James and just as thoroughly empirical. But he is less friendly to revelation and to historical religion.[12] He is thoroughly dominated by the evolutionary theory and completely sold to naturalism.[13] For him, scientific method is the only revelation of reality.[14] Dewey does not talk of revelation of God or of moral codes for he, who has been called the "American Confucius," confines all knowledge to the strictly empirical field. Thus Dewey repudiates not only the transcendant God of historical religion but also the transcendant God of the deists, not only supernatural revelation in a Bible but also the revelation of a supernatural being and his will for men through either innate ideas (Herbert of Cherbury) or through reason reflecting upon nature as created by God (later deists). That is, he rejects the deists' religion of nature along with historical Christianity and other religions that base themselves on a claimed supernatural revelation. What Dewey accepts is simply ethics conceived of in a utilitarian spirit and as a purely natural growth from human experience. Dewey's religion, if it may be called such, is very like the positivist faith of Comte, called the

11) RILEY, I. WOODBRIDGE, *American Philosophy*, p. 320.
12) DEWEY, JOHN, "What I Believe." *The Forum*, March, 1930.
13) DURANT, *The Story of Philosophy*, p. 568.
14) "What I Believe."

"Religion of Humanity," with the ritualistic trimmings omitted. It is humanism as contrasted with both the theism of Christians and the deism of the eighteenth century opponents of historical Christianity. Yet, while Dewey stands just as much opposed to the fundamental principle of deism as to those of theism, he has in common with the deists the rejection of supernatural revelation and the miraculous, the rejection of Christian dogmas and institutions, the making of religion practically identical with ethics and a marked tendency to regard anyone who holds to historical Christianity or to metaphysical philosophy as an antique and a champion of things obsolete and out of place in a modern scientific world.[15] In Dewey, one finds the empiricism of Hobbes, Locke and Condillac, the positivism of Comte, the pragmatism of James, the utilitarianism of John Stuart Mill, the devotion to evolutionary theory of Spencer, the humanism of Walter Lippman and the antagonism to revelation and historical Christianity of the eighteenth century deists.

Humanism has found its clearest expression and its ablest defender in Walter Lippmann. It is closely related to the positivism of Comte. It is dominated by the theory of evolution. It is thoroughly and radically empirical. It affiliates readily with the pragmatism of James and the instrumentalism of Dewey and the behavioristic psychology of Watson. Lippmann's book *A Preface to Morals* has created a real stir in the field of religious philosophy. Lippmann talks much of "the acids of modernity" making impossible for the "modern man" belief in God, in the historical sense of that word, in the Bible and in immortality of the soul as immortality was formerly conceived. There is a boastful intellectual pride in this claim of humanism that it is the only system of religious and ethical thought consistent with modern knowledge and science that reminds of the same boastful spirit among the eighteenth century deists who claimed that they were the enlightened modern men who therefore could not accept the old revelation and religion. Indeed this same boastful spirit of intellectual pride can be found as far back as the day of the second century gnostics who took the name gnostic as a boastful claim that they were the folks who lived by knowledge while others, unenlightened souls, could only live by faith or belief. The deistic hostility to the character of the God of the Old

15) Dewey, John, "What I Believe." *The Forum*, March, 1930.

Testament likewise appears in Lippmann.[16] Though Lippmann goes much farther in the direction of agnosticism or
even atheism than did the deists and though he repudiates
the God of the deists and their natural revelation as well as
the God of the Christian and his supernatural revelation, it
is evident that the "acids of modernity"[17] of Lippmann's
thought include not only radical empiricism and instrumentalism and evolutionary science but also the bitter attacks
upon revelation and historical Christianity which were
made by the deists.[18]

B. THE INFLUENCE OF DEISM UPON NINETEENTH AND EARLY TWENTIETH CENTURY ANTI-CHRISTIAN AGITATION

Most of the philosophical schools of thought of which
cognizance has just been taken not only manifest some influence of the works of the deists but also something of an
anti-Christian spirit. But in them the anti-Christian
element is but a part of an extensive philosophical system.
Attention is now to be directed to the works of men who
made attacking the Bible and historical Christianity more
their main concern. In this study, national boundary lines
need not be given special emphasis.

Throughout the nineteenth century and the first third of
the twentieth century there have continued to be not only
individuals here and there who have disbelieved in the
Christian religion and who have been openly hostile to it
but there have been cliques in smaller villages and more
pretentious clubs and organized societies in larger cities and
in some college and university centers that, under various
names, have carried on an active anti-Bible and anti-Christian propaganda. These individuals, groups and societies
represent a wide variety of attitudes and methods. Some
wish to retain the Bible and the name "Christian" but would
radically revise the former and would change the meaning
of the latter term from its historical one. Some would
wholly discard both Bible and Christianity. Some could be
classed as agnostic, some skeptic, some deistic and some
radically atheistic. Practically all are anti-supernaturalists
and rationalists in theology, if they may be said to have a
theology. Some are cold dispassionate reasoners while

16) LIPPMANN, WALTER, *A Preface to Morals*. New York, The Macmillan Co., 1929. p. 214.
17) *op. cit.*, p. 51.
18) *op. cit.*, pp. 154, 174.

others are bitter and heated disputants. Some approach the subject of religion from the standpoint of some school of philosophy, others from the standpoint of evolutionary scientific theory while others come at the subject of religion from the viewpoint of some social or economic theory like socialism or communism. Nearly all of them like to be considered liberals, rationalists and freethinkers. Few of them like to be called by such names as "Infidel," "Skeptic," "Agnostic" or "Atheist," evidently feeling that some appro- brium attaches itself to these terms. There are exceptions to this, however, in such clubs as the Russian "Society of the Godless" and the recently incorporated organization in America that has branches in a number of universities and that has as its avowed purpose the promotion of atheism. A few anti-Christian clubs have, in a spirit of facetious irreverence, taken such names as "The Society of the Damned." Several nineteenth century organizations incor- porated the term "secularist" into their names to emphasize their lack of interest in extra-mundane matters. Their lead- ers said they did not deal in futures. "Rationalist" socie- ties are common in both England and America. England has a "Rationalist Press Association" that publishes and distributes much anti-Christian literature. "The Truth Seeker Co., Inc." does the same thing in America. "It denies the inspiration and infallibility of the Bible, and asserts the human origin of that book." Joseph McCabe is one of the chief infidel writers for this company as well as for the atheistic publication started in 1933 which, in a few months, has secured several thousand subscribers.

In England, France and America, the small town infidel groups and scattered infidels are mostly given to lampoon- ing and ridiculing Bible stories and Bible characters and haggling over small matters of detail much as many of the eighteenth century deists did and often in nearly the same language. In France, this sort of thing can be traced to Voltaire. In America it goes back through Ingersoll to Paine and Voltaire. In England it goes back to Shaftesbury and Voltaire. This sort of thing sometimes gets into print as in Croffut's pamphlet entitled "Some Funny Bible Stories."

The more weighty attacks upon the Bible and the histori- cal Christian church are generally along either the line of evolutionary scientific theory or of the modern destructive Higher Criticism of the Bible or of monistic philosophy. Evolution, in a Darwinian or modified Darwinian form, is

generally assumed to be true and to be inconsistent with
Bible history and particularly with the Genesis creation
story. Supernaturalism is repudiated and with it miracles,
prophecy and incarnation and the whole doctrine of a
supernaturally inspired book. Reason is made the ultimate
authority in matters of religion as well as everywhere else.
Thus these modern forms of opposition to the Bible and,
historical Christianity have very much in common with the
deists of the eighteenth century but approach their conclusions not from the starting point of a determining conception of God as did the eighteenth century deists but from
the standpoint of a determining conception of nature and
her processes. Though the more recent enemies of the Bible
and Christianity have generally been agreed in their repudiation of supernaturalism and the Bible and the creeds
of the church and any authority other than the human
reason and though they have generally accepted evolution
and monism of either the pantheistic type (Spinoza and
Haldane) or the materialistic type (Hobbes, Priestly, San-
tayana, Watson, et al.), they have varied greatly in their
attitude toward the Bible and Christ and also in what they
propose to substitute for the things of religion which they
have rejected. The position of some is almost entirely negative and destructive. Such offer no substitute for what they
destroy. Some offer a theism based on natural theology
and leaving out Christ. Some offer a naturally achieved
morality as a substitute for religion. Some offer pure
humanism. Some would substitute a humble, reverent contemplation of the sum total of all reality which they sometimes call the Universe and sometimes God. Some would
entirely repudiate the Bible as not only uninspired but full
of what they regard as falsehood and unworthy teachings.
Others would reject only the Old Testament but would retain the New for its high moral teachings, though they
would eliminate the supernatural from it. Most of these
have much in common with deism in their negative attacks
on the Bible. Such as champion a theism based only on
natural theology are almost identical in their position with
eighteenth century deists except that they start their reasoning from the standpoint of evolutionary science rather than
from a scholastic definition of God and his attributes and
that they do not so magnify the element of clerical imposture. Those who discard the Old Testament but hold to the
New after they have eliminated its supernaturalism are

following closely in the footsteps of many deists such as Middleton and Jefferson.

In the first seventy or eighty years of the nineteenth century the tendency among free-thinkers in both England and America was to assume an agnostic (a word used by the scientist Tindall) or skeptic position. In the last fifty or sixty years the tendency of free-thinkers has been to get into the camps of either the pantheizing monists, of the humanists or of the outright atheists. Those who have desired to retain at least some of the Bible and to retain some degree of union with the historical Christian church and to retain the name "Christian" have joined the now powerful "Modernist" faction in the church. Avowed infidelity has perhaps been more common in England than in America.[19] Bradlaugh was the outstanding popular leader of the attack upon Christianity in England about the same time that Robert Ingersoll was the outstanding spokesman for infidelity in America. But such writers as J. M. Robertson and Leslie Stephen were also working on the side of infidelity.

The writings of Rousseau and Voltaire are still widely read in France and perpetuate deistic ideas and sentiments. The influence of the positivism of Comte also still persists. The deistic views and attitudes that derive from these has been modified in France by Freudian psychology, La Marckian and Darwinian evolution theories, as well as by the socialist teachings of men like Saint-Simon and Fourier and by the modern "Higher Criticism of the Bible" in the starting of which the French physician Jean Astruc had an important part. In the direct anti-Christian agitation in France, the influence of the deist Voltaire and of the more radical thinkers La Mettrie and D'Holbach is evident. The influence of the higher criticism and of evolution theory is more apparent in such liberal writers as Renan and Sabatier. In all, there is a strong anti-supernaturalistic attitude that dates back to the eighteenth century deists.

Hostility to Christianity in Germany is chiefly found today in the camp of radical socialists and goes back to Karl Marx and his teaching that religion is the opium by which rulers and their subservient priests seek to keep their servile peoples quiet and obedient. Marx was born in 1818 at a

---

[19] KEYSER, LEANDER S., *A System of Christian Evidence*. Burlington, Iowa, The Lutheran Literary Board, 1924. Third Edition Revised. pp. 60–61. cf. P. M. MUIR'S *Modern Substitutes for Christianity*, GEORGE HENSLOW'S *Present Day Rationalism Critically Examined*, and C. L. DRAWBRIDGE'S *Popular Attacks on Christianity* (1914).

time when deism was still quite prevalent and he evidently
imbibed much of its viewpoint that priests or clergy are the
selfish and unscrupulous corrupters of religion. Some of
the open hostility to Christianity found in Germany today
is traceable chiefly to Darwinian evolution as developed by
the materialist Haeckel. Some, as already indicated, is
traceable chiefly to the line of speculative philospohy. Some
of it is chiefly a development from the radical part of the
"Higher Criticism" of the Bible, the relation of which to
deism will be considered later. In Germany, as in America
and England, there has been a considerable growth of
"modernism" within the church which retains the name
Christian but opposes the supernaturalism of historical
Christianity. The whole world watches with interest and
much concern the rapidly developing Nazi movement in
Germany that is led by Adolf Hitler. This concern is not
only due to the possible consequence of this development to
international peace but also to religion. The centralizing,
autocratic tendencies of the Nazi program seem to distinctly threaten any independence of the church in its relation to
the state and are likely to add a new chapter to the long
story of the relation between church and state. This is a
tendency directly in opposition to the idea of the separation
of church and state and to the principle of religious toleration which were championed by all the deists except Hobbes.
The anti-Jewish attitude of the Nazi regime is also leading
to a marked tendency to repudiate and discard the Old Testament, an attitude that was characteristic of most of the
eighteenth century deists and especially of Thomas Morgan.
In the history of the Bible, attacks upon the Old Testament
have usually been forerunners of attacks upon the New
Testament also. For this reason and because the leading
New Testament characters and writers are almost as much
Jewish as are those of the Old it would seem likely that the
Nazi drift would lead to an anti-Bible and anti-Christian
development, even as the anti-Jewish and anti-Old Testament sentiment among deists of the eighteenth century developed into an anti-Bible and anti-Christian movement.
In the background of this Nazi movement against the Old
Testament lies the deistic attacks of the eighteenth century
and the radical higher criticism of the Bible in the nineteenth century, a criticism which itself rooted back into
eighteenth century deism.

The most astounding and widespread attack upon religion, including not only Christianity but all other particu-

lar or positive religions as well, in all history is taking place in the Bolshevik Soviet Republic that now occupies that vast region that was but recently the Russia dominated by the czars and the eastern orthodox church.   This revolt against religion is but one element in a great revolution that involves also the whole economic, social and political life of the people of Soviet-land.   Lenin, Trotzsky, Stalin, and other founders and leaders of this radical experiment were thoroughly steeped in Marxism with its theory that religion is the opium of the people and that clergy are the tools with which tyrants seek to keep the masses subservient to them.   And, as suggested above, Marx got this conception of the clergy to a large degree from the deistic atmosphere in which he was brought up and educated.   Anti-clericalism and hostility to particular or positive religions and charges that the clergy, working with rulers, developed and main-tained the doctrines and rituals of religion for selfish ends and to keep the people subservient to them, were common characteristics of nearly all the deists.[20]   However, though having this element in common with and indirectly derived from eighteenth century deism, it is not the natural religion of deism that the Soviet government is inculcating, but athe-ism.   As a substitute for the positive religions such as Christianity and Mohammedanism, the Soviet proposes a religious devotion to the communistic principles and pro-gram of the government.   The nearest historical parallel to what Russia is now doing in matters of religion is found in the very temporary experiment of the French when they cast off Christianity for a time during their great Revolution of 1789.   But the thing then substituted was quite different. The rest of the world watches this vast and at times cruel experiment with even more interest and concern than it shows for the Nazi movement in Germany.

Before leaving this subject of modern anti-Christian agi-tation movements and the relation of deism to them it is well to consider the work of a few particular representa-tive men in this field.   By doing so the concrete deistic line of influence can be better pointed out.

1. LESLIE STEPHEN.

In preparing to write his important two volume work, *History of English Thought in the Eighteenth Century,* several editions of which have been published, and his *Free-thinking and Plainspeaking.*   Stephen became thoroughly

---

[20] above, Part II.

familiar with the English deists and their writings. This
familiarity manifests itself in frequent references to them
and many acute and not gentle criticisms of them that occur
throughout both works. He gives his own judgment that
the rationalism of the eighteenth century in England was
"founded upon a decayed system of philosophy" and therefore suffered from a "deeply seated delicacy of constitution."[21] He describes the deist writers as a "ragged regi-
ment" inferior in learning and ability to their opponents
and their works he describes as "but shabby and shriveled
little octavos, generally anonymous, such as lurk in the
corner of dusty shelves, and seem to be the predestined
prey of moths."[22] Woolston, he pillories with the phrase,
"Poor mad Woolston, most scandalous of the deists."[23]
Annet is described as "a rather disreputable link between
Woolston and Thomas Paine."[24] There is something of the
contempt of a British aristocrat and scholar in the sneer
with which Stephen describes Chubb,—"the good Salisbury
tallow-chandler, who ingeniously confesses, while criticising
the Scriptures, that he knows no language but his own."[25]
Stephen speaks of the whole deist controversy, including
both the weapons used in attack and the armor used in
defence, as being as obsolete as medieval castles and knights
in armor.[26] Stephen's own position is that of philosophical
and religious agnosticism.[27] His admiration is for Spinoza,
Hume and Darwin.[28] He speaks with contempt of deists
who "could argue seriously that all the prophets and
apostles were vulgar imposters."[29] But orthodox Christians
are not likely to think much better of Stephen's own position
that the doctrines of Christian theology are but the "conse-
cration of delusive dreams,"[30] that Christ is not divine,[31]
that belief in immortality as well as mystery is to be rejected.[32] Stephen frankly refuses to be called "Christian"
and urges a humanistic religion. The reader of Stephen's

---

21) STEPHEN, *The History of Eng. Thought in the Eighteenth Century*, vol. 1, pp. 33–34.
22) STEPHEN, *The History of Eng. Thought in the Eighteenth Century*, vol. 1, pp. 86, 87.
23) *op. cit.*, vol. 1, pp. 77–78.
24) *loc. cit.*
25) *loc. cit.*
26) *op. cit.*, vol. 1, p. 92.
27) STEPHEN, *Freethinking and Plainspeaking*, p. 371 ff.
28) *op. cit.*, pp. 114, 115. cf. *The Hist. of Eng. Thought*, etc., p. 77 f.
29) *Freethinking and Plainspeaking*, p. 297 ff.
30) STEPHEN, *Freethinking and Plainspeaking*, p. 388.
31) *op. cit.*, p. 391.
32) *op. cit.*, p. 115.

works senses that in spite of his criticisms of the deists he had much in common with them. Though Stephen censures the deists and especially Shaftesbury for the use of ridicule and mockery, he evidently learned the art from them for he practices it himself against the orthodox church viewpoint.[33]

2. JOHN M. ROBERTSON.

Robertson, in preparing his *Short History of Freethought Ancient and Modern* (1899) became thoroughly familiar with the writings of the eighteenth century deists. He admired the English deists and took sharp exception to Stephen's words reflecting upon their worth and dignity as writers.[34] He also shows himself much in sympathy with many of the positions held by the deists.[35] He thinks most of the criticisms of orthodox religion made by Herbert of Cherbury are still valid.[36] He ranks the influence of the writings of Voltaire higher than those of any other man.[37] Indeed Robertson's work is much like the *Discourse of Freethinking* of Collins in form and spirit.

3. W. CAREW HAZLITT.

Hazlitt wrote a bitter attack upon Christianity, the church and the clergy, entitled, *Man considered in relation to God and A Church*, a fifth edition of which appeared in London in 1912. His charges against the clergy are much like those found in the works of most eighteenth century deists but couched in even more violent language. He says, "It is capable of mathematical demonstration that all clergymen are fools or rogues."[38] Like Mandeville, he charged the clergy with being entirely mercenary in spirit. He wrote: "No pay, ladies, no priest. He is a stipendiary officer. It is a question of currency."[39] The aim of the clergy is wealth and power.[40] He frankly says he belongs to no church and wishes to tear down the church.[41] Quite in the tone of the more radical eighteenth century deists he remarks that in the churches "Know-Little clergymen address themselves to

---

[33] *op. cit.*, pp. 88–89, 115, 231, 254.

[34] ROBERTSON, *A Short History of Freethought Ancient and Modern*, pp. 314–317.

[35] *op. cit.*, p. 146 ff.

[36] *op. cit.*, p. 297.

[37] *op. cit.*, p. 338.

[38] HAZLITT, W. CAREW, *Man considered in relation to God and A Church*. London, Bernard Quantich. Fifth Edition, 1912. p. xiii.

[39] *op. cit.*, p. 108.

[40] *op. cit.*, p. xxxvi.

[41] *op. cit.*, pp. 5, 18.

Know-Less audiences."[42])   He calls the church a "drag-chain
and a stumblingblock."[43])   Her property, he claims, "has
been almost entirely acquired by violence or fraud."[44])
Hazlitt is in sympathy with the view of the more radical
"Mortal" deists of the eighteenth century in that he rejects
belief in a future life of rewards and punishments.   The
doctrine of such a life he regards as a "silly ecclesiastical
hoax" of a "mendacious and irresponsible church."[45])   Some
of the eighteenth century deists held Jesus as a man and
moral teacher in highest esteem while others regarded him
as an imposter.   Hazlitt seems to belong to the group that
holds a low opinion of him.   He says Jesus was indiscreet
and inconsistent and failed because he had no aptitude for
affairs, that he made no self-sacrifice but suffered as a political and secular delinquent for the misdemeanor of med-
dling in politics.[46])

Hazlitt, like the deists, asserted belief in and reverence
toward God[47]) but disbelief in any divine interposition in
the way of miracles or answers to prayer.[48])   Miracles of the
Bible he explains away as not really miracles.   The miracle
of the draught of fishes is explained by saying Jesus perceived that there was a school of fish on the other side of
the boat.   The raising of Lazarus is explained by assuming
Lazarus to have been epileptic.[49])   The only value of prayer
is as a moral exercise and discipline.[50])   His view of the
world is stated briefly as follows.   "The earth strikes me as
resembling rather a ball which has been placed by unseen
hands in a certain position, and has been left to roll whither
it lists."[51])

It is often assumed that deism is dead, but evidently
Hazlitt was just one of the deists of the more radical type.
His special fondness was for Voltaire.[52])   Like earlier deists
he brings in the story of Apollonius of Tyana,[53]) in his arguments against Christianity.

42) *Man considered in relation to God and A Church*, p. 15.
43) *op. cit.*, p. 105.
44) *op. cit.*, p. 39.
45) *op. cit.*, p. iv.
46) *op. cit.*, pp. 16, 203.
47) *op. cit.*, p. 5.
48) *op. cit.*, p. 226.   cf. pp. 75, 200.
49) *op. cit.*, p. 200.
50) *op. cit.*, p. 75.
51) *op. cit.*, p. 226.
52) *op. cit.*, pp. 134, 139.
53) *op. cit.*, p. 198.

4. ROBERT G. INGERSOLL.

During the last half of the eighteenth century, no other agitator against the Bible and Christianity gained the eminence and influence in the United States that was attained by the eloquent orator Ingersoll. By his speeches, he scattered his views widely. His written works greatly extended the reach of his influence. Around him rallied nearly all who were unfriendly to the Bible and the Christian religion. He and the earlier deist Thomas Paine became the leading authorities of all infidel groups. The Dresden Edition of his works occupies twelve large volumes.

Ingersoll sounded the praises of Hume, Spinoza and especially of Voltaire and Paine.[54] His works abound in references to Voltaire and Paine and contain some references showing familiarity with the earlier eighteenth century deists.[55]

Ingersoll not only praised the deists and quoted them much but he also agreed with them fully on many matters. Like them he repudiated miracles. Like them he regarded the Bible as a book naturally and not supernaturally produced and as a book full of errors and mistakes. He liked to talk and write about the "mistakes of Moses." Like them he spoke and wrote much about the cruelties of the Bible and against such Bible stories as those of the fall of man, of the resurrection of Christ and also of his ascension.[56] Like them he heaped ridicule upon the stories of the Bible about such characters as Abraham, Lot, David, Elijah and Elisha.[57] Like them he was especially unfavorable to the church teaching concerning the death or atonement of Christ.[58] As with the deists, so too with Ingersoll, much of the work done was negative or destructive in character. He evidently thought it important to remove things that he felt to be inconsistent with truth. He wrote, near the beginning of his works, "The destroyer of weeds, thistles and thorns is a benefactor, whether he soweth grain or not."[59]

But though extensive sections of Ingersoll's work were little more than republications of the works of earlier deists, he himself was not a deist but an agnostic, or, perhaps an

[54] INGERSOLL, ROBERT G., *The Writings of Robert G. Ingersoll.* New York, C. P. Farrell, Dresden Edition, 1900. 12 vols. vol. 1., pp. 129, 138 ff.; vol. 4, pp. 358–391, 159 ff.; vol. 5, pp. 447–524; vol. 7, p. 18; vol. 8, p. 28 f.; vol. 11, p. 482.
[55] *loc. cit.*
[56] *op. cit.*, vol. 1, pp. 15, 443; vol. 2, pp. 15 ff.; 400 ff., 433 ff.
[57] *op. cit.*, vol. 2.
[58] *Writings of Robert G. Ingersoll*, vol. 2, p. 369 ff. cf. vol. 1, p. 16.
[59] *op. cit.*, vol. 1, title page.

atheist. Unlike the deists he repudiated the very idea of a creation.[60] He regarded God as but a man made invention, saying, "An honest God is the noblest work of man."[61] At times he was definitely opposed to belief in a future life while at other times he seemed a bit uncertain and agnostic on that point.[62]

In so far as deism was an anti-Bible and anti-Christian movement, it was popularized in recent times by Ingersoll. However he repudiated its positive element with the exception of the one point that he agreed with the deists in emphasizing morality rather than doctrine or ritual.[63]

5. CLARENCE S. DARROW.[64]

Clarence Darrow (1857-), noted criminal lawyer, is probably the most widely known and ablest of the living champions of agnosticism and infidelity in America. He gained great fame as a lawyer by his skilled defence of noted socialist and communist agitators. He increased it by his work as attorney for the young atheists Loeb and Leopol᾿ in the notorious Frank murder case. He attracted still wider attention when he became the chief legal opponent of William Jennings Bryan in the far-famed *Scopes trial* at Dayton, Tennessee, in which the right to teach evolution was the issue. He also has lectured and debated on politics, prohibition, science and religion in almost every state of the Union, always on the radically liberal side of every issue. He has sought to spread his views still further by his books which include an autobiography in which he frankly states and argues for his agnostic or even atheistic views and a work entitled *An Eye For An Eye* which is an attack upon the Mosaic legislation of the Old Testament.

Darrow is not a deist, but an agnostic or atheist. He repudiates both the *Natural Religion,* which the deists championed, and the *Supernatural Religion* of the opponents of deism who championed revelation. He regards religion as but a development from magic. Like the more radical of the deists he repudiates and argues against the doctrine of

---

[60] *Writings of R. G. Ingersoll,* vol. 2, p. 366; vol. 4, p. 5 ff.; vol. 2, pp. 237–259; vol. 12, p. 341; vol. 6, p. 61.

[61] *op. cit.,* vol. 1.

[62] *op. cit.,* vol 6, pp. 52–55 ff.

[63] *op. cit.,* vol. 1, p. 443.

[64] C. S. Darrow is not to be confused with Floyd L. Darrow. F. L. Darrow also is decidedly anti-Christian and anti-supernaturalistic in viewpoint, rejecting all miracles and regarding the Gospels as wholly unhistorical. vid. DARROW, FLOYD L., *Miracles, A Modern View.* Indianapolis, Bobbs-Merrill Co., 1926. pp. 49, 87, 92, and esp. p. 187, where deistic influence is indicated.

immortality. He sees no evidence in nature of design or of
a Creator. It is in his attitude toward and attacks upon
revelation and in his satirical witticisms against the clergy
that he is at one with the deists.[65]

It is not difficult to trace the route by which deistic influence reached Darrow. He writes:[66] "Neither of my parents
held any orthodox religious views. They were both readers
of Jefferson, Voltaire and Paine; both looked at revealed
religion as these masters taught.—My father was the village
infidel—."

C. THE INFLUENCE OF DEISM UPON THE MODERN
CRITICAL STUDY OF THE BIBLE

During the last two centuries two important branches of
Bible study have been developed. These are known as
"Higher Criticism" and "Lower Criticism." Higher criticism is that branch of Bible study which seeks to ascertain
the age, authorship, character, sources and value of the
documents which compose the Bible. It seeks these ends
primarily by a study of the documents themselves but does
not hesitate to call into its service the sciences of geography,
history, ethnography and archæology. Lower criticism is
that branch of Bible study that seeks to determine the
correct text of the original writers of the various books that
compose the Bible. Both of these are entirely legitimate
and valuable branches of Biblical scholarship which may be
and have been pursued by both very conservative and orthodox Christian scholars and very liberal and unorthodox
men. In the popular mind and language, however, the distinction between "Higher" and "Lower" critics is entirely
lost sight of and the term "Higher Critics" is applied to
liberal and radical scholars in either the field of the Higher
or the Lower criticism whose conclusions are not regarded
as "orthodox." The term "Higher Critic" thus becomes the
equivalent of "Destructive Critic."

Modern enemies of the Bible and of historical Christianity
naturally draw upon not only philosophical systems which
are unfavorable to Christianity and upon scientific theories,
such as some forms of the theory of evolution, which are
unfavorable to Christianity and the Bible, and upon the
various unfriendly criticisms advanced by older enemies of
the faith, but also draw upon the conclusions of these more

---

[65] DARROW, C., *The Story of My Life*. N. Y. and London, C. Scribner's
Sons, 1932. pp. 77, 383, 387 ff., 411, 412 ff.

[66] *op. cit.*, p. 14.

recent destructive critics for material in the making of their own attack upon conservative Christianity. Some of those making this use of the work and "results" of the destructive critics are themselves openly enemies of the whole Christian faith while others would retain for themselves the name "Christian" and also would claim that they have a more correct and a more profitable viewpoint concerning the Bible and its use and value than do those more conservative groups who repudiate the work and methods of these destructive critics.[67] Thus the Higher and Lower criticism have become an important factor in the present day conflict between Christianity and infidelity and also in the conflict between the conservative and liberal branches within the Christian church.

The development into elaborate branches of Biblical scholarship of the Higher and Lower criticism, especially the Higher criticism, is traceable rather directly to the age of the English deists and to a large extent to the influence of the work of those deists. Evidence for this statement will follow. Arising from this source and in the atmosphere of deism and with the deistic hostility to the Bible, conceived of as a supernatural revelation, all about it in its early development, it is not strange that the "Higher criticism" early gained the reputation of being "Destructive" and unfavorable to the Bible and orthodox Christianity. Thus, through the channel of the still very influential work of the Bible critics, Higher and Lower, the influence of eighteenth century deism is still at work.

A study of the history of "Bible Criticism" and especially of the "Higher Criticism" of the Bible shows that deism had a considerable influence upon the early development of these lines of Biblical scholarship. The antisupernaturalism of the deists led them not only to reject the miracles of the Bible but also to reject the church doctrine of the inspiration of the Bible. Having rejected these, the deists felt the necessity for supplying some plausible theory of the natural origin of the Bible and of its contents. This led to a study of the origin of the Books of the Bible, to investigations of questions of canon and authorship. These were investigations in the field of Higher Criticism. It also led to discussions of text, interpolations, corruption of text and modes of transmission of documents. This was the field of the Lower Criticism.

---

[67] Fosdick, Harry Emerson, *The Modern Use of the Bible.* New York, The Macmillan Co., 1924.

Thomas Hobbes was the first of the deists to enter extensively upon these lines of discussion. He discussed both the
canon and the transmission of the Scriptures from the standpoint of an anti-supernaturalist.[68]   Following Hobbes,
Toland discussed the canon of Scripture in his *Amyntor*.
Shaftesbury argued that the Bible should be subjected to
criticism just as are other books and himself criticised it
severely.[69]   A crude, elementary form of Higher Criticism
is also found in Collins' treatment of prophecies. All of
these assumed the truth of antisupernaturalism, rejecting
the notion of a supernatural revelation, just as most of the
Higher Critics of later times have done.

The main development of Bible criticism took place, not
in England among the deists, but on the continent and
especially in Germany. The early impetus given by Hobbes
to the examination of the canon of Scripture and to the
questions of content, authorship, transmission and value of
the Scriptures led Spinoza to take up and carry further
these lines of study. This famous Dutch Jewish philosopher
who was much under the influence of Hobbes not only carried on Bible investigation in the spirit of Hobbes but also
transmitted the influence of Hobbes' work to Germany
where Spinoza had great influence as a philosopher and
where the Higher Criticism had its full development. In
1753, Jean Astruc, a freethinking French physician who had
much in common with English deists in his attitude toward
the Bible and supernaturalism, published his *Conjectures
Sur La Genese*,[70] *etc.*, in which he seized upon what is said
about the different names of God in Exodus 6:3 and with
that as a "clue" started the division of Genesis and the
Pentateuch into hypothetical documents ascribed to various
authors.[71]   Later Higher Critics have taken this docu-
mentary theory and with many and great changes and
elaborations upon it have worked out a naturalistic explanation of the origin, authorship and value of various parts
of the Old Testament. Because of his part in this development Astruc has been called the "Father of Higher Criticism" although he has scarcely more claim to that title than

68) above, p. 75.
69) above, p. 128. cf. GIZYCKI, *Die Philosophie Shaftesbury's*. Leipzig und Heidelberg, C. F. Winter'sche Verlagshandlung, 1876. pp. 166,
169.
70) ASTRUC, JEAN, *Conjectures Sur La Genese*, etc. Bruxelles, Chez
Fricx, Imprimeur de Sa Majeste, 1753.
71) *op. cit.*, p. 17.

Spinoza or Hobbes.[72]   As noted above,[73] the writings of
English and French deists were first largely spread in such
German university centers as Tübingen, Leipsic, Halle, Jena
and Göttingen.   It was in these centers also, and more
especially in Tübingen which soon gave its name to a radical school of Bible criticism and liberal theology, that the
Higher Criticism had its fullest development and expression.
There seems to be a direct connection between these two
facts.   Cheyne, himself a leading English Higher Critic, in
his book on the *Founders of Criticism,* justly points out the
great indebtedness of the early schools of criticism to English deism.   James Orr points out that much in the works of
the Higher Critics is already found as vigorously stated in
the works of such deists as Morgan, Bolingbroke and
Paine.[74]   German Higher Critics first applied their critical
methods of study to the Old Testament.   Leading German
Higher Critics in this field include such names as De Wette,
Vatke, Eichhorn, Ewald, Graf and Wellhausen.   Eichhorn
seems to have first given the name "Higher Criticism" to
this branch of scholarly investigation.   These men, though
all "Higher Critics," represent different schools of Higher
Criticism.   The school most influential in recent times is
the so-called Graf-Wellhausen school.   F. C. Baur and D. F.
Strauss applied the methods of the Higher Criticism to the
New Testament.

As deism first attained its fuller development in England
and then spread to France, Germany, America and other
lands, so Higher Criticism developed first and most fully in
Germany and then spread to other countries.   Kuenen in
Holland, Renan in France, Colenso, Cheyne and Driver in
England, H. P. Smith, Foster and Kent in America are a
few of the many representatives of this form of Criticism
as it has spread from Germany to other lands.   Thus,
through its influence in the beginning and early development of Biblical criticism, eighteenth century deism extends
its influence widely down to the present time.   Many people
of today who do not even know the names of such deists as
Toland, Collins, Hobbes and Bolingbroke do know and are

---

[72] How the Higher Criticism, thus begun, developed to its present
large proportions and wide influence can be read in *An Outline of Christianity. The Story of Our Civilization.*   New York, Bethlehem Publishers, Inc., Dodd, Mead & Co., 1926.   5 vols.   vid. especially vol. 4, pp. 350–
394.

[73] above, pp. 191–193.

[74] ORR, JAMES, *The Bible Under Trial.*   New York, A. C. Armstrong
& Son, 1907.   Second Edition, p. 17.

much influenced by the writings of such Bible critics as Wellhausen, Driver and Kent. Even more are influenced by writers who, though not themselves Higher Critics, accept as valid the conclusions of such critics.

Higher and Lower critics insist that the Bible be subjected to examination and criticism upon the same plane as any other ancient book. Orthodox friends of the Bible do not object to this. Destructive critics also insist that only a purely naturalistic explanation of the origin and contents of the books of the Bible can be allowed. No unique supernatural inspiration by God is conceded to Bible writers. The best of them are regarded only as men of unusual spiritual wisdom and insight who, out of a varied and rich experience of life made valuable moral and religious "discoveries." But these are "discoveries" and not "revelations" from God with divine authority and infallibility. No miracle and no prophecy that would require the miraculous element of a direct revelation from the all-knowing God is allowed. Miracle stories are explained in various ways as exaggerations or myths or crafty inventions, or interpolations or superstitions. Miraculous prophecy is disposed of by making the date of the writing as a whole which contains it later than the event or by insisting the prophetic passage is an interpolation of late date or by putting a different interpretation upon the prophetic passage that removes the miraculous foresight from it. This refusal of the destructive critics to allow any supernaturalism in the Bible is the point at which the influence of deism upon Biblical criticism is most apparent. It is to this antisupernaturalism in the assumptions of the critics that the orthodox friends of the Bible object. They maintain that such critics are assuming the truth of the very thing they have to prove if claims as to authorship, date, value and content of various parts of the Bible are to be established. Another important principle in the work of the negative or destructive critics is the assumption of the truth of an evolutionary view of religious history. It is assumed that any passage of high ideals and lofty spiritual insight must be late and only passages of lower ethical ideals and less noble religious insights are conceded an early date. This element in much modern Bible criticism is naturally enough connected with the antisupernaturalism that rejects revelation and talks only of naturally attained religious discoveries. However, this bringing of an evolution principle into Bible criticism is not an influence of deism upon Bible criticism but rather an influence that comes from the prestige of the doctrine of evolution that arose at a later date than the deists.

The negative or destructive Higher Criticism retains not a few of the methods of the deists in dealing with particular Bible prophecies and miracles. But it brings in an evolutionary explanation of the history of Bible books and religion which is not found in the deists. It also drops most of the deistic charges of deliberate and selfish corruption of the Bible and religion by priests. It is much more scholarly than was deism and also puts much more emphasis on languages and language study. Yet there remains in it quite enough that reminds of the deistic source in which it had its origin and of which it can rightly be regarded as one of the fruits.

D. THE INFLUENCE OF DEISM UPON PRESENT DAY "MODERNISM" IN RELIGION

The terms "Modernism" and "Modernist" were first used to designate a liberal movement and group within the Roman Catholic Church. Two of its most prominent leaders and representatives were the Frenchman Loisy and the Englishman George Turrell. They claimed to represent the world of up-to-date scientific thought and revealed a bias against supernaturalism. They did not wish, however, to separate from the church. But in 1907 the Pope condemned the movement as "The compendium and poisonous essence of all heresies." A false philosophy was declared to be at the root of the heresies of the modernists in history, dogma and Bible criticism. Its leaders were condemned by name and the whole movement was vigorously suppressed. How much of its spirit continues under cover within the church cannot be known.

About the time of the suppression of this thought movement within the Roman Catholic Church it became common practice to designate a somewhat like spirited liberal element within the various branches of the Protestant Church as "Modernists" and their viewpoint as "Modernism." A few religious conservatives wrote books and pamphlets naming and emphasizing what they regarded as fundamental articles of the Christian faith. A few conservatively led church organizations also issued statements of what they considered fundamental and essential Christian doctrines. This soon led to the practice of designating Protestant religious conservatives as "Fundamentalists." Thus began the alignment of Protestants into "Modernists" and "Fundamentalists." Between these two antagonistic schools of religious thought there exists a less vocal group of considerable size whose members do not wish to be considered as either Fundamentalists or Modernists. They protest sympathy and general agreement in doctrine with the Fundamentalists but disagreement with the combative, dogmatic, intolerant and exclusionist spirit that they find characteristic of most Fundamentalists. They disagree with the Modernists in doctrine but would let them stay in the church, letting the church be an "inclusive" organization in which men of differing theological viewpoints would work together in peace for the moral and social progress of the world. This rather large group has no accepted name like the other two factions but is often referred to as the "Middle-of-the-Road" or "Pacifist" or "Inclusionist" group. It usually votes with the Modernists in Church conventions, conferences and assemblies. There are some who are in the main in sympathy with Modernist views but who dislike the name because it is associated often with more radical opinions with which they do not sympathize. They would rather be considered just as liberal, broad-minded, up-to-date Christians. There are also some who are in most points in full sympathy with the Fundamentalist position but who do not like the pugnacious spirit of some of the outstanding Fundamentalist leaders and who do not agree with the particular pre-millennial doctrine of the second coming of Christ on which those leaders insist. These prefer to be considered as simply conservative, orthodox Christians rather than as Fundamentalists. It is to be borne in mind that schools of thought invariably have within them adherents some of whom are more radical and some more conservative than others. There were deists who disliked to be called by that term because they had little sympathy with more radical deists and there were radical deists who gloried in the term in its most radical connotation. So there are "Modernists" and "Fundamentalists" who are radical representatives of these schools and who glory in the name while there are others who dislike the designation applied to them because of the connotation of the term.

Although representatives of "Modernist" and "Fundamentalist" schools of religious thought can be found in all lands, the lines have been more sharply drawn in America than elsewhere. Therefore Modernism and the influence of deism upon it can best be studied by examining the teach-

ings of outstanding Modernists in America. Lyman Abbott,
Henry Preserved Smith, C. A. Briggs and Washington Glad-
den were forerunners of the Modernist movement and entertained views much akin to those of present day Modernists.
However, the term "Modernist" had not yet come into cur-
rent use in their day to designate that liberal school of religious thought. Harry Emerson Fosdick, William Pierson
Merrill, Rufus M. Jones, Francis McConnell, Henry Sloane
Coffin, Shailer Matthews, and William E. Hocking are
prominent leaders among American Modernists. The
Christian Century is the outstanding Modernist religious
journal. Among prominent Fundamentalists who oppose
Modernism are such men as Riley, G. Machen, W. B. Greene,
C. E. Macartney and S. G. Craig. *Christianity Today* is
perhaps the outstanding Fundamentalist religious journal.

The Fundamentalist does, as Dr. Snowden says,[75] believe
that the foundations of truth and life are of primary importance and to be well guarded. He is invariably a man of
conservative temperament who is slow to give up the old
and slow to accept the new. The Modernist, on the other
hand, is invariably a man of liberal and adventurous temperament who gives up the old easily and accepts the new
readily. The Modernist is likely to regard the Fundamentalist as much too slow in giving up what the Modernist is
sure is obsolete and therefore he charges him with medievalism.[76] The Modernist also regards the Fundamentalist
as altogether too slow in accepting the theories and conclusions and discoveries of more recent philosophy, science
and Bible criticism. Because of this he is prone to regard
the Fundamentalist as an obscurantist and to read him out
of the ranks of intelligent and scholarly men. The Modernist claims for himself and his school of thought the honorable distinction of being open-minded, scholarly, intelligent and up-to-date. The Fundamentalist charges the Modernist with intellectual pride, with unfairness, with a much
too great readiness to take up with the latest scientific theories that are likely soon to prove unsound and temporary,
with a much too great alacrity in giving up facts and doctrines that are essential to a vital and full-orbed Christianity
though no completely established facts of science or history
require such surrender, and with seeking to substitute for
Christianity what is essentially a different religion while

75) SNOWDEN, JAMES H., *Old Faith and New Knowledge.* Cornwall,
N. Y., Harper & Bros., 1928. p. 18.
76) SNOWDEN, *Old Faith and New Knowledge*, p. 18, footnote.

still using the Christian nomenclature and bearing its in-signia. This last charge of duplicity and of being traitors to the Christian faith while remaining within the Christian camp is, of course, only made against the more extreme Modernists. In the heated controversies between these two schools of religious thought there has been, as in most past religious disputes, altogether too much resort to *ad homi-nem* arguments.

Inclusionists, like Mr. Snowden, are prone to define Fundamentalism and Modernism as "principles and processes and not results and doctrines" and to think of them as simply the conservative and liberal types of thought within the Church each of which has much worthy achievement to its credit, each of which is essential to the well-being of the Church, each of which is loyal to the essentials of Christianity, and therefore each of which should have a place in an inclusive Church.[77] But this is a conception of the two schools of thought which an Inclusionist and religious pacifist as between the disputants would like to hold rather than the meaning of the terms as those terms are used and understood by the common people who use them. And, after all, popular usage, not partisan likes and dislikes, must determine the definition of terms. While the distinction between conservative and liberal does remain in the terms as popularly used, there is also associated with each term, in that usage, a doctrinal connotation. The Fundamentalist is a man who accepts the unique supernatural inspiration of the Bible by God so that its message and history is the infallible and authoritative Word of God, who believes that the Bible contains miracles and supernatural prophecy and that these actually took place, who believes in the Virgin Birth of Christ, in the deity of Christ as a person in the eternal triune Godhead, in the second coming of Christ, in the vicarious atonement of Christ on the cross, in his bodily resurrection from the dead on the third day, and who believes in a future general bodily resurrection of the dead. There are many other doctrines on which nearly all who are called Fundamentalists agree such as the doctrine of the Fall and of the Holy Spirit. On a few of even the above named doctrines, especially of the doctrine of the atonement and of the second coming of Christ, there is some variety of viewpoint among Fundamentalists. Some regard the second coming of Christ as premillennial, others as post-millennial and still others as amillennial. The acceptance

---

[77] SNOWDEN, *Old Faith and New Knowledge*, pp. 19–27.

of the doctrine of the supernatural inspiration and authority of the Bible and the acceptance of the miraculous element in the Bible are probably the two most characteristic points in the positive beliefs of Fundamentalists of all denominations. Fundamentalists are unitedly agreed in rejecting the main conclusions of the Negative or Destructive Higher and Lower Critics of the Bible and opposed to the antisupernaturalistic assumptions of those critics. Most Fundamentalists are unfavorable to and many of them definitely reject the evolutionary theory that makes man a biological descendant from lower forms of life. Fundamentalists are agreed that Christianity is the final and absolute religion which should be propagated among all peoples and which should displace all other religions. Fundamentalists tend to emphasize the importance of doctrines and of being sound in doctrine.

"Modernism," as popular usage determines the meaning of that term, is at odds with most of the positions of the Fundamentalists as given above. Modernists minimize the importance of creeds and doctrines and magnify the importance of the manner and spirit of a man's living. For them, Christianity is not a creed but a way of life. Modernists do not like to speak of Christianity as true and of other religions as false nor do they like to have Christian missionaries seeking to supplant other religions with Christianity. They speak rather of Christianity as perhaps the best among many religions each of which has much of good in it to share with peoples of other faiths. They would not have Christianity seek to replace other religions but to live side-by-side with them, receiving the good things they have to impart and sharing with them the best things Christianity has to give.[78] Most Modernists are favorable to and many of them definitely accept the evolutionary theory that makes man a biological descendant from lower forms of life. While doing this they usually dismiss the Genesis story of creation as a Babylonian or Chaldean myth of little value and no authority. All Modernists accept some and many of them accept a large part of the conclusions of the negative or destructive Higher and Lower critics of the Bible. There is a general tendency among them to share the evolutionary view of the Bible critics as to the growth of the Bible and of Bible religion. They also incline to share the antisupernaturalism of the critics. Some are much more radical at

---

[78] *Re-Thinking Missions.* New York and London, Harper & Brothers, 1932.

this point than others. All Modernists reject the high doctrine of the supernatural inspiration, the inerrancy and the
infallibility of the Bible which is championed by Fundamentalists. They still speak of inspiration but by it they
mean an inspiration not differing in kind but only in degree
from the inspiration of great poets and philosophers outside the Bible field. It is not an inspiration that makes all
of the Bible the word of God with the weight of Divine
authority back of it. Modernists seldom have much to say
about the second coming of Christ but those that do speak
of it often reject the idea of his physical re-appearance. A
considerable proportion of Modernists are either agnostic
about or else definitely disbelieve in the Virgin Birth of
Christ. Many Modernists also express themselves as dis-
believers in the bodily resurrection of Christ. Most Modernists still write or speak as if they were believers in the
divinity or deity of Christ. But in some cases these terms
"divinity" and "deity" are used with a different meaning
than that which the Fundamentalist gives them. For these
Modernists all men are divine or have the divine in them
and Christ differs from other men in degree rather than in
kind. This is not deity in the sense of being a member of
the triune Godhead. Though not all Modernists openly reject Trinitarianism, the trend of Modernism is away from
Trinitarianism and toward Unitarianism, a Unitarianism
that is often pantheistic in tone. Whereas Fundamentalists
accept the priestly sacrifices and the prophetical ethical
utterances of the Bible as alike from God, the Modernist
contemns the priest and his sacrifices and esteems the
prophet whom he sets over against the priest. The Fundamentalist regards the bloody Passover, Sin-Offering and
Trespass-Offering as God-ordained types of the vicarious
atonement made by Christ on the cross of Calvary. The
Modernist regards such bloody sacrifices as relics of bar-
baric heathenism, rejects the conception of Christ's death
being a vicarious atonement or propitiation for sin, regarding it rather as just a noble martyr death, and repudiates
the Fundamentalists' conception of the way of salvation as
a repulsive "Bloody Religion." The Modernist does not
talk much about personal salvation but, in so far as he does,
he seems to regard it as an ethical attainment of the individual which is accepted by a merciful God who needs no
propitiating. The Fundamentalist regards ethical living as
a fruit rather than a root of salvation. It is characteristic
of Fundamentalism to stress personal salvation and that

through the atoning death of Christ. It is characteristic of Modernism to emphasize the social side of religion and to discuss problems of the social and industrial life and such problems as those of war and peace and race relations. Of course Fundamentalists do not entirely neglect the social side of religion nor do Modernists entirely neglect personal religion. But there is a marked difference of emphasis.

Fundamentalists generally regard Paul very highly, recognizing in him the great theologian among the writers of the Bible and the one who did most to formulate Christian doctrine. Modernists are inclined to think less highly of Paul just because he did give Christianity a doctrinal cast. They would go "back to Jesus' 'and away from Paul.

Both Modernists and Fundamentalists desire to unify our growing experience in knowledge and life. In the unifying process, the Fundamentalist is sure of the facts and doctrines of an inspired revelation, is sure that no facts discovered or yet to be discovered by science will prove inconsistent with the teachings of revelation, and is sure that any scientific theory or discovery that is inconsistent with them will not stand the test of time and further light. He points with much pleasure to the way in which the spade of the archæologist confirms the trustworthiness of revelation.[79] He is slow to cast off long held and tested doctrines. He is slow to accept new theory. On the other hand, in the unifying process, the Modernist refuses to believe that there is an inspired and inerrant revelation of doctrines and facts or that there is any list of facts and doctrines handed down from the past that is so absolutely established that no past, present or future scientific discovery can hope to modify or replace them. Indeed he believes that many of the doctrines and facts of history that the Fundamentalist regards as completely established have already been made obsolete or proved not facts by scientific discoveries and that many doctrines and items of religious history now commonly held may in the future have to be given up as new light breaks from the scientist's laboratory and the historian's study. He has little or no veneration for creeds of the past. He is inclined to readily modify them or give them up entirely. He has great respect for modern science and scientists. He is ready to quickly accept the newest scientific claim or theory. He prefers the new to the old. The Fundamentalist, on the other hand, is inclined to think that old doctrines, like old wines, are likely to be the better.

---

[79] HAMILTON, *The Basis of Christian Faith*, pp. 172–193.

If a comparison is made between the position and attitude of the present day Modernist and the eighteenth century deist, it will be found that they have many points in common and a few at which they differ. Both are boastful of their wide awake, up-to-date intelligence and inclined to read their opponents out of the list of intelligent and scholarly men. Both are boastful that they are free, untrammeled thinkers. Both hold in low esteem the creeds and traditions of the past and hold in high esteem the scientific thought of the present. Both reject the idea of a supernatural and authoritative revelation. Both are inclined to claim that their own views are the result of the latest scientific knowledge and discovery while as a matter of fact the views of both are in the main as old as the times of Celsus, Porphyry, Arius and Pelagius. Both are inclined to set the New Testament against the Old, the Prophets against the Priests, Christ against Paul and in doing so to undermine any high doctrine of Bible inspiration. Both like to claim themselves as of the party of the prophets and of Christ as against the priests and doctrinal Paul. Both are inclined to set the God of the New Testament over against the God of the Old and to talk about the cruelties of the Old Testament. Both hold in low esteem the sacrifices of the Old Testament. Both reject the doctrine that Christ's death was a vicarious propitiatory sacrifice and atonement and maintain that it was simply a martyr death. Both disbelieve in the doctrine of the Fall and the consequent depravity of man and are inclined to ridicule the Bible story of the Fall. Both have a strong bias against belief in miracles and supernaturalism and both single out much the same list of Bible miracles for negative criticism and ridicule, and the criticisms and ridicule is much the same in each. Both attack the doctrine of the Virgin Birth of Christ and in their attack both make use of heathen stories of gods having marital relations with men. Both make use of the miracle stories of other religions to discredit the Bible miracle stories. Both make special attacks upon the Bible miracle of the bodily resurrection of Jesus and this because both sense the fact that this is a citadel of supernaturalistic religion. Both make religion almost entirely a matter of ethics. Both argue against supernatural or miraculous prophecy in the Bible but the method of disposing of the prophetic passages is different because the Modernist makes use of the Higher Criticism which was not yet developed in the eighteenth century. Both make use of Comparative Religion to show that there is good in all religions and that Christianity is not the only true or final religion. The science of Comparative Religion as used by the deist was much less developed than that used by the Modernist. The deist used it in order to disparage and to lead to the discarding of all positive religions in behalf of natural religion whereas the Modernist uses it in advocating the discarding of no positive religion.

There is certainly enough in common between eighteenth century deism and twentieth century Modernism to indicate that the latter is in a large measure a continuation of or a fruit of the former. Later an attempt will be made to show how the deistic influence came down into Modernism.

However, Modernism is not to be considered as just a twentieth century repetition of eighteenth century deism. There are some striking differences between the two. Deism represents an exaggerated and extreme doctrine of the transcendance of God whereas most Modernists are inclined to stress the doctrine of the immanence of God, in some cases to the point of becoming pantheistic. Deism had a decidedly medieval scholastic flavor in its methods of argument and quotation from ancient authorities, whereas the tone and flavor of Modernistic writings is scientific. Though the deists were very friendly to the science they knew in their day, that science was in a very embryonic state as compared with present day science. Such sciences as that of Comparative Religion and of Biblical Criticism were then just beginning. Psychology and Sociology were then hardly yet in existence as sciences. Biology and Geology were also in a very undeveloped state. The doctrine of evolution, though known, had not been developed and had not assumed anything like the dominant influence in the thinking of men that it has since attained. Each of these more recently developed sciences exercises a very large influence upon the thought of Modernists and tends to make their conceptions and reasoning differ to quite an extent from those of the deists. While Modernists and deists are generally in agreement in rejecting supernatural revelation, miracles and sacrificial ordinances, the reasons which they advance for doing so, differ greatly. The deists' main line of reasoning against these was based on his conception of God and creation. He thought of God as an infinite and perfect machinist who in making a machine, the world, would make such a perfect machine that it would require no further attention from Him. To allow need for a supernatural revelation or miracles seemed to the deist a denial of the conception of

God as an infinite and perfect Creator. And it also seemed to the deist that to admit a supernatural revelation or miracles known only to a part of mankind was inconsistent with the idea of the impartiality of God. These are not the lines of reasoning used by the Modernist against revelation and miracles. He argues rather from the widely observed uniformity of nature and from the idea that the uniformity of nature is a principle which science must assume as an axiom if it is to build any superstructure. Secondary arguments against both revelation and miracles, such as setting one claimed revelation in opposition to another, ridiculing particular miracle stories, paralleling Bible miracles and Bible claims to supernatural revelation with similar miracles and claims in other faiths, are common to both deists and Modernists. The objection to bloody sacrifices and to the doctrine of the vicarious propitiatory sacrifice of Christ that they are inconsistent with the kind and merciful character of God is urged by both deist and Modernist. But the deistic explanation of the origin and transmission of these claims to revelation and these miracles and sacrifices and doctrines as the work of cunning, fraudulent and self-seeking priests and clergy is urged by but very few Modernists. Indeed the bitter anticlericalism of deism is largely missing from Modernism. Modernism looks to other theories of origin for these elements in the Bible and in religion.

Were the main sources of influence that have worked to produce Modernism to be named the following would be the more prominent among them: (1) the liberal line of theology down through the centuries including Arianism, Pelagianism, Socinianism, Arminianism, and Unitarianism; (2) the negative or destructive Biblical criticism, both Higher and Lower; (3) the work of enemies of revelation and of historical Christianity such as Celsus and Porphyry, the deists, skeptics, atheists of the eighteenth century and the agnostics like Ingersoll and Darrow of the nineteenth and twentieth centuries; (4) modern science and sciences including especially biology and geology and astronomy with their theory of evolution and the newer sciences of sociology, psychology and comparative religion. Of these it is likely that deism, Biblical criticism and evolutionary theory have had the most influence upon the development of Modernism. Since Biblical criticism in its negative aspects is, as shown above, itself a fruit of deism, its influence upon Modernism constitutes an indirect influence of deism. Since Darrow, Ingersoll and the nineteenth century agnostics were, as also shown above, largely influenced by earlier deists, their influence upon Modernism also constitutes an indirect influence of the deists. In so far as the later theological liberalism of such schools as transcendentalism and unitarianism and the latitudinarians were themselves the results of the influence of the deists, their influence upon Modernism likewise becomes an indirect influence from the earlier deism. In addition to these very important indirect lines of influence by which deism has reached and affected Modernism, there is also undoubtedly a direct influence of the deists themselves upon at least some prominent Modernist leaders. This is more easily traced than the indirect lines of influence and can best be shown by an examination of the works of some of these Modernists.

1. HARRY EMERSON FOSDICK.

Probably no other man in America is more generally recognized as a leading Modernist than Fosdick. Mention his name and Modernism comes to mind. Mention Modernism and his name immediately suggests itself. He is a man of finest personality and of unusually fine gifts as a speaker and writer. He has been a favorite preacher at University centers. His many books have an unusually wide circulation. He regularly addresses great throngs from his New York pulpit. His voice is listened to by millions over radio networks. Whether speaking over the radio or from his pulpit or in conference or through the pages of his books, Fosdick is always and everywhere the outspoken champion of Modernism in religion. Although a Baptist minister, he preached regularly for some time in the First Presbyterian church of New York City as an associate minister of the Church. While doing so he preached a sermon on the theme, "Shall the Fundamentalists Win?" which attracted wide attention and criticism that reached even the floor of the Presbyterian General Assembly and that finally led to the termination of his irregular ecclesiastical relationship with the New York Presbyterian Church. Soon he became pastor of the large new Riverside Baptist Church of New York from whose pulpit he continues his presentation of Modernist doctrines and principles. A comparison of his views with those of the deists shows some differences but shows much in common. His references to the deists indicate that he was familiar with their viewpoint and with the writings of at least some of the leading deists. He criticizes eighteenth century deism for its "sterile frigidity" and

for its putting God "in exile."[80]   He rightly notes that the
newer liberalism emphasizes the immanence rather than
the transcendance of God.[81]   He is not in sympathy with
the attitude of such deists as Toland who tried to read
mystery out of religion if not out of the universe itself.   He
insists that much of the mysterious remains[82] and quotes
with approval a saying of the inventor Thomas Edison that
"No one knows one seven-billioneth of one per cent about
anything."[83]

Yet, though there are these points of divergence from the
position of the deists in Fosdick's viewpoint, he has much in
common with the deists and shows much of their influence.
He readily accepts most of the Higher Critics' conclusions
about the Bible.   He says that as a result of the work of
these Higher Critics, "We can tell when and in what order
the deposits were laid down whose accumulated results
constitute our Scriptures."[84]   In this connection it will be
recalled that the Higher Criticism was itself one of the
fruits of deism and was largely dominated by deistic antisupernaturalism.   He readily rejects the orthodox view of
Bible inspiration and authority and bluntly says, "Of course
the Bible is not an inerrant book."[85]   He is quite in sympathy with the deistic hostility to miracles and uses much the
same lines of argument in seeking to explain stories of particular miracles recorded in the Bible.   He says that to
modern men "Miracles are antecedently improbable, stories
of them seem in general unreliable, reliance on them seems
practically undesirable, and so in the end the whole matter
becomes pretty much unbelievable."[86] He thinks the Church
of the eighteenth century found itself cornered in a dangerous position by its championing of Bible miracles.[87]   He
does not fail to make use of the argument against Bible
miracles which the deists were wont to use when they pointed to miracles in other religions and especially to the story
of Apollonius of Tyana.   Fosdick writes, "The modern man
knows that no kind of miracle is related in Scripture the
counterpart of which cannot be found repeatedly in the

[80] FOSDICK, HARRY EMERSON, *The Modern Use of the Bible*.   New
York, The Macmillan Co., 1924.   p. 264 f.
[81] *loc. cit.*
[82] FOSDICK, HARRY EMERSON, *Adventurous Religion and other Essays*.
New York and London, Harper and Bros., 1926.   p. 159.
[83] *op. cit.*, p. 154.
[84] *The Modern Use of the Bible*, p. 6.
[85] *Adventurous Religion*, etc., p. 96.
[86] *The Modern Use of the Bible*, p. 155.
[87] *op. cit.*, p. 154.

records of other religions."[88]   After Locke and others had referred to miracles and miraculous prophecy as proofs and supports of supernatural revelation, the deists, especially Collins and Woolston, had attacked these supports by explaining them away by various methods and especially by the use of an allegorical explanation. Fosdick also writes of "allegorical interpretation"[89] and "pious fraud,"[90] though not making this charge nearly so strongly as did the deists. He also seeks to get away from the literal acceptance of the miracles by asking, "What, if any, was the vital spiritual experience that our forefathers were trying to express by their category of miracle?"[91]   The following statement by Fosdick reminds one much of the attitude toward miracles and the methods of dealing with particular miracles that were shown and used by the deists. "Joshua making the sun stand still may be poetry and the story of Jonah and the great fish may be parable: the miraculous aspects of the plagues in Egypt and the magic fall of Jericho's walls may be legendary heightenings of historical events: the amazing tales of Elijah and Elisha may be largely folk-lore: and, in the New Testament, finding a coin in a fish's mouth to pay the temple tax, or walking on water, or blasting a tree with a curse, may be just such stories as always have been associated with an era of outstanding personalities and creative spiritual power. Certainly, I find some of the miracle-narratives of Scripture historically incredible."[92]   In connection with his discussion of miracles, Fosdick refers to the eighteenth century deists and particularly to Tillotson and to Conyers Middleton's *Free Enquiry*,[93] a fact that suggests that the likeness of his views to those of the deists was derived, at least in part, from them rather than accidental. Fosdick's statement that "miracles are apriori improbable" and "historically unreliable" is just a happy way of stating the exact position of the deists on miracles.

There are other likenesses between the position of Fosdick and that of the deists. Like them, he emphasizes toleration.[94]   Like them, he stresses ethical religion to the rejection of forms and creeds and the disparagement of creedal religion. Like them, he with most other Modern-

---

88) *The Modern Use of the Bible*, p. 151.
89) *op. cit.*, p. 67 f.
90) *op. cit.*, p. 132.
91) *op. cit.*, p. 156.
92) *The Modern Use of the Bible*, p. 164.
93) *op. cit.*, pp. 152–153.
94) *Adventurous Religion and other Essays*, p. 215 ff.

ists[95]) rejects the doctrine of the fall and depravity of man
and the doctrine of salvation by the vicarious propitiatory
atoning death of Christ. On the doctrines that concern the
person of Christ, it is common for Modernists to use language more nearly like that of the more orthodox element
of the Church than did the deists and Fosdick is more conservative in this respect than many other Modernists. He
frequently uses the term "God in Christ" and asserts his
belief in Christ's deity. Since it is not uncommon for
Modernists to speak of the divine in man and of the divine
in Christ as of the same kind and only differing in degree,
there has been some doubt whether or not Fosdick intends
to assert the deity of Christ in the orthodox trinitarian
sense of that word. Especially is this true because of his
expressions concerning the doctrine of the Virgin Birth of
Christ which he does not specifically deny though the tenor
of his remarks on the doctrine are unfavorable to it. He
repeats the old deist line of argument against it that the
ancient world and other religions were wont to believe in
virgin births of their great ones.[96]) His statement that "The
deification and worship of the religion's founder is no
peculiarity of Christianity"[97]) is quite in line with the argumentation of the deists against the deity of Christ and is
certainly not calculated to increase faith in that deity. He
speaks of God's character being revealed in Christ but also
as being revealed in every other form of goodness.

Although Fosdick is probably the most outstanding American representative of modernism in religion, many other
prominent and influential leaders of American thought such
as Bishop McConnell of the Methodist Episcopal Church,
Shailer Matthews of Chicago University, Henry Sloan Coffin
of Union Theological Seminary, New York City, are modernists with views and attitudes akin to those of Fosdick.[98])
Many text-books now widely used in Departments of Bible
and Departments of Religion in colleges and universities
and also many textbooks used in Theological seminaries

95) Compare Fosdick's sermon, *Shall the Fundamentalists Win?* with
George A. Gordon's views, also Modernistic, as expressed in his book,
Religion and Miracles (Boston and New York, Houghton Mifflin Co.,
1910), pp. LXIV, 214.
96) Vid. the pamphlets, *Christianity According to Dr. Fosdick*, by S. G.
Craig, and *The Deadline of Doctrine Around the Church*, by J. M. Gray.
97) FOSDICK, H. E., *As I See Religion*. New York and London. Harper and Brothers, 1932. p. 35.
98) Vid. such works as SHAILER MATTHEWS' *The Church and the
Changing Order* (New York, Macmillan Co., 1907), and *The Gospel and
the Modern Man* (New York, Macmillan Co., 1910).

and in Sunday School Teacher Training institutes represent the modernist viewpoint. Such texts as *The Old Testament Speaks* by C. S. Knopf and *The Career and Significance of Jesus* by W. B. Denny, both published in 1933, are notably of this type, as are older works by such authors as Kent and Weigle and Eiselen. Some of these are more liberal and depart farther from the conservative orthodox viewpoints than does Fosdick and others are less liberal than he is.

CHAPTER VIII

THE CONCLUSION—SUMMARY AND CRITICISM

THE fore-going study of deism has sought first of all to define and describe what is meant by the term deism. In doing this it was indicated that deism has much in common with theism, from which it began to separate in the sixteenth century. It was indicated that deism admits the existence of a God and a creation and that it emphasizes the transcendance of God. It also puts emphasis on the reign of natural law and is antagonistic to supernaturalism. It was pointed out in this connection that historically the deists gave much more attention to the negative corollaries of their main doctrine than to the setting forth or proving that doctrine itself.

Having defined deism, an attempt has been made to indicate the main source of influence that brought about the rise and development of deism. It was found that these were numerous and that some of them led back into the remote past while others were contemporary with the rise of deism itself. Among the major influences discovered and presented were the works of early pagan opponents of Christianity such as Celsus and Porphyry, the Reformation with its quarrels and wars, the advance in science, including the new geographic and astronomical discoveries, and, perhaps most fundamental of all, the scholastic conception of God somewhat modified by new scientific concepts that made the creator a great mechanic. The main position of deism seemed to be the result of men attempting to fit a conception of God inherited from the Schoolmen into a developing scientific conception of the world.

While deism formulated itself first into something of a system in France, it had its early complete development and greatest growth in England. This was not strange in view of the fact that English thought had long been inclined toward the more empirical and scientific views as exemplified in such men as Roger and Francis Bacon.

Having studied the meaning and sources of deism, an attempt has been made in Part II to study the actual history of English deism in the works of its leading literary representatives. In this connection it was necessary to study the

works of a few men other than deists because of their great
influence with deists and upon deistic thought. The most
notable man of this class was Locke. The most notable
writers among the deists themselves in the long period during which deism spread but slowly, were Herbert of Cherbury, Thomas Hobbes and Charles Blount. Then, with
Locke's influence potent, there came a rapid flowering of
deism in England with a large number of writers, the most
famous and important of which were John Toland, Anthony
Collins, the Earl of Shaftesbury, and Matthew Tindal. Following about half a century of this flourishing period of
deism there came a period of rapid decline. During this
period deistic writers tended to greater radicalism and their
thought was largely a gathering together of ideas already
found in earlier deistic writers. But while some, such as
Bolingbroke and Chubb and Morgan were spreading deistic
ideas among the masses, a skeptical note that was inimical
to the foundation principle of deism was appearing in the
works of two writers, Henry Dodwell, Jr., and David Hume.
But even before the influence of these writers was felt,
deism seemed to be showing signs of exhaustion and soon
its decay began to be evident.

In closing the study of this third or period of decline in
English deism, an attempt was made to indicate the causes
that operated to bring about that decline. Among the important causes noted were divisions among the deists themselves, the exhaustion of the subject, the undermining effect
of the new skeptical philosophy, the strong and sometimes
able literary opposition to deism on the part of apologists
in the churches, the effects of the great religious revival and
the turning of the people to pressing political and military
interests.

But though deism was soon practically dead in England,
it spread to France and then to Germany and America. As
an important distinct thought movement it had practically
ended with the eighteenth century. But its influence has
carried on into philosophical and theological thought of the
nineteenth and twentieth centuries. That influence has
been traced in Part III of this work. The influence of
eighteenth century deism has been found showing itself to
some extent in the works of individual philosophers and in
certain schools of recent or present day philosophical
thought. A still greater evidence of the influence of eighteenth century deism is found in the history and teachings
of much of modern Bible criticism, especially of the so-called

Destructive Higher Criticism. But the most direct and extensive influence of deism upon later thought is discovered in the views and writings of various infidel and anti-Christian groups from the day of the deists themselves down to the present time. Some evidence of deistic influence and of the perpetuation of certain deistic ideas and attitudes is also found in that liberal wing of present day Christianity known as "Modernism." Thus the deism of eighteenth century England, having been largely instrumental in producing the somewhat later deistic movements of France, Germany and America, and having almost ceased to exist as a distinct deistic school of thought, has nevertheless continued to exercise a not inconsiderable influence upon the thought of the two and a half centuries that have elapsed since it itself ceased to flourish. It became one of the major influences in shaping thought-trends of later days.

In purpose and character, this study of *English Deism: Its Roots and Its Fruits* has been historical rather than polemic. In order that the position of the deists might be clearly perceived and understood, the author has presented the views and arguments of all the outstanding deists with considerable fullness of detail although doing so has involved an amount of repetition of ideas likely to try the patience of the reader. No such full presentation of the many replies made to the deists could be given in the limits of this work. It should not be forgotten, however, that the replies far outnumbered the works of the deists and also outweighed them in scholarship and erudition in the judgment of even so liberal a critic as Leslie Stephen.[1] To renew the controversy now either on the side of the deists or of their opponents would be as foolish as for present day Englishmen and Frenchmen to try to fight over again the battles of the Napoleonic wars. The controversialist could find a better field for his valor by entering the religious controversies of the present day such as the controversy between the conservative and destructive critics of the Bible or between the fundamentalists and modernists or between believers in Christianity and enemies of that faith. Therefore no extended or detailed criticism of either the deists or their opponents will be entered upon here. However, some general criticisms are in order.

Undoubtedly there were many individuals and some whole branches of the Christian church in the time of the

---

[1] STEPHEN, *History of English Thought in the Eighteenth Century*, vol. 1, pp. 86–88.

deists which were putting altogether too much emphasis on
forms and rituals and ceremonies in religion and were giving altogether too little place to the ethical element. The
deistic attitude was a corrective of this evil. Unfortunately
the deists went to the opposite extreme of failing to recognize the legitimate place and value of some ritual. One is
likely to discover something of the same types of extremes
today in the modernist-fundamentalist controversy.

The best friend of the Bible and of Christianity and of the
Christian church, if well-informed, must admit that there
have been and are still some clergymen and priests of religion who have been or are selfish, some who have been too
ready to lend themselves as tools to ambitious political and
industrial leaders, and even a few who have not been above
perverting truth and doctrine for selfish ends. This was true
in the times of Elijah and Jeremiah and of Jesus. It was
true in the medieval age, in the age of the deists, and is still
true today. It cannot be denied that there have been and
that there still are such things found among the clergy as
selfishness, ambition, subserviency and even dishonesty.
Clergymen as a class would be the first to admit and the
most sincere in regretting that this is so. They would admit that this evil has been a great stumblingblock in the
way of the advance of true religion and that any clergyman
who is guilty of these faults does great harm to religion.
They would admit also that this evil does require diligent
watchfulness lest it introduce elements of unworthy doctrine or ritual into religion and religious worship. They
would say that what the deists said and what present day
infidels often say against clergymen should be a warning to
all clergymen how much harm to the cause of religion can
come from any departure on the part of a single clergyman
from the path of loyalty to truth and right. The anticlericalism of the deists drove home these lessons. Their attacks
had some element of truth in history to justify them. But
what no clergymen need admit is that all or most clergymen
are of the base type that the deist pictured them as being.
And what no informed and conscientious person will admit
for a moment is that practically all the rituals and doctrines
and practices of the church and of positive religion owe
their origin to clerical corruption and degeneracy. Religion
and its rites and ordinances and doctrines have far deeper
and nobler roots than this. The bitter anticlericalism of the
deists led them to be utterly unfair to the clergy as a class

and to an explanation of the history of religion that is almost entirely unsound and superficial.

The deistic attack upon supernaturalism, including Bible miracles, the inspiration of the Bible as a supernatural revelation from God and the incarnation and deity of Christ was not built upon a very strong foundation. The modern infidel who denies any divine creation, though he may be equally in error with the deist, occupies a stronger position in attacking these doctrines than did the deist. The deist having admitted the stupendous miracle of creation itself could not deny the possibility of the miraculous. All he could do was to argue from what he believed was God's nature and from what he believed was God's purpose in creation and from the nature of the historical evidence for any particular claimed miracle. But anyone could answer him by challenging his right to claim his conception of God or his idea of God's purpose in creation to be the correct one. How could he prove that God had the will to make a perfect and complete universe all at once rather than to make a universe that would gradually develop toward perfection under his control through the ages? What right had he to assume that God was like a master-mechanic watchmaker who tries to see how perfect a machine he can make so that it will run without any interference from him? Might not God have made a universe with the desire to have fellowship and intercourse with the parts of it that possess spiritual capacities for communion with him? The deists made much of an argument against revelation or miracles or salvation through Christ on the ground of the impartial nature of God. They argued that since these were not, according to the teaching of their opponents, and could not be, in the very nature of things, given equally to all men, it would be inconsistent with the impartial nature of God to give them to any. But many of them immediately weakened their own argument by suggesting that revelation or the Bible was given not to reveal a way of salvation or new truths in religion but only to correct abuses and errors that had come in through priestcraft. But to admit a revelation even for the correction of error would be to admit supernaturalism. And to admit that some had such revelation to correct error and abuses while others did not have it would be to impugn the impartiality of God just as surely as if he gave a new revelation. Moreover the evident inequalities in the gifts and opportunities of men would raise as much difficulty with the idea of impartiality as would a special revelation. The opponent of the deist could answer the deist at this point with the word "Hath not the potter power over the clay; of the same lump to make one vessel unto honor, and another unto dishonor?" (Rom. 10:21). Over against the deists' arguments against the historical evidence for the revelation and miracles and doctrines he rejected, the opponent of deism could point out the many and extensive arguments in favor of the truthworthiness and credibility of the Bible as revelation from God and could also show how frail a basis the deistic charge of fraud rested upon. In dealing with advocates of antisupernaturalism today, the champion of revelation and supernaturalism has an advantage over the eighteenth century opponent of the deists for the work of the Bible critics and the spade of the archeologist has supplied him with many and strong arguments in support of the historical trustworthiness of the Bible.

The deistic refusal to admit any mystery in religion is a position that has lost ground with the passing of the years. Today a modernist like Fosdick is not only quite ready to admit that there is, but that there must remain much of mystery in religion. When men of the intelligence and the rich acquaintance with the secrets of nature possessed by Thomas A. Edison make statements to the effect that nobody knows one seven-billionth of one per cent about anything, the fact that religion contains some mystery will hardly weigh against it as it did with the eighteenth century deists.

Butler's *Analogy,* while it would be of no value in argument with an atheist or with anyone who does not admit a creator of Nature and her laws, was a very cogent answer to the deists who admitted a creator and claimed that Nature and her laws were the only revelation of God. Butler ably showed that the objections which many of the deists urged against revealed religion and elements of it would weigh just as heavily against the religion of nature and the revelation through nature which the deists championed.

The deists largely failed to realize to what an extent they had gained their conceptions of God and morality from revelation and revealed religion. They disowned the source of things they cherished.

The deists claimed to be discarding a religion of doctrines and rituals for a religion of ethical principles alone. Yet their own lives for the most part were not good adver-

tisements for their natural religion and as their propaganda
spread public morality declined. This was true in England
where social morality was in a very deplorable condition
till an improvement was brought about by the great religious revival led by Whitefield and the Wesleys which began as deism started upon its rapid decline. A similar decline in public and private morality came also with the
growth of deism in France, Germany and America. As seen
above, Benjamin Franklin, though greatly enamored as a
youth with the teachings of the deists, came to regard the
deists and their teachings with some suspicion because he
noticed that their influence upon morality did not appear
to be wholesome. Deism did not stand well the application
of the Master's test, "By their fruits ye shall know them."

In their efforts to disparage the Bible as revelation, the
deists often showed themselves very prejudiced and unfair
in criticism. Their strictures upon such Bible characters as
Abraham, David and Paul showed an utter lack of appreciation of the true greatness of these men in spite of their
faults,—faults which the Bible records themselves plainly
admit. The deists failed altogether to notice that the fact
of the inclusion of the stories showing the faults of these
great heroes of the Jewish people and the Christian church
in the records of their lives points to the honesty and trustworthiness of those who first made the records and also of
those who have transmitted them. Dishonest Jewish and
Christian historians would hardly have recorded so fully the
faults of their heroes such as Abraham, Moses, David, Jacob,
Peter, Paul and John, nor would they have preserved the
record of their own faultiness as peoples as is done in the
Bible. In setting prophet against priest, the deists failed to
note that the prophetic protest was not against the sacrifices
and other rituals of religion as such but against divorcing
these from the ethical elements of religion. In setting the
New Testament against the Old, the deists again failed to
note that it was not against the real teaching of the Old Testament properly interpreted that the New protested but
against perverted interpretations of and additions to the
Old Testament. In setting Jesus against Paul the deists entirely failed to realize that Paul's teachings are in embryo
in Jesus' acts and words and that Paul has but given the
logical development of Jesus' religion. Also the deists failed
to see that there is not disagreement between Paul and

James and that each of these is only guarding against an incorrect interpretation of the other. The deists entirely failed to take note of the marvelous unity of the Bible in structure, theme, ethical teaching, symbolism, and emphasis.

Leslie Stephen was right when he said deism suffered from a delicacy of constitution due to its being founded on a faulty philosophy. Its conceptions of God and of creation and of God's purposes in creation were faulty. The deist found himself side by side with the Christian while fighting against atheism and for belief in God and a creation. But he found himself aligned with the atheist when attacking revelation and Christian doctrine. His starting point of admitting a supernatural creation certainly left him in a weaker position for an attack upon miracles and the supernatural than that occupied by the atheist.

The deists weakened their own position by their failure to agree with one another just as the position of Christianity is weakened in confronting an enemy by the disunion and disagreement of Christians. Some deists claimed their doctrines to be innate ideas while others denied all innate ideas and said their doctrines were rational inferences based on such universally known and clear facts as to be irresistible. But whether these doctrines were to be regarded as innate ideas or plain truths that every man must infer by reason, they all insisted that the doctrines were plain. Yet they differed in doctrine, some claiming a future life and some denying. Thus the disagreement cast doubt upon the plainness and clearness and inescapability of their doctrines. Some of the deists praised the New Testament highly and heaped honors upon Christ as the greatest of ethical teachers while others accused the New Testament as well as the Old and Christ as well as other Bible characters of low ethics and dishonesty. This division again weakened the position of the deists in meeting their Christian opponents.

The main trend of recent religious thought has been in the direction of emphasizing the immanence of God. Indeed the tendency in many writers is to go so far in this direction as to almost or altogether involve the giving up of the conception of the transcendance of God and the going over from theism to pantheism. Even radical Bible critics and modernists who share much of the bias of the deists against miracles and the supernatural incline today to emphasize the doctrine of the immanence of God. This present day emphasis on the immanence of God springs out of both the soil of modern science and modern philosophy. Deism involved the complete negation of the immanence of God and the putting of the fullest emphasis on his transcendance. In this respect deism is entirely out-of-line with modern religious thought trends.

The deists while criticizing and ridiculing the Bible story of the Fall, showed a lack of appreciation of the great problem of human depravity and had no explanation to offer for that depravity. When criticizing sacrifices and the Bible doctrine of the atonement, they objected that these tended to be made a substitute for good living and even to be an encouragement to presumption in evil doing. That sacrifices and the atonement could be so incorrectly and superficially understood as to involve this danger is apparent. But as taught by the church in connection with such other doctrines as those of the Holy Spirit, regeneration, and sanctification, this danger is eliminated. The deist never seemed to grasp the idea that, in the orthodox Christian view, morality is not the root or basis of salvation but a fruit or product of it, that Christians seek to do the right thing not because hoping thus to escape punishment and win reward but because their Holy Spirit regenerated and guided natures delight in the good. There is in the Christian teaching a mystic element which the coldly rationalistic minds of the deists simply could not see or grasp. Deists had little appreciation of the real nature, the real roots and the profound richness and value of religion in human life. They themselves lacked that spiritual experience which alone gives spiritual discernment.

Deism, from the standpoint of the believer in the Bible and Christianity and the Christian church, did religion and morality a great disservice by weakening or destroying faith in the Bible, in Christ and in the ministers of religion, and by lowering public morals. It also did a great disservice in the promoting of an irreverent attitude. Yet, by causing men to examine with a new thoroughness the Bible documents and their history, by drawing attention to the abuses of Christian doctrine, by sharply and clearly pointing out superstitions and evils of conduct that had become connected with religion and the church and thus preparing for their removal, and by calling forth many able works in the fields of Christian Evidences, the deists did, perhaps unintentionally, do the Christian religion a real service. The believer is likely to see in this but another illustration of the truth that the infinite God overrules the wrath and malice of men to His praise and to the advancement of righteousness and truth. But, whether for good or ill, the deists with their keen, clever, but superficial, rationalism, lived their lives, thought their thoughts, filled their niche in the intellectual structure being erected by man through the ages, and made their contribution to the great stream of human thought.

FINIS.

BIBLIOGRAPHY

BIBLIOGRAPHY

[NOTE. Many of the works of the deists were published anonymously and often without indication of publisher or place or date of publication. When any of these items concerning a work is known it is inserted in the following references to such works. Note is taken of the absence of any such item in the original work. References are usually given in footnotes by giving volume and page of the work cited. But an exception to this rule is taken in reference to such works as Locke's great Essay, many editions of which have been published with the same text. In such cases it was thought best to follow the usual practice by giving book, chapter, and paragraph.]

ADAMS, JOHN, *The Life and Works of John Adams* (compiled by his grandson Charles P. Adams). Boston, 1856. Ten vols.

ANNET, PETER, *The History and Character of St. Paul Examined.* London, F. Page. (Pub. anonymously and without date.)

ANNET, PETER, *The History of the Man after God's Own Heart.* London. (Pub. not indicated. Originally published anonymously and without date.) 1766. "A New Edition."

ANNET, PETER, *The Resurrection of Jesus Considered; In Answer to the Tryal of the Witnesses.* London. Printed for the Author, 1744. (The author published this work anonymously, using the penname, "Moral Philosopher").

An Outline of Christianity. The Story of Our Civilization. Bethlehem Publishers, Dodd, Mead and Company, 1926. 5 Vols.

ASTRUC, JEAN, *Conjectures Sur La Genese,* etc. Bruxelles, chez Fricx, Impremeur de Sa Majeste, 1753.

BACON, FRANCIS LORD, *The Essays of Lord Bacon.* Philadelphia, Henry Altemus. (Date not given.)

BACON, ROGER, *Opus Majus.* London. (Edited by S. Jebb). 1733.

BENTLEY, RICHARD (using penname "Phileleutherus Lipsiensis"), *Remarks Upon Late Discourse of Free-Thinking.* London. (Publisher not given.) 1737.

BLAKEY, R., *History of Moral Science.* London, James Duncan. 1833.

BLOUNT, CHARLES, *Miscellaneous Works of Charles Blount, Esq.,* containing: 1. *Oracles of Reason.* 2. *Anima Mundi, or the Opinions of the Ancients concerning Man's Soul after this Life, according to unenlighten'd Nature.* 3. *Great is Diana of the Ephesians, or the Original of Priestcraft and Idolatry, and of the Sacrifices of the Gentiles,* etc. Also *Life of Author and Vindication of his death.* (Place of pub. and publisher not given.) 1695.

BLOUNT, CHARLES, *The Two First Books of Philostratus,* Concerning the *Life of Apollonius Tyaneus: Written Originally in Greek, and Now Published in English: Together with Philological Notes Upon each Chapter, by Charles Blount, Gent.* London. Printed for Nathaniel Thompson. 1680.

BOCCACCIO, GIOVANNI, *The Decameron or Ten Days' Entertainment of Boccaccio.* New York, Albert and Charles Boni. 1925. Fine Paper Edition.

BOGARDUS, EMORY S., *A History of Social Thought.* Los Angeles, J. R. Miller. 1929. 2nd Edition.

BOLINGBROKE, HENRY ST. JOHN, VISCOUNT, *The Works of Lord Boling-broke, with a Life.* Philadelphia, Carey and Hart, 1841. 4 vols. (The first edition of Bolingbroke's works was given out in five vol-umes by David Mallet in the year 1754, three years after Boling-broke's death.)

BROWNE, SIR THOMAS, *Religio Medici, Letter to a Friend,* etc. And *Christian Morals.* London. Macmillan & Co., 1885.

BROWNE, SIR THOMAS, *The Works of Sir Thomas Browne.* London, Faber and Groyer, Limited; New York, W. E. Rudge, 1928. 6 vols.

BUDDEUS, JOAN F., *Theses Theologicæ De Atheismæ Et Superstitione.* Jenæ, Apud John F. Brelckium, 1717.

BURTT, EDWIN ARTHUR, *The Metaphysical Foundations of Modern Phys-ical Science.* New York, Harcourt, Brace & Co., Inc.; London, Kegan Paul, Trench, Trubner & Co., Ltd., 1927.

BURY, J. B., *A History of Freedom of Thought.* New York, Henry Holt & Co.; London, Williams and Norgate, 1913.

CHARRON, PIERRE, *Of Wisdome.* (Place of publication and publisher not given), 1601. Translated by Sampson Lennard.

CHUBB, THOMAS, *The Posthumous Works of Mr. Thomas Chubb.* Lon-don, R. Baldwin, 1748. 2 vols.

COLLINS, ANTHONY, *A Discourse of Free-Thinking, Occasion'd by the Growth of a Sect call'd Free-Thinkers.* London. (Published with-out the name of author or publisher), 1713.

COLLINS, ANTHONY, *A Discourse on the Ground and Reason of the Chris-tian Religion.* (Published without name of author, publisher, place of publication, or date), 1724.

CRAIG, SAMUEL G., *Christianity according to Dr. Fosdick.* (A pamphlet reprinted from *The Presbyterian.*)

DARROW, CLARENCE, *The Story of My Life.* New York and London, G. Scribner's Sons, 1932.

DARROW, FLOYD L., *Miracles, A Modern View.* Indianapolis, Bobbs-Mer-rill Co., 1926.

D'AUBIGNÉ, J. H. M., *History of the Reformation in the Sixteenth Cen-tury.* New York, William L. Allison, 1882.

DEWEY, JOHN, *What I Believe. The Forum,* March, 1930.

DODWELL, HENRY JR., *Christianity Not Founded on Argument; and the True Principle of Gospel-Evidence Assigned: In a Letter to a Young Gentleman at Oxford.* London. Printed for M. Cooper, 1743. The 3rd Edition. (The first edition was published anonymously in 1742, the author being generally known.)

DUCHESNE, MONSIGNOR LOUIS, *Early History of the Christian Church.* New York, Longman Green & Company, 1909. (A trans. of the 4th Edition.)

DURANT, WILL, *The Story of Philosophy.* New York, Simon and Schus-ter, 1927.

FARRAR, A. S., *A Critical History of Free Thought in Reference to the Christian Religion.* New York, D. Appleton & Co., 1882.

FISHER, GEORGE PARK, *History of the Christian Church.* New York, Charles Scribner's Sons, 1903.

FLINT, ROBERT, *Agnosticism.* New York, Charles Scribner's Sons, 1903.

FLINT, ROBERT, *Anti-Theistic Theories.* Edinburgh and London, William Blackwood and Sons, 1879.

FOSDICK, HARRY EMERSON, *Adventurous Religion and Other Essays.* New York and London, Harper and Brothers, 1926.

Fosdick, Harry Emerson, *As I See Religion*. New York and London, Harper and Brothers, 1932.

Fosdick, Harry Emerson, *The Modern Use of the Bible*. New York, The Macmillan Co., 1924.

Franklin, Benjamin, *Autobiography of Benjamin Franklin*. Boston, Ginn & Co., 1891. (Edited by D. H. Montgomery.)

Franklin, Benjamin, *Writings of Benjamin Franklin*. New York, The Macmillan Co., 1907. Ten vols.

George, Edward Augustus, *Seventeenth Century Men of Latitude, Forerunners of the New Theology*. New York, Charles Scribner's Sons, 1908.

Gibbon, Edward, *The Decline and Fall of the Roman Empire*. New York and London, The Co-Operative Publication Society. (Date of edition not given.) Six vols.

Gizycki, Georg von, *Die Philosophie Shaftesbury's*. Leipzig and Heidelberg, C. F. Winter'sche Verlagshandlung, 1876.

Gordon, George, A., *Religion and Miracles*. Boston and New York, Houghton Mifflin Co., 1910.

Gosse, Edmund, *Sir Thomas Browne..* London, Macmillan and Co., Limited, 1905.

Gray, James M., *The Deadline of Doctrine Around the Church*, (a pamphlet). Chicago, Moody Bible Institute, 1922.

Green, John Richard, *History of the English People*. New York, The Edward Publishing Company. (Date not given.) Four vols.

Guizot, M. and De Witt, *France*. New York and London, The Co-Operative Publication Society, 1876. 8 vols.

Haldane, J. S., *The Sciences and Philosophy*. Garden City, New York, Doubleday, Doran & Co., Inc., 1929.

Hamilton, Floyd E., *The Basis of Christian Faith*. New York, George H. Doran Co., 1927.

Hamilton, J. G. R. (Editor), *The Best Letters of Thomas Jefferson*.

Harnack, Adolf, *Die Mision und Ausbreitung des Christentums in ersten Drei Jahrhunderten.* Leipzig, J. C. Hinrich's'sche Buchhandlung, 1902.

Hazlitt, W. Carew, *Man Considered in Relation to God and a Church*. London, Bernard Quantich, 1912. Fifth Edition.

Herbert, Eduard, Baron de Cherbury en Angleterre, *De la Verité*. (Publisher and place of publication not given. Place probably Paris.) 1639. Third Edition.

Herbert of Cherbury, Edward Lord, *The Antient Religion of the Gentiles, and Causes of their Errors Considered*. London, John Nutt, 1705. (First published by Isaac Vossius in Amsterdam in the year 1663.)

Herbert of Cherbury, Edward Lord, *The Autobiography of Edward Lord Herbert of Cherbury, with Introduction, Notes, Appendices, and a Continuation of the Life by Sidney Lee*. London, George Routledge and Sons, Limited; New York, E. P. Dutton & Co., 1906. Second Edition. Revised.

Hobbes, Thomas, *The English Works of Thomas Hobbes of Malmesbury*. London, John Bohn, 1839. (The *Leviathan* is vol. 3 in this edition of Hobbes' works.)

Hume, David, *An Enquiry Concerning the Human Understanding, and An Enquiry Concerning the Principles of Morals*. Oxford, Clarendon Press, 1894.

Hume, David, *Essays, Literary, Moral and Political*. London, Ward, Lock & Co., Limited. (Date not given.)

Infidelity. Comprising JENYN'S *Internal Evidence*, LESLIE'S *Method*, LYTTLETON'S *Conversion of Paul*, WATSON'S *Reply to Gibbon and Paine*, a Notice of HUME on *Miracles*, and an Extract from WEST on *The Resurrection*. New York, American Tract Society. (Date not given.)

INGERSOLL, ROBERT G., *The Writings of Robert G. Ingersoll.* New York, C. P. Farrell. Dresden Edition. 1900. 12 vols.

JEFFERSON, THOMAS, *The Works of Thomas Jefferson.* 10 vols.

JOHNSON, W. J., *George Washington the Christian.* (Place not given.) The Abingdon Press, 1919.

KANT, IMMANUEL, *Critique of Practical Reason.* London, New York, etc., Longmans, Green & Co., Limited. Sixth Edition. 1927.

KANT, IMMANUEL, *Critique of Pure Reason.* New York, The Macmillan Co., 1925.

KEYSER, LEANDER S., *A System of Christian Evidence.* Burlington, Iowa, The Lutheran Literary Board. 3rd Edition, Revised. 1924.

LECHLER, G. V., *Geschichte Des Englischen Deismus.* Stuttgart und Tuebingen, J. G. Cotta'scher Verlag, 1841.

LELAND, JOHN, *A View of the Principal Deistical Writers that have appeared in England in the last and present Century, With Observations upon them, and some account of the answers that have been published against them.* London. Printed for T. C. Cadell, Jr., and W. Davies, 1798. Fifth Edition. 2 vols.

LESLIE, CHARLES, *A Short and Easie Method with the Deists. Wherein the Certainty of the Christian Religion is Demonstrated, by Infallible Proof from Four Rules, which are incompatible to any imposture that ever yet has been, or that can possibly be.* London, J. Applebee, 1723. Eighth Edition. (The first edition was published anonymously.)

LESSING, GOTTFRIED EPHRAIM, *Nathan der Weise.* Boston, D. C. Heath & Co., 1905.

LIPPMANN, WALTER, *A Preface to Morals.* New York, The Macmillan Co., 1929.

LOCKE, JOHN, *The Works of John Locke.* London. Printed for W. Olridge and Son, etc., etc., 1812. 11th Edition. 10 vols.

Essay Concerning Human Understanding. Vols. 1, 2, 3.

Replies to the Bishop of Worcester. vol. 4.

Of Civil Government. vol. 5.

Letters on Toleration. vol. 6.

The Reasonableness of Christianity. vol. 7.

A Discourse on Miracles. vol. 9.

LORD, JOHN, *Beacon Lights of History.* (Second Series.)

MACHIAVELLI, NICOLO, *The Prince.* London, George Routledge & Sons, Ltd; New York, E. P. Dutton & Co., 1883.

MANDEVILLE, BERNARD DE, *The Fable of the Bees; or Private Vices Public Benefits.* London, Allen and West; Edinburgh, J. Mundell & Co., 1795. (This larger work contains *The Grumbling Hive, or Knaves Turned Honest*, which was written about 1706.)

MATTHEWS, SHAILER, *The Church and the Changing Order.* New York, The Macmillan Co., 1907.

MATTHEWS, SHAILER, *The Gospel and the Modern Man.* New York, The Macmillan Co., 1910.

MIDDLETON, CONYERS, *An Introductory Discourse to a Larger Work.* London, R. Manby and H. S. Cox, 1747.

MIDDLETON, CONYERS, *Free Inquiry into the Miraculous Powers, Which are supposed to have subsided in the Christian Church.* London, R. Manby and H. S. Cox, 1749.

MONTAIGNE, MICHEL DE, *The Essays of Montaigne.* New York, A. L. Burt Co. (Date of publication not given.) Translated by Charles Cotton and Edited by W. Carew Hazlitt. 2 vols.

MORGAN, THOMAS, *The Moral Philosopher, In a Dialogue Between Philathes a Christian Deist, and Theophanes a Christian Jew.* In Which the Grounds and Reasons of Religion in General, and particularly of Christianity, as distinguished from the Religion of Nature: the Different Methods of conveying and proposing Moral Truth to the Mind, and the necessary Marks, or Criteria on which they must all equally depend; the Nature of positive Laws, Rites, and Ceremonies, and how far they are capable of Proof as of standing perpetual Obligation; with many other matters of utmost consequence in Religion, are fairly considered, and debated, and the Arguments on both Sides impartially represented. London. Printed for the Author, 1738. The Second Edition Corrected.

Nicene and Post-Nicene Fathers of the Christian Church. New York, The Christian Literature Company, 1890. Second Edition.

NINDE, E. S., *George Whitefield.* New York, The Abingdon Press, 1924.

NOACK, LUCIUS, *Die Freidenker in der Religion, oder die Repraesenten der religioesen Aufklaerung in England, Frankreich und Deutschland.* Bern, Jent und Reinert, 1853-1855. Drei Bande. I. England. II. Frankreich. III. Deutschland.

O'LEARY, DE LACY, *Arabic Thought and its Place in History.* London, Kegan Paul, Trench, Trubner & Co., Ltd.; New York, E. P. Dutton & Co., 1922.

ORR, JAMES, *The Bible Under Trial.* New York, Armstrong and Sons, 1907. Second Edition.

OWEN, JOHN, *The Skeptics of the French Renaissance.* London, Swan Sonnenschein & Co.; New York, The Macmillan Co., 1893.

OWEN, JOHN, *The Skeptics of the Italian Renaissance.* London, Swan Sonnenschein & Co.; New York, The Macmillan Co., 1893. Second Edition.

PAINE, THOMAS, *The Age of Reason, Being An Investigation of True and Fabulous Theology.* New York, G. P. Putnam's Sons, 1907. (First published in Paris in 1794.)

PERRIERS, BONAVENTURE DES, *Cymbalum Mundi, ou Dialogues Satyriques Sur differens Sujets.* Amsterdam, Prosper Marchaud, 1537.

Re-Thinking Missions. New York and London, Harper and Brothers, 1932.

RILEY, I. WOODBRIDGE, *American Philosophy.* New York, Dodd, Mead & Co., 1907.

RILEY, I. WOODBRIDGE, *American Thought from Puritanism to Pragmatism and Beyond.* New York, Henry Holt & Co., 1923.

ROBERTSON, JOHN M., *A Short History of Freethought Ancient and Modern.* London, Swan Sonnenschein & Co., Ltd.; New York, The Macmillan Co., 1899.

ROOP, HERVIN U., *Christian Ethics or the Science of Christian Living.* New York, Chicago, London, and Edinburgh, Fleming H. Revell Co., 1926.

ROUSSEAU, JEAN JACQUES, *Emile, or Treatise on Education.* New York, D. Appleton & Co., 1901.

ROUSSEAU, JEAN JACQUES, *The Social Contract, or the Principles of Political Rights.* New York and London, G. P. Putnam's Sons, 1893. Second Edition, Revised.

SCHAFF, PHILIP, *History of the Christian Church*. New York, Charles Scribner's Sons, 1905. Eighth Edition. 7 vols. (Vol. 3 used in this work.)

SCHNIZ, ALBERT, *Vie et Oeuvres de J. J. Rousseau*. Boston, New York, and Chicago, D. C. Heath & Co., 1921.

SHAFTESBURY, ANTHONY, EARL OF, *Characteristics of Men, Manners, Opinions, Times*, etc. London, Grant Richards, 1900. 2 vols. (The first edition of this often issued work appeared in London in 1711.)

SHAFTESBURY, ANTHONY, EARL OF, *The Life, Unpublished Letters and Philosophical Regimen of Anthony, Earl of Shaftesbury*. London, Swan Sonnenschein & Co., Limited; New York, The Macmillan Co., 1900.

SNOWDEN, JAMES H., *Old Faith and New Knowledge*. Cornwall, New York, Harper and Brothers, 1928.

SORLEY, W. R., *A History of English Philosophy*. Cambridge, Cambridge University Press, 1920.

SPINOZA, BENEDICT DE, *The Chief Works of Benedict de Spinoza*, translated from the Latin with an Introduction by R. H. M. Lewes. London, G. Bell & Son, 1908.

STEPHEN, LESLIE, *Free Thinking and Plain Speaking*. New York and London, G. P. Putnam's Sons, The Knickerbocker Press, 1905.

STEPHEN, LESLIE, *History of English Thought in the Eighteenth Century*. New York, G. P. Putnam's Sons; London, Smith, Elder & Co., 1902. Third Edition. 2 vols.

STODDARD, W. O., *The Lives of the Presidents*. 3rd Edition.

STRONG, A. H., *Systematic Theology*. Philadelphia, The Judson Press, 1912.

The Ante-Nicene Fathers. Buffalo, The Christian Literature Company, 1885-1886.

The Writings of Benjamin Franklin. (Smyth, Editor.) New York, The Macmillan Company, 1907. 10 vols.

TINDAL, MATTHEW, *Christianity as Old as the Creation; or The Gospel a Republication of the Religion of Nature*. London. (Publisher not given.) 1730.

TOLAND, JOHN, *Amyntor; or a Defense of Milton's Life*. London, John Darby, 1699.

TOLAND, JOHN, *Christianity Not Mysterious; or, a Treatise shewing That there is nothing in the Gospel Contrary to Reason, nor above it; and that no Christian Doctrine can be properly Called a Mystery. To which is added An Apology for Mr. Toland in relation to the Parliament of Ireland, ordering this book to be burnt*. London. (Publisher not given.) 1702. (First published anonymously in 1696.)

UEBERWEG, FRIEDRICH, *Grundriss der Geschichte der Philosophie*. Berlin, Ernst Siegfried Mittler und Sohn, 1883. Sechste Auflage.

UHLHORN, G., *The Conflict of Christianity With Heathenism*. New York, Charles Scribner's Sons, 1879. (Translated, with the Author's sanction from the Third German Edition, by E. C. Smyth and C. J. H. Roper.)

VOLTAIRE, F. M. A., *The Works of Voltaire*. Paris, London, and New York, E. R. Du Mont. Collector's Edition. 1901. 42 vols.

WEBER, ALFRED, *History of Philosophy*. New York, Charles Scribner's Sons, 1905.

WHITEHEAD, ALFRED NORTH, *Religion in the Making*. New York, The Macmillan Company, 1926.

WHITEHEAD, ALFRED NORTH, *Science and the Modern World*. New York, The Macmillan Company, 1925.

WILLSTACH, PAUL (Editor), *The Correspondence of John Adams and Thomas Jefferson, 1812-1826*. Indianapolis, Bobbs-Merrill, 1925.

WOOLASTSON, WILLIAM, *The Religion of Nature Delineated*. London, Samuel Palmer, 1726.

WOOLASTSON, WILLIAM, *The Religion of Nature Delineated*. Glasgow, Une & Co., 1746. Seventh Edition.

WOOLSTON, THOMAS, *The Works of Thomas Woolston*. London. Printed for J. Roberts, 1733. 5 vols.

"Wycliffe," *The People's Right Defended*, to which is added *A Discourse on Transsubstantiation by Archbishop John Tillotson*. Philadelphia, W. F. Geddes, 1831.

INDEX

INDEX

Abbott, Lyman, 252.
Adams, John, 202, 204, 231.
Agnostic, 235, 237, 243, 244, 259.
Allegory, 33-34, 132-133, 139, 141, 143, 230, 262.
Allen, Ethan, 204, 217, 219.
Annet, Peter, 33, 42, 43, 150-152, 240.
Anti-clericalism, 17, 37, 65, 102, 126, 131, 133, 135, 138, 139, 146, 156, 175, 183, 195, 236, 241, 245, 259, 268-269.
Arianism, 34, 35, 45, 59, 90, 91, 257, 259.
Arminianism, 35, 59, 231, 259.
Astruc, Jean, 237, 247.
Atheist, 77, 181, 212, 235, 244.

Bacon, Francis, 30, 130, 212, 223, 265.
Bacon, Roger, 54, 223, 265.
Bahrdt, C. F., 194.
Basedow, J. B., 194.
Baur, F. C., 248.
Bayle, 180, 181, 185, 188.
Blount, Charles, 18, 27, 30, 34, 37, 39, 40, 41, 42, 43, 45, 53, 84, 109-113, 141, 149, 187, 266.
Bodin, Jean, 29, 46, 49, 59, 180.
Bolingbroke, 27, 30, 37, 39, 47, 50, 67, 100, 103, 155-158, 187, 202, 248, 266.
Bradlaugh, 237.
Briggs, C. A., 252.
Browning, Robert, 225.
Browne, Thomas, 61, 79-81, 114.
Butler's Analogy, 140, 172, 225, 270.
Byron, 225.

Canon of Scripture, 75, 118, 121, 133, 152.
Celsus, 39, 41-43, 44, 59, 109, 145, 257, 259, 265.
Charron, Pierre, 29, 46, 49, 50, 143, 180.
Cherbury, Herbert of, 18, 35, 37, 39, 40, 42, 44, 52, 59, 60, 61-69, 87, 89, 110, 114, 118, 130, 140, 149, 174, 179, 192, 207, 213, 214, 232, 241, 266.
Cheyne, 248.
Christian Century, 252.
Christianity Today, 252.

Chubb, Thomas, 31, 53, 152-155, 187, 240, 266.
Coffin, H. S., 252, 263.
Colenso, Bishop, 248.
Collins, Anthony, 33, 34, 37, 39, 40, 42, 53, 79, 82, 86, 129-134, 149, 187, 190, 206, 219, 230, 262, 266.
Columbus, Christopher, 25.
Comparative Religion, 64, 257-258.
Comte, 224, 227-228, 232, 233, 237.
Copernicus, 27-28, 49, 113, 156.
Craig, S. G., 252.
Croffut, 235.

Damned, Society of the, 235.
Darrow, Clarence S., 244-245, 259.
Darrow, Floyd, 244.
Deism:
—Corollaries of, 13-14.
—Criticism of, 267-274.
—Definition of, 13-18, 167.
—Duration of, 18-19.
—Exhaustion of, 174.
—Five Principles of, 62-63.
Democritus, 37.
Denny, W. B., 264.
De Veritate, 18, 29, 60, 61, 187, 189.
De Wette, 248.
Dewey, John, 232-233.
Diderot, 181, 185, 187, 188, 212, 227.
Dippel, 189.
Dodwell, Henry Jr., 18, 149, 150, 155, 160-165, 173, 174, 175, 266.
Driver, 248, 249.
Drummond, 225.

Edelman, J. C., 189.
Edison, Thomas, 261, 270.
Edwards, Jonathan, 203, 231.
Eichorn, 248.
Emerson, R. W., 231.
Epicurus, 37, 70.
Evolution, 224, 230, 235, 236, 237, 238, 245, 254.
Ewald, 248.

Flint, Robert, 13, 14.
Fosdick, H. E., 252, 260-263, 270.
Foster, 248.

287